Essential Latin
Grammar

Gregory Klyve

For UK order enquiries: please contact Bookpoint Ltd,
130 Milton Park, Abingdon, Oxon OX14 4SB.
Telephone: +44 (0) 1235 827720. *Fax:* +44 (0) 1235 400454.
Lines are open 09.00–17.00, Monday to Saturday, with a 24-hour
message answering service. Details about our titles and how to
order are available at www.teachyourself.com

For USA order enquiries: please contact McGraw-Hill Customer
Services, PO Box 545, Blacklick, OH 43004-0545, USA.
Telephone: 1-800-722-4726. *Fax:* 1-614-755-5645.

For Canada order enquiries: please contact McGraw-Hill
Ryerson Ltd, 300 Water St, Whitby, Ontario L1N 9B6, Canada.
Telephone: 905 430 5000. *Fax:* 905 430 5020.

Long renowned as the authoritative source for self-guided
learning – with more than 50 million copies sold worldwide –
the *Teach Yourself* series includes over 500 titles in the fields of
languages, crafts, hobbies, business, computing and education.

British Library Cataloguing in Publication Data: a catalogue record
for this title is available from the British Library.

Library of Congress Catalog Card Number: on file.

**First published in UK 2002 as Teach Yourself Latin Grammar
by Hodder Education,** part of Hachette UK, 338 Euston Road,
London NW1 3BH.

First published in US 2002 by The McGraw-Hill Companies, Inc.

This edition published 2010.

The *Teach Yourself* name is a registered trade mark of Hachette UK.

Copyright © 2002, 2003 2010 Gregory Klyve

Typeset by MPS Limited, A Macmillan Company.

Printed in Great Britain for Hodder Education, an Hachette UK
Company, 338 Euston Road, London NW1 3BH, by XXX.

The publisher has used its best endeavours to ensure that the URLs
for external websites referred to in this book are correct and active
at the time of going to press. However, the publisher and the author
have no responsibility for the websites and can make no guarantee
that a site will remain live or that the content will remain relevant,
decent or appropriate.

Hachette UK's policy is to use papers that are natural, renewable
and recyclable products and made from wood grown in sustainable
forests. The logging and manufacturing processes are expected to
conform to the environmental regulations of the country of origin.

Impression number   10 9 8 7 6 5 4 3 2 1

Year   2014 2013 2012 2011 2010

Contents

Credits

Front cover: © Oxford Illustrators Ltd

Back cover: © Jakub Semeniuk/iStockphoto.com, © Royalty-Free/Corbis, © agencyby/iStockphoto.com, © Andy Cook/iStockphoto.com, © Christopher Ewing/iStockphoto.com, © zebicho – Fotolia.com, © Geoffrey Holman/iStockphoto.com, © Photodisc/Getty Images, © James C. Pruitt/iStockphoto.com, © Mohamed Saber – Fotolia.com

Meet the author

I have been an enthusiast of the classical world since my early teenage school years in Wales when I first encountered the Romans and their language. I survived the kinaesthetic methods of my teacher who used to hurl books and wooden board rubbers at her pupils' heads, and was hooked on Latin for life.

My family moved to Blackpool in 1975 where I attended Blackpool Collegiate Grammar School. After doing O-levels in 1978 I concentrated on Latin, Greek and Ancient History for A-level and, following in the footsteps of my inspiring teacher, went to Exeter College, Oxford where I obtained a BA in Literae Humaniores (Classics) in 1984 and, after a break in teaching, a doctorate in Greek Tragedy in 1995.

I have taught classical subjects at various schools and tutorial colleges since 1984 and have been Head of Classics at Sevenoaks School in Kent and The Leys School in Cambridge. I have been teaching part-time at St Mary's School in Cambridge since 2008.

In addition to teaching, I write scripts for sketches, plays and short films and I am the co-author, with C.G. Oakley, of a comic novel The Legend of Perseus (Byronic Books 1989).

Only got a minute?

Latin is the language used by the ancient Romans whose city, traditionally founded in 753 BCE, grew to dominate the Mediterranean and, at its height, most of Europe, including Britain, until the fifth century CE.

As a result of this political domination Latin became a common European tongue and was still used as the formal language of administration, scholarship, the law, the church, medicine and science for centuries after the Roman empire declined. Indeed, Latin is alive today, from mottoes to gardening and from joke books to the news on the internet. Latin's continued usefulness lies not only in its logical structure and conciseness of expression, but also in the fact that its paneuropean history has made it the basis of the Romance languages: Italian, French, Provençal (Occitan), Spanish, Catalan, Galician, Portuguese, Romansch and Romanian.

Of equal value to historians and linguists, a knowledge of Latin will also be of great use to students of literature, as the cultural impact of Roman writers can be traced through the Middle Ages, the Renaissance, the Enlightenment and the Romantic Movement.

Learning Latin is fun. As languages go it has only a small number of irregular forms and many of the words are recognizable as there is usually at least one English word derived from every Latin word. The main difference between English and Latin is that Latin is an *inflected* language (like German and Russian) which means that *the meaning or use of a word can be altered by changing its ending*. One result of this is that Latin word order is not the same as English word order, but more like Yoda's from *Star Wars*: **multum hilaritatis erit** = *much of fun it will be* (i.e. *it will be a lot of fun*).

10 Only got ten minutes?

The Latin language developed in and around the city of Rome in the area of Italy called Latium (modern Lazio). The city's tradition is that it was founded by king Romulus in 753 BCE and proved a successful place of refuge which attracted exiles, refugees and political dissidents from the surrounding regions.

In 510 BCE (traditional date), the Romans expelled their kings and established a republic ruled by two consuls, elected annually. Under this invigorated republic the Romans eventually came to dominate not only their neighbours but the entire Italian peninsula, challenging other powers in the Mediterranean, notably Carthage (in modern Tunisia) in the West and the Greek states in the East. By 146 BCE, with destruction of Carthage and Corinth, the Romans had become masters of the Mediterranean. With no other enemies in sight, the Romans turned on each other and the republic destroyed itself in a series of brutal civil wars until Augustus became master of the Roman world after his defeat of Antony and Cleopatra at the Battle of Actium in 31 BCE. Thereafter the Roman world was ruled by emperors, a regime known as the Principate.

The empire reached its height in the first decade of the second century CE under the emperor Trajan. Facing sociopolitical pressures from within and geopolitical pressures from without, in 285 BCE the Roman world was divided under Diocletian into the Western and Eastern empires, centred on Rome and Byzantium (later Constantinople, now Istanbul) respectively. Christianity was legalized by Constantine in 313 CE and soon became the official state religion. The Western empire finally collapsed in 476 and the last significant Roman from the East, the jurist and emperor Justinian, died in 565.

The Romans left behind not only the infrastructure of empire, notably roads and civic settlements and institutions, but also an immense cultural legacy whose influence is still felt strongly today. Their language endured and continued, with variations, to be used as a common European tongue until the Enlightenment as well as forming the basis of the Romance languages.

The remains of Classical Latin literature which have survived are as old as the third century BCE. Much of the best Latin owes an enormous amount to the literary influences of the Greeks. The surviving literature can be (roughly) divided into early, which includes the comedies of Plautus and Terence (220–160 BCE); the Ciceronian (or early golden) age 80–43 BCE, including Cicero, Caesar, Sallust, Lucretius and Catullus; the Augustan (or late golden) age 43 BCE–14 CE, including Virgil, Horace, Ovid and Livy and the silver age 14–120 CE including Seneca, Pliny, Tacitus, Juvenal, Lucan, Martial and Statius.

Vulgar Latin, or colloquial Latin, was the the Latin spoken by ordinary people, rather than written by authors. Only a few examples of it survive in written form, from 'low' literature, e.g in the comedies of Plautus and Terence and in Petronius' *Cena Trimalchionis*. Vulgar Latin developed in different forms in the culturally diverse provinces of the empire and eventually became the basis of the Romance languages Italian, French, Provençal (Occitan), Spanish, Catalan, Galician, Portuguese, Romansch and Romanian. Vocabulary, pronounciation and grammar changed, to suit the region, while the neuter gender and the system of case endings was lost. Word order came to resemble what we now use in English. Even a cursory comparison of basic words in the Romance languages shows a clear debt to Latin.

Medieval Latin is the term used for the version of the language which was used by educated people for scholarly, legal, literary, scientific, administrative and theological purposes during the Middle Ages. Spelling and pronouciation differ from Classical Latin. The collection of poems *Carmina Burana* is written in Medieval Latin, as are the works of the Venerable Bede and the scholar Roger Bacon.

The most obvious example of Latin's continued survival since the ancient world, and of its use in a daily, modern context, has been the Ecclesiastical Latin used by the Roman Catholic Church. Spoken in ceremonies and written in official documentation, it grew out of Late Latin and was used by clerics to speak to their flocks, both in services, including sermons or homilies (Latin **sermo humilis** = *common talk*), and for theological and administrative purposes. The Latin translation of the bible (by St Jerome, and others, in the fourth century CE) is known as the Vulgate (Latin **editio vulgata** = *popular edition*, from the Latin **vulgus** = *crowd*). Ecclesiastical Latin differs from Classical Latin in having a simpler form of syntax, some different vocabulary and a word order a little closer to that of English and the Romance languages.

Latin is the official of the Holy See in the Vatican City. At the Second Vatican Council (1962–5) the use of vernacular languages instead of Latin for church services was approved, but the persistence of Latin has been impressive and recently it has enjoyed something of a revival in the Catholic church.

During the Renaissance educated writers, particularly of the Humanist movement, tried to cleanse the language of medieval and vulgar forms and modelled their Latin on the authors from the 'Golden Age'. Their efforts enjoyed much success and their influence on education is still felt in the texts we study in schools today. Among the authors of Renaissance Latin are Dante, Petrarch, Boccaccio and Erasmus.

New Latin is a term used to describe the version of Latin used between the sixteenth and nineteenth centuries for scholarly and scientific works. The scientific terms created during this period survive today in scientific terminology, particularly in the taxonomy (classification) of plants and animals, and also in medical, pharmaceutical and biological terms. Prominent authors of New Latin are Sir Thomas Moore, John Milton, Sir Isaac Newton, Nicolaus Copernicus, Johannes Kepler, Galileo Galilei, Francis Bacon, Carolus Linnaeus (who invented biological classification), René Descartes and Baruch Spinoza.

Latin is an inflected language (sometimes also called a radical language) which means that the endings of words change according to their usage. We have something like this in English. We usually change the end of a noun if we want it to refer to more than one thing; e.g. *one cat: several cats*. We change some nouns depending on whether they are masculine or feminine; e.g. *emperor* and *empress*. We sometimes alter the endings of our verbs depending on who is performing the action; e.g. *I run, he runs*. We also change our pronouns (*I*, *he*, *she*, *it*, *we*, *they* and *who*) depending on how they are being used in a sentence; e.g. *I chase him then he chases me*. In this sentence both *I* and *me* refer to the same person (myself) but the words are different because they are used differently. In '*I chase him*' I am performing the action but in '*then he chases me*' I am having the action performed upon me. Normally, however, we do not change the forms of words in English but rely upon word order to make our meaning clear.

In Latin things are different. It is a language in which the start of a word, usually called the *stem* (sometimes also called the *root*), does not usually change but the endings of almost all words (sometimes also called *inflections*) do change according to how those words are being used. Word order is, therefore, not as important in Latin as it is in English and the verb usually comes at the end of a sentence. At first this can seem confusing but it is really a bit like a jigsaw puzzle. When you translate you must take care not to be too influenced by the word order. You will need to look up the meanings of the words and then check their endings to find out how each one is being used, just like finding the corners, edges and middle of a jigsaw.

As Latin is available to all and spoken as a mother tongue by none, it retains a neutrality and independence almost unique among languages. Its universality can be seen in the weekly news broadcasts produced by the Finnish Broadcasting Corporation on the internet (**nuntii latini**), some of which are ingenious and amusing.

Introduction

How to use this book

Essential Latin Grammar takes you through the principal elements of Classical Latin grammar in a graded series of units, starting with explanations and details of how Latin words are formed (known technically as **accidence**), from simple forms of verbs, through nouns, prepositions, adjectives, adverbs, conjunctions and pronouns to more complex forms of verbs, ending with an examination of the normal constructions found in Latin sentence structure (known technically as **syntax**). After the units on grammar there are some sections on Roman dates, money, weights and measures, names, history and the use of Latin today. It has been designed so that you can dip into the book at any point to study a particular piece of grammar, or progress through the book unit by unit from the beginning. It is assumed that you have access to a dictionary and that you will accumulate your own bank of Latin vocabulary as you work. Almost all the Latin words are translated for you. Remember that a dictionary will give all the various meanings of a word and you will need to pick the right one for the context.

You can consolidate your knowledge by attempting the exercises which accompany each unit. These exercises are geared to that particular unit and contain tests on the grammar point which is being examined. Exercises may also contain simple grammatical elements met in previous units as the book progresses. A key with all the answers is provided at the back of the book.

The contents of each unit will vary in size and difficulty. However, clear cross-references are made to other units which further explain any important item which is mentioned but is not under direct scrutiny.

It is assumed that the reader does not have a knowledge of the technical terms used in grammar and so explanations for all of these are provided at appropriate points.

If you are only just starting Latin, then try to become familiar with grammatical terms as you meet them in the course of the units. Most importantly, do not worry if the terms seem long winded. You will be able to cope with simple sentences fairly quickly. The wonderful thing about the Latin language is that it has a completely logical structure. Simply follow the examples and consolidation exercises carefully and remember that you are doing it at your own speed so there is no pressure of time and that you can always return to any unit to refresh your memory.

If you already have some knowledge of Latin and are using this book for revision purposes or because you need to read Latin documents for work or pleasure, or just to brush up what you know, then you will find the layout straightforward. Exhaustive detail has been deliberately avoided as this can be very confusing. If you are reading a work of Latin literature, then you should always use a good published commentary on the work. This book does not examine things like literary techniques or the metres of Latin verse.

One very important thing to remember throughout is that there is no word for '*a*' or '*the*' in Latin.

Latin sentences usually have a number of **clauses**. A clause is a group of words which form a sense unit and have a verb. One clause is always more important than the others and is called the **main clause**. The others are called **subordinate clauses** (see 1T for a detailed account). The main clause is the one which will stand on its own and still make sense. Subordinate clauses do not make complete sense on their own. The verb of the main clause is called the **main verb** of a sentence.

Insight

A clause is a part of a sentence with its own verb. Main clauses can stand on their own; subordinate clauses cannot: in 'I ate the cakes which my mother had made', 'I ate the cakes' is a complete sentence in its own right; 'which my mother had made' is a subordinate clause (in this case a relative clause), which cannot stand on its own.

Abbreviations:

abl.	ablative	**nom.**	nominative
acc.	accusative	**n.**	neuter
dat.	dative	**pl.**	plural
f.	feminine	**s.**	singular
gen.	genitive	**voc.**	vocative
m.	masculine		

1

Alphabet, pronunciation and terminology

Alphabet and pronunciation

There are 24 letters in the Latin alphabet. The Romans had no j or w. In writing, capitals are used for proper nouns, adjectives and numerals, not to start sentences.

A Pronunciation
There are no silent letters in Latin and long vowels take about twice as long to say as short ones.

A <u>a</u> as in f<u>a</u>ther when long, but as in <u>a</u>ct when short

B <u>b</u> as in <u>b</u>ut

C <u>c</u> as in <u>c</u>ut, not as in church, cider or loch

D <u>d</u> as in <u>d</u>og

E <u>e</u> as in pr<u>e</u>y when long, but as in j<u>e</u>t when short.

F <u>f</u> as in <u>f</u>ather

G <u>g</u> as in <u>g</u>oat, not as in genius

H <u>h</u> as in <u>h</u>ave

I <u>i</u> as in mach<u>i</u>ne when long, as in p<u>i</u>t when short and as <u>y</u> in <u>y</u>et when used as a consonant

K <u>k</u> as in <u>k</u>ing (this Greek letter [kappa] was used only in words of Greek origin)

L <u>l</u> as in <u>l</u>ong

M <u>m</u> as in <u>m</u>other

N <u>n</u> as in <u>n</u>ewt, but, before c, g and qu it is pronounced <u>ng</u>, as in si<u>ng</u>

O **o** as in t**o**ne (although the French **o** in ch**o**se is closer) when long, as in h**o**t when short

P **p** as in **p**at

Q **q** as in **q**ueen and always followed by u, as in English

R **r** is always rolled, as in Italian

S **s** as in **s**un, not as in was, treasure or sugar

T **t** as in **t**op, not as in motion

U **u** as in f**oo**d when long but as in p**u**t when short

V **w** as in wine, although the Hindi pronunciation of **v** is closer

X **x** as in a**x**e, not as in exact

Y **y** as in the French v**u** (this Greek letter [**upsilon**] was used only in words of Greek origin)

Z **z** as in **z**oo (this Greek letter [**zeta**] was used only in words of Greek origin)

B Diphthongs are combinations of vowels making one sound. In Latin they are all long:

ae pronounced **ai** as in **ai**sle, e.g. pr**ae**da → *booty*
au pronounced **ou** as in h**ou**se, e.g. **au**rum → *gold*
oe pronounced **oi** as in b**oi**l, e.g. p**oe**na → *penalty*
ei pronounced **ei** as in r**ei**gn. Only found in the exclamations **ei**! **ei**a! h**ei**a! → *oh! aha!*
eu pronounced **ew** as in p**ew**, e.g. s**eu** → *whether*
ui pronounced **wea** as in **wea**k, e.g. h**ui**c → *to this*

The diphthongs **ei, eu** and **ui** are rare. Mostly when these vowel combinations are found they are pronounced separately, as in **tui** → *yours* (pronounced two-ee), **fluit** → *it flows* (flew-it), **mei** → *mine* (meyee) and **deus** → *god* (de-yus). When the u follows the letter **q** it is pronounced **w**, as in English.

C Consonantal i and u

▶ In some Latin words the letter **i** is pronounced as the consonant **y** at the beginning or even in the middle of words, e.g. con*i*ungo (*I join together*: pronounced con-yungo) and *i*am (*already*: pronounced yam). In the English derivatives of many of these words the consonantal i becomes the letter j, e.g. juvenile comes from **iuvenis** (*young man*), judicial comes from **iudicium** (*judgement*), joke comes from **iocus** (joke) and the name Julius from **Iulius**.

▶ The Romans made no distinction between **v** and **u** when writing so, for example, in an inscription you might find **EQVVS** for **equus** → *horse*. Some published texts still make no distinction so you may find **uinum** for **vinum** → *wine*.

D When t, c or p are followed by an h, they are called aspirated consonants **th**, **ch** and **ph**. They come from the Greek letters *theta*, *chi* and *phi* and exist in Latin words which come from Greek. They should be pronounced as an emphasized version of the letters without the h but in practice th and ph are often pronounced as in the English <u>th</u>in and <u>ph</u>oto and ch as in the Scottish lo<u>ch</u>.

E Length of vowels and syllables
▶ In English the stressed vowel of a word is usually lengthened while unstressed ones are not, e.g. *c<u>i</u>der*, *b<u>o</u>redom*. In a Latin word, however, any of the vowels may be either long or short. In dictionaries and textbooks the long vowels are usually marked out by a line over the top of the vowel called a macron (¯). In some cases, it is important to know whether a vowel is long or short, especially in verse, but when you come to read Latin documents you will not find any distinguishing marks over long vowels. In this book there are no marks used over vowels for the exercises and readers do not need to include them. In the explanatory matter, long syllables are marked when they are of importance.
▶ The length of a **syllable**, as opposed to a vowel, is important to know for verse. A syllable is **long** if it has a long vowel or a diphthong, or ends in two consonants, the letter x or a single consonant if the next word also begins with a consonant. All other syllables are **short**.

F Stress accent
▶ In Latin the stress accent (ictus) falls on the first syllable of two syllabled words, e.g. <u>pa</u>ter → *father*. It falls only rarely on the last syllable, e.g. il<u>lic</u> → *to there* (for il<u>lice</u>).
▶ In words of more than two syllables the ictus is on the last but one (**penultimate**) syllable if that syllable is **long**, e.g. cor<u>rup</u>tum → *corrupted*, but on the one before that (**antepenultimate**) if it is short, e.g. mi<u>li</u>tibus → *for the soldiers*.

Verbs: essential terminology

Verbs refer to actions (e.g. *I carry*) **and are divided into four categories, depending on their usage: moods, voices, tenses and persons.**
Brief explanations follow of the terms which you will meet most often when studying verbs. It is important to be familiar with them but do not expect to understand them all straight away.

G Mood
There are four moods. The first three are called **finite** moods because each part of the verb in these moods is limited to a particular **person** (see J).

▶ The **indicative mood** is generally used for making statements and asking questions (e.g. *Grass grows. Where is he going?*). The **main verb** (see Introduction) of a Latin sentence will usually be in the indicative mood.
▶ The **imperative mood** is used to give commands (Unit 11).
▶ The **subjunctive mood** is used mainly as a verb in **subordinate clauses** (see T), often to express anticipated or conditional actions. On the less common occasions when it is a main verb, it usually expresses a wish and is often found in mottos (Unit 9).
▶ The **infinite mood** is so called because no part of the verb is limited to a particular **person** (see J). This mood includes the **infinitive** (Unit 11), **participle, gerundive, gerund** and **supine** (Unit 10).

H There are two **voices:**

....

Insight
Verbs have two 'voices', *active* and *passive*. In the active voice, the subject carries out the action of the verb; in the passive voice the subject experiences the action of the verb. In English the sense of the passive is conveyed by the verb *to be*
(Contd)

and a participle: '*The man was <u>bitten</u> by the dog.*' In Latin the sense of the passive is conveyed by verb endings.

> ▶ The **active** voice is used when the **subject** (Unit 4A2) of the sentence or clause is performing the action of the verb, e.g. *The elephant chases the mouse.*
> ▶ The **passive** voice (Unit 8) is used when the subject is experiencing the action of the verb, e.g. *The elephant is chased by the mouse.*

I There are six **tenses** (see Unit 2):

A **tense** refers to the time when the action of a verb takes place.

▶ **Present** (Unit 2A–F)	▶ **Perfect** (Unit 2L–R)
▶ **Imperfect** (Unit 2J–K)	▶ **Future perfect** (Unit 2U–W)
▶ **Future** (Unit 2G–I)	▶ **Pluperfect** (Unit 2S–T)

A tense can be either active or passive as well as being either indicative or subjunctive. By convention, if mood and voice are not stated then the tense is indicative and active.

J Person
In each **tense** six **persons** can perform the action:

1st person singular:	I
2nd person singular:	you (when one person performs the action)
3rd person singular:	he, she, it (depending on the context)
1st person plural:	we
2nd person plural:	you (when two or more people perform the action)
3rd person plural:	they

In English we sometimes use a pronoun before the verb (we walk, she sits etc.). In Latin this is not needed because the ending of the verb changes to let us know who is doing it. These endings are called **personal endings** (see under the units on separate tenses).

K Principal parts

The principal parts of a Latin verb enable us to recognize the various parts of that verb when we meet it in our reading and tell us what conjugation a verb belongs to.

When you look for a verb in your dictionary you will find four Latin words in the entry, followed by the meaning. Sometimes they are written out in full (e.g. **porto, portare, portavi, portatum**: *I carry*) or they can be abbreviated (e.g. **porto -are -avi -atum**: *I carry*). These are called the **principal parts** because their **stems** are the bases for every form of that verb. Learn every principal part when you meet a verb.

1 The 1st person singular of the present (**indicative active**) (Unit 2B), e.g. **porto**: *I carry*.
2 The **present (active) infinitive** (Unit 11B), e.g. **portare**: to carry.
3 The 1st person singular of the perfect (**indicative active**) (Unit 2N), e.g. **portavi**: *I carried*.
4 The **supine** (e.g. **portatum**) which ends in **-um** and has no equivalent in English (Unit 10G), or, occasionally, as in the Cambridge Latin Course, the **perfect passive participle** (Unit 10C), e.g. **portatus**: *carried*.

L Conjugation (See Unit 2)

A **conjugation** is a group of verbs which share similarities in appearance (not in meaning or usage). There are four in Latin and you can identify which conjugation a verb belongs to by examining the endings of its first two **principal parts**:

▶ The **first conjugation** verbs end in **-o -āre**, like port<u>o</u> port<u>āre</u> (*carry*) (Unit 2C).
▶ The **second conjugation** verbs end in **-ēo -ēre**, like hab<u>ēo</u> hab<u>ēre</u> (*have*) (Unit 2D).
▶ The **third conjugation** verbs end in **-o -ere**, like reg<u>o</u> reg<u>ere</u> (*rule*) (Unit 2E).
  N.B. Some verbs of the third conjugation end **-io -ere**, like cap<u>io</u> cap<u>ere</u> (*take*) (Unit 2E).

▶ The **fourth conjugation** verbs end in **-io -īre**, like aud**io** aud**īre** (*hear*) (Unit 2F).

M Verbs taking a **direct object** in the **accusative** are called **transitive**; others are called **intransitive**. (See Units 4B1 and 4D2.)

Nouns: essential terminology

Brief explanations follow of the terms which you will meet most often when studying nouns, and other words which decline. It is important to be familiar with them but do not expect to understand them all straight away.

N A **noun** is the name of a person, place, thing or quality. **Proper nouns** are used for the names of particular people or places, e.g. Caesar or Rome. **Concrete nouns** name things which exist in the physical universe (e.g. table or elephant), while **abstract nouns** name qualities that exist only as a mental concept (e.g. wisdom or mercy).

O Number
If a noun is referring to one thing, it is **singular**. If it refers to more than one thing it is **plural**. Some nouns only have a plural, e.g. **arma** (*arms*), **nuptiae** (*marriage*) and **moenia** (*city walls*). Some have only a singular, e.g. **aurum** (*gold*).

> **Insight**
> The term 'case' is grammatical shorthand for the different situations that alter the endings of nouns and adjectives. English has the remnants of a case system in its pronouns.

P Case (see Unit 4)
Latin nouns have six cases, in the singular and plural, which are different forms of the noun used in different contexts. They are:

- **Nominative** (Unit 4A1–3)

  This case is used for the **subject** of sentences and for the **complement**. It is the 'name' of the noun and is the case you will find first in a dictionary entry.

- **Vocative** (Unit 4A4)

  The vocative is the case used when someone is addressing someone else directly. It is almost always the same as the nominative.

- **Accusative** (Unit 4B1–6)

  The accusative is used for the **direct object** of verbs, after certain **prepositions**, for expressing duration of time or motion towards something and adverbially.

Insight

Prepositions are words like *in*, *through*, *with* that describe the relationship of one noun/pronoun to another.

- **Genitive** (Unit 4C1–8)

  The genitive case is used to denote possession (of) but it has a very wide range of meanings beyond this and it contains the **stem** of the noun (see R below).

Insight

Latin nouns can be split into a stem, which carries the meaning, and an ending, which denotes the function of the word in the sentence. This gives Latin great flexibility in word order.

- **Dative** (Unit 4D1–7)

  The dative case is used for the **indirect object** (to or for), but it has a very wide range of meanings beyond this.

- **Ablative** (Unit 4E1–17)

  The ablative expresses means, association or separation (by, with or from), but it has a very wide range of meanings beyond these. It is also used after certain prepositions.

There is also a specialized case called the **locative** which is used to denote 'at' a particular place (Unit 4F).

Q Gender

▶ In English, nouns which have genders are those which are obviously either male or female, like man, woman, boy, girl, stallion, mare and so on. Sometimes we also apply gender to inanimate objects like calling a ship, a country or even a car 'she'.

▶ In Latin all nouns have a gender. There are three: **masculine**, **feminine** and **neuter**. Names of men and men's occupations are **masculine**, as the names of women and women's occupations are **feminine**, but otherwise, there is no general rule which can be given as to why a noun has one gender or another. Some nouns which include both male and female are said to be of **common** gender. The gender of a noun will always be given in a dictionary and should be learnt along with the meaning.

R Dictionary entries

When you look a Latin noun up in a dictionary you will find the **nominative** case first, followed by the **genitive case** (or its ending), the **gender** (usually abbreviated) and finally the meaning, e.g. **ira, irae** f. *rage*. The **genitive** is a very important case because the **stem** of a noun is that part of the noun which comes before the **genitive ending**. You can also tell what **declension** a noun belongs to from the genitive ending.

S Declensions (see also Unit 3)

A declension is a group of nouns which share similarity in appearance but not in meaning. There are five declensions in Latin and we can identify them from the genitive ending which is the same for all members of that declension.

These are the **endings** for the nominative and genitive singular of the five declensions:

▶ **First declension** nouns: mostly feminine. (Unit 3A–C)
    nominative ending -a   genitive ending - ae
▶ **Second declension** nouns: mostly masculine and neuter. (Unit 3D–I)
    nominative ending usually **-us**, **-ius**,   genitive ending -ī
    or **-er** for masculine and **-um** for neuter

▶ **Third declension:** all genders are found in this declension. (Unit 3J–N)

 nominative ending: there is a great   genitive ending **-is**
 variety of endings for this case.

▶ **Fourth declension** nouns: mostly masculine with some feminines and neuters. (Unit 3O–Q)

 nominative ending **-us** for   genitive ending **-ūs**
 masculine and feminine and
 -u for neuter

▶ **Fifth declension** nouns: all feminine except for one masculine (**dies:** *day*). (Unit 3R)

 nominative ending **-es**   genitive ending **-eī**

NB Do not confuse this genitive ending with that of the second declension whose nominative never ends in **-es**.

Subordinate clauses

T Simple sentences make a statement or ask a question in the **indicative,** express a wish in the **subjunctive** or give an order in the **imperative.**

▶ In **complex** sentences we encounter more than one clause and one clause almost always has a more important status than the other(s). This is called the **main clause** and the others are called **subordinate clauses.** The arrangement of these clauses is called syntax (Units 13–16).

▶ The **main clause** can stand on its own and still make sense whereas a **subordinate clause** cannot, e.g. *While I was cooking dinner, the dog stole the cakes.* In this sentence you can identify the main clause, which is *the dog stole the cakes*, because it can stand on its own and still make sense. However, the other clause, *while I was cooking dinner*, does not make complete sense on its own and so is a subordinate clause. The important idea in the sentence is that the dog stole the cakes while the subordinate clause simply sets the main clause in a context.

It tells us at what point the dog stole the cakes and what else was going on at the time.

▶ Latin sentences are usually much longer than English ones, sometimes as long as a paragraph. They may therefore contain a large number of subordinate clauses. When you are translating into English, it is a good idea to split a Latin sentence up into a number of smaller English ones to avoid a cumbersome result.

▶ Subordinate clauses in English are usually linked to the main clause by a conjunction and this is frequently the same in Latin.

U The key to understanding subordinate clauses lies in the verbs. Each subordinate clause is governed by its own verb. That verb is commonly a **finite** one, often a subjunctive, as in **final clauses** and **consecutive clauses** (Unit 14), **clauses of fearing** and **clauses of doubting** (Unit 16) and **indirect questions** (Unit 15). Indicative verbs are found in some subordinate clauses like **causal** and **concessive clauses** (Unit 16). However, the verb may also be a participle, as in the case of the **ablative absolute** (Unit 13) or an infinitive, as in the **indirect statement** (Unit 15).

Once you have identified the main verb (or verbs) and clause of a sentence, look for all the other verbs which will be the foundations of the subordinate clauses.

V Relative clauses (Unit 13) are also called **adjectival clauses** because they qualify a word or idea in another clause, like an adjective. **Relative particles** like **ubi** (*where*) **also introduce adjectival clauses.**

W Those clauses known as **adverbial clauses** qualify the main clause like an adverb, answering questions such as *how?*, *why?* or *when?*

▶ **Consecutive clauses** (Unit 14): *so that, with the result that*
▶ **Final clauses** (Unit 14): *in order that*
▶ **Causal clauses** (Unit 16): *because*
▶ **Temporal clauses** (Unit 13): *when, until*
▶ **Conditional clauses** (Unit 14): *if, unless*

- ▶ **Concessive clauses** (Unit 16): *although, even if*
- ▶ **Clauses of proviso** (Unit 16): *provided that*
- ▶ **Comparisons** (Unit 16): *as, as if, as though*
- ▶ **Clauses of fear** (Unit 16): *lest*

X The **indirect statement, indirect question, indirect command** and **indirect wish** (Unit 15) are called **substantival clauses** because they stand like a noun in relation to the main verb.

Y Sequence of tenses

The tense of the Latin verb in a subordinate clause is not necessarily the same as it would be in English. In Latin something called the **sequence of tenses** is applied. There are exceptions to it but the broad principle is that:

- ▶ If a verb is in the present, future or future perfect indicative or the imperative or in the present or perfect subjunctive, then it is said to be in **primary sequence**.
- ▶ If a verb is in the imperfect or pluperfect indicative or subjunctive, then it is said to be in **historic sequence**.
- ▶ The perfect indicative tense straddles these definitions. If it is used to mean, e.g. *I have eaten* then it has some reference to the present and so is **primary**. If it is used simply to mean e.g. *I ate*, then it has no reference to the present and so is **historic**.
- ▶ If the main verb is **primary**, then it is followed by a verb in a primary tense in the subordinate clause. On the other hand, if a main verb is **historic**, it is followed by a verb in a historic tense in the subordinate clause.
- ▶ In subordinate clauses, the present and imperfect subjunctive tenses are used for incomplete action, while the perfect and pluperfect subjunctive tenses are used for completed action.

Points to remember

1 Latin uses the Greek letters th (theta), k (kappa), y (upsilon), ph (phi) and ch (chi) only when writing words of Greek origin.

2 There are no silent letters in Latin. Everything is pronounced.

3 Latin verbs have four moods: indicative, imperative, subjunctive, and infinitive.

4 Latin verbs have six tenses: present, future, imperfect, perfect, future perfect and pluperfect.

5 Latin verbs have two voices: active and passive.

6 Latin verbs and nouns have two numbers: singular and plural.

7 Latin verbs are grouped into four separate conjugations which share similarities in formation but not in meaning. The conjugation of each may be identified from the present infinitive (the second principal part of the verb).

8 Latin nouns come in three genders: masculine feminine and neuter.

9 Latin nouns are grouped into five separate declensions which share similarities in appearance but not in meaning. The declension of each may be identified from the genitive singular.

10 Latin sentences generally have one main clause and one or more subordinate clauses.

2

Tenses (indicative active)

Present tense

Endings and the first conjugation.

A The **present tense** refers to actions which occur in the present. We can express this in different ways in English, e.g. *I am going to school, I go to school,* or even, *I do go to school.* These English expressions have slightly different meanings. Latin, however, only uses one word for all three versions and so the particular meaning must be worked out from the context.

B In English we sometimes use a pronoun, e.g. *we, you, or they,* to explain who is performing an action before using the verb itself (e.g. *we wait*). In Latin this is not always done because the endings of the verb change to let us know who is performing the action. These endings are called **personal endings.** These are the personal endings for the present tenses of all the conjugations:

1st person singular	**-o**	*I*
2nd person singular	**-s**	*you* (singular)
3rd person singular	**-t**	*he/she/it*
1st person plural	**-mus**	*we*
2nd person plural	**-tis**	*you* (plural)
3rd person plural	**-nt**	*they*

C The **first conjugation** verbs can be recognized by the characteristic letter **a** which occurs in the present infinitive -**are** (the second principal part), e.g. labor*a*re (*to work*), am*a*re (*to love*), ambul*a*re (*to walk*) and port*a*re (*to carry*).

The **present stem** (for **stem** see Introduction, p. 3) of these verbs also ends in -**a** and this can be seen in all the persons except the 1st person singular.

> ## Insight
> Latin verbs can be split into a stem, which carries the meaning, and an ending, which denotes the person, tense, mood, voice etc. For example, in **porto**, *I carry*, **port-** is the stem and **-o** conveys the sense of '*I*', present tense, indicative, active.

▶ This is the present tense of the **first conjugation**. Notice the characteristic letter **a** at the end of the stem before all personal endings except the first. Remember also that in English there are different ways of expressing the present tense. The verb used in the example is **porto -are -avi -atum**: *carry*:

1st person singular	**porto**	*I carry / am carrying*
2nd person singular	**portas**	*you (s.) carry / are carrying*
3rd person singular	**portat**	*he/she/it carries / is carrying*
1st person plural	**portamus**	*we carry / are carrying*
2nd person plural	**portatis**	*you (pl.) carry / are carrying*
3rd person plural	**portant**	*they carry / are carrying*

Second, third and fourth conjugations.

D The **second conjugation** can be recognized by the characteristic long letter **e** in the present infinitive -*ē*re (second principal part). Notice also that there is an e in the stem before all of the personal endings in the present tense, e.g. hab*e*o hab*e*re (*have*) and ten*e*o ten*e*re (*hold*).

habeo	*I have*	habemus	*we have*
habes	*you* (s.) *have*	habetis	*you* (pl.) *have*
habet	*he/she/it has*	habent	*they have*

E The third conjugation is recognizable by the short letter **e** in the present infinitive -*ere* (second principal part), e.g. **ago ag̱ere** (*do*), **rego reg̱ere** (*rule*) and **dico dic̱ere** (*say*). In the present tense these verbs have a letter **i** before the personal endings, except the 1st person singular (*I*) and the 3rd person plural (*they*).

ago	*I do*	agimus	*we do*
agis	*you* (s.) *do*	agitis	*you* (pl.) *do*
agit	*he/she/it does*	agunt	*they do*

▶ There are some verbs which are technically in the **third conjugation** but which have an **i** before all the personal endings in the present tense and so resemble the fourth conjugation (see F), e.g. **cap̄io cap̱ere** (*take*), **fac̄io fac̱ere** (*make*) and **iac̄io iac̱ere** (*throw*).

capio	*I take*	capimus	*we take*
capis	*you (s.) take*	capitis	*you* (pl.) *take*
capit	*he/she/it takes*	capiunt	*they take*

F The **fourth conjugation** is distinguished by the letter **i** in the present infinitive -*ire* (second principal part) and before all of the personal endings, e.g. **aud̲io aud̲ire** (*hear*), **custod̲io custod̲ire** (*guard*).

audio	*I hear*	audimus	*we hear*
audis	*you* (s.) *hear*	auditis	*you* (pl.) *hear*
audit	*he/she/it hears*	audiunt	*they hear*

Future tense

First and second conjugations.

G The **future tense** refers to actions that will happen in the future. In English we usually use the words *will* or *shall* before the verb, e.g. *I shall go*. Normally, the word *shall* is used before the 1st person (singular and plural) and the word *will* is used before the 2nd and 3rd persons (singular and plural). However, when special emphasis is intended, the words are used the other way round, e.g. *You **shall** go to the ball, Cinderella.* We also use the present tense of the verb *to go* plus an infinitive to indicate future plans (e.g. *I am going to buy a computer*). In Latin the ending of the verb changes.

H In the **first** and **second conjugations** the **future** endings (placed on the **present stem**) are:

1st person singular	**-bo**	1st person plural	**-bimus**
2nd person singular	**-bis**	2nd person plural	**-bitis**
3rd person singular	**-bit**	3rd person plural	**-bunt**

▶ The future tense of the **first conjugation** is as follows. Notice that the stem contains the characteristic letter **a** which distinguishes this conjugation.

portabo	*I shall carry*
portabis	*you* (s.) *will carry*
portabit	*he/she/it will carry*
portabimus	*we shall carry*
portabitis	*you* (pl.) *will carry*
portabunt	*they will carry*

▶ The future tense of the **second conjugation** is as follows. Notice that the stem contains the characteristic letter **e** which distinguishes this conjugation.

habebo	*I shall have*
habebis	*you* (s.) *will have*
habebit	*he/she/it will have*
habebimus	*we shall have*
habebitis	*you* (pl.) *will have*
habebunt	*they will have*

Third and fourth conjugations.

I In the **third** and **fourth conjugations** the endings of the **future tense** (placed on the present stem) are:

1st person singular	**-am**	1st person plural	**-ēmus**
2nd person singular	**-ēs**	2nd person plural	**-ētis**
3rd person singular	**-et**	3rd person plural	**-ent**

▶ The future tense of the **third conjugation** is as follows. Be careful not to confuse the future tense of the third conjugation with the present tense of the second conjugation (see D).

agam	*I shall do*
ages	*you* (s.) *will do*
aget	*he/she/it will do*
agemus	*we shall do*
agetis	*you* (pl.) *will do*
agent	*they will do*

▶ The future tense of verbs in the **third conjugation** which resemble those in the fourth conjugation, like **capio** (see E), keeps the letter **i** before the endings. For example:

capiam	*I shall take*
capies	*you* (s.) *will take*
capiet	*he/she/it will take*
capiemus	*we shall take*
capietis	*you* (pl.) *will take*
capient	*they will take*

▶ The future tense of the **fourth conjugation** is as follows. Notice the characteristic letter **i** before the endings.

audiam	*I shall hear*
audies	*you* (s.) *will hear*
audiet	*he/she/it will hear*
audiemus	*we shall hear*
audietis	*you* (pl.) *will hear*
audient	*they will hear*

Imperfect tense

J Imperfect means incomplete and the **imperfect tense** is used for actions in the past which did not get finished, went on regularly, lasted for some time before they ended or only just got started; as opposed to single actions which were completed in one go (see L). There is a variety of ways of using an imperfect tense in English:

▶ 'I was locking the stable door when the horse bolted.' I did not finish locking the door so the action is imperfect.
▶ 'I used to lock the stable door whenever the horse bolted.' I habitually locked the door so the action is imperfect.

We can use the simple past tense if it is clear that the action took place over a period of time, e.g. 'I wrote in my diary every day.'

K The **personal endings** of the **imperfect tense** for all the conjugations are:

1st person singular	**-bam**	1st person plural	**-bamus**
2nd person singular	**-bas**	2nd person plural	**-batis**
3rd person singular	**-bat**	3rd person plural	**-bant**

▶ The imperfect tenses are as follows:

First conjugation		Second conjugation	
portabam	*I was carrying*	habebam	*I was having*
portabas	*you* (s.) *were carrying*	habebas	*you* (s.) *were having*
portabat	*he/she/it was carrying*	habebat	*he/she/it was having*
portabamus	*we were carrying*	habebamus	*we were having*
portabatis	*you* (pl.) *were carrying*	habebatis	*you* (pl.) *were having*
portabant	*they were carrying*	habebant	*they were having*

Third conjugation		Fourth conjugation	
agebam	*I was doing*	audiebam	*I was hearing*
agebas	*you (s.) were doing*	audiebas	*you (s.) were hearing*
agebat	*he/she/it was doing*	audiebat	*he/she/it was hearing*
agebamus	*we were doing*	audiebamus	*we were hearing*
agebatis	*you (pl.) were doing*	audiebatis	*you (pl.) were hearing*
agebant	*they were doing*	audiebant	*they were hearing*

Perfect tense

Formation and first conjugation.

L The **perfect tense** refers mostly to single, completed actions in the past. In English we use either the past tense on its own or together with the verbs *have* or *did*, e.g. *I carried, I have carried* or *I did carry*. There is an important difference between saying *I carried* and *I have carried*. 'I have carried' suggests that the action took place in the past (often the recent past) and that its consequences are still important in the present, e.g. *I have opened the box* suggests that the contents of the box are now of immediate interest in the present. *I opened the box* could refer to any time in the past and does not have the same suggestion that the contents of the box are of immediate relevance to the present.

M The perfect tense is formed from the **third principal part** (see Unit 1K) which is the 1st person singular of the perfect indicative active. The **perfect stem** is that part of the word before the ending -i.

N The **personal endings** for the **perfect tense** of all conjugations are:

1st person singular	**-ī**	1st person plural	**-imus**
2nd person singular	**-istī**	2nd person plural	**-istis**
3rd person singular	**-it**	3rd person plural	**-ērunt**

O First conjugation

▶ As a general rule the perfect stem of the first conjugation ends in -**av**-:

portavi	*I carried/have carried*
portavisti	*you* (s.) *carried/have carried*
portavit	*he/she/it carried/has carried*
portavimus	*we carried/have carried*
portavistis	*you* (pl.) *carried/have carried*
portaverunt	*they carried/have carried*

▶ Some common verbs of the **first conjugation** have different perfect stems, but their endings are always the same, e.g. **do, dare**, *dedi*, **datum** (*give*), **sto, stare**, *steti*, **statum** (*stand*) and **seco, secare**, *secui*, **sectum** (*cut*).

Second, third and fourth conjugations.
P Second conjugation

▶ As a general rule the **perfect stem** of the **second conjugation** ends in -**u**-:

habui	*I had/have had*	habuimus	*we had/have had*
habuisti	*you* (s.) *had/have had*	habuistis	*you* (pl.) *had/ have had*
habuit	*he/she/it had/has had*	habuerunt	*they had/have had*

▶ Some common verbs of the **second conjugation** have different perfect stems, but their endings are always the same, e.g. **fleo, flere**, *flevi*, **fletum** (*weep*), **rideo, ridere**, *risi*, **risum** (*laugh*) and **mordeo, mordere, momordi, morsum** (*bite*).

Q Third conjugation

▶ The **perfect stem** of the **third conjugation** has a variety of endings, mostly consonants. In some verbs the vowel of the stem also changes, as in our model verb **ago, agere**, *egi*, **actum** (*do*):

egi	*I did/have done*	egimus	*we did/have done*
egisti	*you* (s.) *did/have done*	egistis	*you* (pl.) *did/have done*
egit	*he/she/it did/has done*	egerunt	*they did/have done*

▶ The variety of **stems** can be seen from this selection: **premo, premere,** *pressi,* **pressum** (*press*); **rego, regere,** *rexi,* **rectum** (*rule*); **colo, colere,** *colui,* **cultum** (*worship*); **cresco, crescere,** *crevi,* **cretum** (*grow*); **peto, petere,** *petivi,* **petitum** (*seek*); **cado, cadere,** *cecidi,* **casum** (*fall*); **acuo, acuere,** *acui,* **acutum** (*sharpen*) and **capio, capere,** *cepi,* **captum** (*take*).

R Fourth conjugation

▶ The perfect stem of the fourth conjugation is usually **-iv-** or **-i-**:

audivi *or* audii	*I heard/have heard*
audivisti *or* audiisti	*you* (s.) *heard/have heard*
audivit *or* audiit	*he/she/it heard/has heard*
audivimus *or* audiimus	*we heard/have heard*
audivistis *or* audiistis	*you* (pl.) *heard/have heard*
audiverunt *or* audierunt	*they heard/have heard*

▶ Some of these verbs have different perfect stems, e.g. **aperio, aperire,** *aperui,* **apertum** (*open*); **haurio, haurire,** *hausi,* **haustum** (*drain*) *and* **venio, venire,** *veni,* **ventum** (*come*).

Pluperfect tense

S The **pluperfect tense** is expressed in English by using *had* before the past participle of the verb to indicate an action which occurred at two stages back in the past, e.g. *When the horse had bolted, I shut the stable door*. The shutting of the door took place in the past and the horse bolting took place at a stage even further back in the past, so the pluperfect is used.

T The **pluperfect tense** is formed by adding the following **personal endings** onto a verb's **perfect stem** (see M):

1st person singular	**-eram**	1st person plural	**-eramus**
2nd person singular	**-eras**	2nd person plural	**-eratis**
3rd person singular	**-erat**	3rd person plural	**-erant**

▶ The following are examples of the **pluperfect tense** from each conjugation:

First conjugation		Second conjugation	
portaveram	*I had carried*	habueram	*I had had*
portaveras	*you* (s.) *had carried*	habueras	*you* (s.) *had had*
portaverat	*he/she/it had carried*	habuerat	*he/she/it had had*
portaveramus	*we had carried*	habueramus	*we had had*
portaveratis	*you* (pl.) *had carried*	habueratis	*you* (pl.) *had had*
portaverant	*they had carried*	habuerant	*they had had*

Third conjugation		Fourth conjugation	
egeram	*I had done*	audi(v)eram	*I had heard*
egeras	*you* (s.) *had done*	audi(v)eras	*you* (s.) *had heard*
egerat	*he/she/it had done*	audi(v)erat	*he/she/it had heard*
egeramus	*we had done*	audi(v)eramus	*we had heard*
egeratis	*you* (pl.) *had done*	audi(v)eratis	*you* (pl.) *had heard*
egerant	*they had done*	audi(v)erant	*they had heard*

Future perfect tense

U The **future perfect tense** refers to an action which will have taken place by a certain time in the future. In English, as the name of the tense suggests, we use the auxiliary verbs *will* (the future element) and *have* (the perfect element), e.g. *They will have decided by the end of the day.*

V The **future perfect tense** is formed by adding the following **personal endings** onto a verb's **perfect stem** (see M):

1st person singular	**-ero**	1st person plural	**-erimus**
2nd person singular	**-eris**	2nd person plural	**-eritis**
3rd person singular	**-erit**	3rd person plural	**-erint**

W The following are examples of the future perfect tense from each conjugation:

First conjugation		Second conjugation	
portavero	*I shall have carried*	habuero	*I shall have had*
portaveris	*you (s.) will have carried*	habueris	*you (s.) will have had*
portaverit	*he/she/it will have carried*	habuerit	*he/she/it will have had*
portaverimus	*we shall have carried*	habuerimus	*we shall have had*
portaveritis	*you (pl.) will have carried*	habueritis	*you (pl.) will have had*
portaverint	*they will have carried*	habuerint	*they will have had*

Third conjugation		Fourth conjugation	
egero	*I shall have done*	audi(v)ero	*I shall have heard*
egeris	*you (s.) will have done*	audi(v)eris	*you (s.) will have heard*
egerit	*he/she/it will have done*	audi(v)erit	*he/she/it will have heard*
egerimus	*we shall have done*	audi(v)erimus	*we shall have heard*
egeritis	*you (pl.) will have done*	audi(v)eritis	*you (pl.) will have heard*
egerint	*they will have done*	audi(v)erint	*they will have heard*

The verb 'to be'

X The verb **sum, esse, fui** (there is no supine (see Unit 10G))
(*to be*) is irregular in formation. The **indicative** tenses follow.
For the **subjunctive** tenses and other moods, see Unit 12P.

▶ Present tense

sum	*I am*
es	*you* (s.) *are*
est	*he/she/it is*
sumus	*we are*
estis	*you* (pl.) *are*
sunt	*they are*

▶ Future tense

ero	*I shall be*
eris	*you* (s.) *will be*
erit	*he/she/it will be*
erimus	*we shall be*
eritis	*you* (pl.) *will be*
erunt	*they will be*

▶ Imperfect tense

eram	*I was*
eras	*you* (s.) *were*
erat	*he/she/it was*
eramus	*we were*
eratis	*you* (pl.) *were*
erant	*they were*

▶ Perfect tense

fui	*I have been*
fuisti	*you* (s.) *have been*
fuit	*he/she/it has been*
fuimus	*we have been*
fuistis	*you* (pl.) *have been*
fuerunt	*they have been*

▶ Pluperfect tense

fueram	*I had been*
fueras	*you* (s.) *had been*
fuerat	*he/she/it had been*
fueramus	*we had been*
fueratis	*you* (pl.) *had been*
fuerant	*they had been*

▶ Future perfect tense

fuero	*I shall have been*
fueris	*you* (s.) *will have been*
fuerit	*he/she/it will have been*
fuerimus	*we shall have been*
fueristis	*you* (pl.) *will have been*
fuerint	*they will have been*

Y Word order

▶ At the beginning of a sentence without a specific **subject** (see Unit 4A2), e.g. **est canis in horto:** *there is a dog in the garden.*

▶ After a subject; immediately after or at the end of a clause (see Introduction), e.g. **canis est in via,** or **canis in via est:** *a dog is in the street.*

Notice the difference in meaning when the verb comes at the beginning.

▶ With a noun and its complement (see Unit 4A3), e.g. **Caesar imperator erat** → *Caesar was a general.*

1 Who is performing the action of these verbs?
e.g. **laboramus** (work) → *we work*

a orant (*beg*)
b dat (*give*)
c curas (*care*)
d poto (*drink*)
e probamus (*approve*)
f paratis (*prepare*)
g das (*give*)
h stamus (*stand*)
i laborat (*work*)
j potant (*drink*)

2 Write out the present tense of these verbs.
e.g. **ambulo** (*I walk*), **ambulo, ambulas, ambulat, ambulamus, ambulatis, ambulant**

a servo (*I save*)
b comparo (*I procure*)
c loco (*I place*)
d concito (*I hurl*)
e voco (*I call*)
f computo (*I reckon up*)
g muto (*I change*)
h pugno (*I fight*)
i adflo (*I breathe upon*)
j amo (*I love*)

3 Translate these verbs into Latin.
e.g. *he cares* → **curat**

a we call
b you (s.) are working
c I approve
d he approves
e they are drinking
f you (pl.) care

g she is calling
h it walks!
i I stand
j they care

4 Write the present infinitive (second principal part) of these verbs and say what it means.

e.g. **do** (*I give*) → **dare** *to give*

a puto (*I think*)
b cogito (*I ponder*)
c lanio (*I mangle*)
d mando (*I command*)
e praetervolo (*I fly past*)
f claro (*I explain*)
g demonstro (*I show*)
h fatigo (*I exhaust*)
i coacto (*I force*)
j appello (*I pronounce*)

5 What conjugation do these verbs belong to?

e.g. **cogo cogere** (*to compel*) → third

a emunio emunire (*to strengthen*)
b mordeo mordere (*to bite*)
c perfrico perfricare (*to scratch*)
d sternuo sternuere (*to sneeze*)
e revincio revincere (*to tie up at the back*)
f perficio perficere (*to finish*)
g adsentio adsentire (*to agree*)
h converto convertere (*to turn around*)
i debeo debere (*to owe*)
j invigilo invigilare (*to be awake*)

6 Translate the following verbs.

e.g. **ambulo et** (*and*) **specto** → *I walk and watch*

a currimus et superamus
b dormitis et stertitis
c quaerit et servat
d vides et credis
e sciunt et tacent
f inspicio et probo
g fugiunt et lacrimant
h doceo et discitis
i ridetis et luditis
j salimus et canimus

7 Write out the present tenses of the following verbs. You will need to check the infinitive to find out what conjugation the verb belongs to.

e.g. **servio servire** (*I serve*), servio, servis, servit, servimus, servitis,
   serviunt

   a aperio aperire (*I open*)   **f** teneo tenere (*I hold*)
   b peto petere (*I seek*)   **g** facio facere (*I make*)
   c advenio advenire (*I arrive*)   **h** vasto vastare (*I destroy*)
   d video videre (*I see*)   **i** libro librare (*I balance*)
   e discedo discedere (*I depart*) **j** fugio fugere (*I flee*)

8 Write down the present infinitive (second principal part) of these verbs and say what it means.

e.g. **anticipo** (*I anticipate*) → **anticipare** *to anticipate*

   a nubo (*I marry*)   **f** implico (*I entwine*)
   b mereo (*I deserve*)   **g** paco (*I pacify*)
   c arcesso (*I summon*)   **h** sero (*I sew*)
   d claudico (*I limp*)   **i** statuo (*I set up*)
   e gero (*I carry*)   **j** voveo (*I vow*)

9 Write out the future tenses of the following verbs. Remember to look up their infinitives to check which conjugation they belong to.

e.g. **moneo** (*I advise*), monebo, monebis, monebit, monebimus,
   monebitis, monebunt

   a aedifico (*I build*)   **f** crepo (*I creak*)
   b misceo (*I mix*)   **g** sto (*I stand*)
   c ardeo (*I burn*)   **h** fundo (*I secure*)
   d mulceo (*I soothe*)   **i** narro (*I relate*)
   e sono (*I sound*)   **j** horreo (*I shudder*)

10 Translate these future tenses into Latin. Remember to look up words you do not know yet.

The word **sed** → *but* is included in this exercise.

e.g. **equitabimus sed ambulabitis** → *we shall ride but you will walk*

   a monebunt et suadebunt   **d** manebimus et spectabimus
   b portabitis sed ambulabimus **e** nuntiabunt sed tacebimus
   c vocabunt et servabunt   **f** flebit et lugebit

g ardebo sed mulcebis   **i** narrabo et spectabitis
h horrebunt et terrebimus   **j** aedificabit sed delebunt

11 Translate the following into Latin. The verb you should use is given in brackets.

e.g. *she will work* (**laboro**) → **laborabit**

a I shall ponder (**cogito**)   **f** it will please (**placeo**)
b we shall fly (**volo**)   **g** you (s.) will owe (**debeo**)
c they will alter (**muto**)   **h** I shall announce (**nuntio**)
d you (pl.) will mourn (**lugeo**)   **i** they will call (**voco**)
e she will warn (**moneo**)   **j** you (pl.) will have (**habeo**)

12 Translate the following into English. There is a mixture of present and future tenses in this exercise.

e.g. **stupet et ridebunt** → *he is amazed and they will laugh*

a dant sed debebitis   **f** aedificant sed delebimus
b pulsabunt et vocabo   **g** cogito sed pugnabunt
c pacas et tacebunt   **h** stat et manebit
d portamus sed aedificabitis   **i** paro et probabitis
e ambulas sed festinabimus   **j** comparabimus et computabitis

13 Write out the future tenses of the following verbs. Remember to look up their infinitives to check which conjugation they belong to.

e.g. **salio** (*I leap*), **saliam, salies, saliet, saliemus, salietis, salient**

a cingo (*I surround*)   **f** facio (*I make*)
b scribo (*I write*)   **g** iacio (*I hurl*)
c claudo (*I shut*)   **h** rapio (*I seize*)
d colo (*I cultivate*)   **i** dico (*I say*)
e peto (*I seek*)   **j** aperio (*I open*)

14 Translate these future tenses into English. Remember to look up words you do not know.

The words **sed** → *but*, **et** → *and* and **non** → *not* are included.
e.g. **curretis et ludemus** → *you will run and we shall play*

a dicam et credetis
b arcessemus sed non audient
c fodietis et traham
d non dormiet
e incipietis sed non perficietis
f fugient sed resistemus
g aperiam sed claudet
h quaerent sed non invenient
i discedes et adveniam
j adsentiemus sed dissentietis

15 Translate the following into Latin. The verb you should use is given in brackets.

e.g. *they will not leap* (**salio**) → **non salient**

a I shall dig (**fodio**)
b they will not begin (**incipio**)
c you (s.) will not play (**ludo**)
d he will agree (**adsentio**)
e I shall run (**curro**) but you (s.) will resist (**resisto**)
f they will arrive (**advenio**)
g she will capture (**capio**)
h you (pl.) will not believe (**credo**)
i we shall not yield (**cedo**)
j they will sleep (**dormio**) but we shall drag (**traho**)

16 Translate the following into English. There is a mixture of present and future tenses in this exercise.

e.g. **dormit et custodient** → *he is sleeping and they will guard*

a resistetis et non cedetis
b claudo sed aperient
c non adveniemus
d currit sed non fugiet
e ludis sed fodiam
f scribunt et non ludent
g non dicent
h peto et inveniam
i dicit sed non credetis
j scribis et non audies

17 Write out the imperfect tenses of the following verbs. Remember to check the infinitives to see which conjugation they belong to.

e.g. **scribo** (*I write*), **scribebam, scribebas, scribebat, scribebamus, scribebatis, scribebant**

a maneo (*I remain*)
b munio (*I fortify*)
c ceno (*I dine*)
d coquo (*I cook*)
e rego (*I rule*)
f venio (*I come*)
g lenio (*I soften*)
h ambulo (*I walk*)
i pono (*I put*)
j sedeo (*I sit*)

18 Translate these imperfect tenses into English. Remember to look up words which you do not know.

The words **sed** → *but*, **non** → *not* and **et** → *and* are included.

e.g. **laborabamus et fodiebamus** → *we were working and digging*

a sedebamus sed non dormiebamus

b pugnabatis et resistebatis

c audiebas et spectabas

d coquebam sed cenabant

e ambulabat et canebat

f tenebant et vocabant

g dicebas et non tacebant

h trahebam et gemebam

i ludebamus sed non ridebamus

j aedificabam et portabatis

19 Translate the following into imperfect tenses in Latin. The verb you should use is in brackets.

e.g. *we were writing and they were playing* → **scribebamus et ludebant**

a I slept (**dormio**) but they were not quiet (**taceo**)

b we spoke (**dico**) and they listened (**audio**)

c you (s.) did not watch (**specto**)

d I arrived (**advenio**) but you (pl.) departed (**discedo**)

e he used to agree (**assentio**)

f we were dragging (**traho**) and they were digging (**fodio**)

g she stood (**sto**) but we sat (**sedeo**)

h he summoned (**arcesso**) and you (s.) came (**venio**)

i we used to laugh (**rideo**) and they used to cry (**fleo**)

j I did not see (**video**)

20 Translate the following into English. There is a mixture of present, future and imperfect tenses.

e.g. **pulsabat et aperient** → *he was knocking and they will open*

a imperabat et parebatis

b non mutabit

c parabam, coquis et cenabunt

d resistebamus sed fugitis

e non scribebat

f portabamus, fodimus et aedificabimus

g currebam sed ambulas

h horrebant et timebamus

i sedebant et dormient

j dabatis et accipiebam

34

21 What is the third principal part of the following verbs? Write out the word in full. The verbs are from different conjugations.

e.g. terreo (*I frighten*) → terrui

a timeo (*I fear*)

b paro (*I prepare*)

c rego (*I rule*)

d cubo (*I lie down*)

e facio (*I make*)

f traho (*I drag*)

g tango (*I touch*)

h spargo (*I scatter*)

i frango (*I break*)

j sentio (*I feel*)

22 Write out the perfect tenses of the following first conjugation verbs. Remember that you will need to look up the verb to find the third principal part.

e.g. sto (*I stand*), steti, stetisti, stetit, stetimus, stetistis, steterunt

a demonstro (*I show*)

b seco (*I cut*)

c do (*I give*)

d curo (*I care for*)

e veto (*I forbid*)

f iuvo (*I help*)

g ambulo (*I walk*)

h mico (*I glitter*)

i amo (*I love*)

j neco (*I slay*)

23 Translate the following perfect tense first conjugation verbs into English.

e.g. stetimus → *we stood*

a aedificavistis

b dederunt

c appellavi

d servavisti

e locavimus

f comparaverunt

g paravit

h oravi

i secuisti

j vetuimus

24 Translate the following into the perfect tense of the first conjugation in Latin. The verb you should use is in brackets.

e.g. *they have walked* (ambulo) → ambulaverunt

a they hoped (**spero**)

b we have loved (**amo**)

c I gave (**do**)

d they have shown (**demonstro**)

e you (pl.) have forbidden (**veto**) **h** I have built (**aedifico**)
f it has stood (**sto**) **i** you (s.) have swum (**no**)
g she has related (**narro**) **j** he has called (**voco**)

25 It is important to be able to find out which verb a particular perfect stem belongs to. Use your dictionary to find out which verb the following perfect tenses come from and translate the verb. You should look for a verb which starts with the same few letters and check the third principal part. This will take some patience but do not give up because you will be practising a very important skill. There is a mixture of conjugations in this exercise.

e.g. **movi** → **moveo** (*I move*)

a credidi	**f** vinxi
b vetui	**g** sedi
c veni	**h** custodivi
d vidi	**i** tenui
e potavi	**j** fugi

26 Write out the perfect tenses of the following verbs. There is a mixture of conjugations.

e.g. **scribo** (*I write*), **scripsi, scripsisti, scripsit, scripsimus, scripsistis, scripserunt**

a quaero (*I seek*)	**f** ludo (*I play*)
b cedo (*I yield*)	**g** vinco (*I conquer*)
c pono (*I put*)	**h** curro (*I run*)
d effluo (*I rush out*)	**i** rideo (*I smile*)
e rumpo (*I burst*)	**j** deleo (*I destroy*)

27 Translate the following into the perfect tense in Latin. The verb you should use is in brackets.

e.g. *we have heard* → **audivimus**

a he has found (**invenio**)	**d** I dragged (**traho**)
b they have seen (**video**)	**e** we have worshipped (**colo**)
c you (pl.) have waited (**maneo**)	**f** you (s.) have said (**dico**)

g they led (**duco**)
h she has captured (**capio**)
i it has thundered (**tono**)
j they have pondered (**cogito**)

28 Translate the following perfect tenses into English. Remember to look up the verb carefully.

e.g. **timuerunt** → *they feared*

a effluxit
b pressistis
c lusi
d quaesiverunt
e risisti

f duxit
g collocavimus
h posuimus
i ceperunt
j posuisti

29 Write out the pluperfect tenses of the following verbs.

e.g. **sentio** (*I feel*), **senseram, senseras, senserat, senseramus, senseratis, senserant**

a mordeo (*I bite*)
b titillo (*I tickle*)
c solvo (*I undo*)
d postulo (*I demand*)
e emano (*I leak out*)

f capto (*I try to capture*)
g mitto (*I send*)
h reduco (*I lead back*)
i statuo (*I establish*)
j verbero (*I beat*)

30 Translate the following pluperfects into English. Remember to check which verb they come from.

e.g. **posueram** → *I had placed*

a monueratis
b comparaverant
c ceperam
d amaveramus
e cucurreras

f luserat
g inspexeratis
h concesserant
i foderas
j vetueram

31 Translate the following into Latin. The verb you should use is in brackets.

e.g. *you* (pl.) *had slept* → **dormiveratis**

a we had stood (**sto**)
b you (s.) had waited (**maneo**)

c I had thought (**puto**)
d they had caught (**capio**)

e she had escaped (**effugio**)　　**h** I had sat (**sedeo**)
f it had slept (**dormio**)　　**i** he had guarded (**custodio**)
g you (pl.) had thrown (**iacio**)　　**j** we had placed (**pono**)

32 Translate the following into English. This exercise contains a mixture of perfect and pluperfect tenses. Remember to check the verbs in your dictionary.

e.g. **mansi sed discesseras** → *I remained but you* (s.) *had left*

a non celaveram sed fleverunt　　**f** ambulaverunt sed cucurreramus
b dormivit et laboraveratis　　**g** docuerat et audiverant
c aedificaveramus sed deleverunt　　**h** spectaveras sed non vidisti
d portaverant et foderamus　　**i** non mutaveratis
e clauserat sed aperui　　**j** coxeram et cenaverunt

33 Write out the future perfect tenses of these verbs.

e.g. **mitto** (*I send*), **misero, miseris, miserit, miserimus, miseritis, miserint**

a cano (*I sing*)　　**f** praebeo (*I offer*)
b accipio (*I receive*)　　**g** compleo (*I fill*)
c verto (*I turn*)　　**h** veho (*I convey*)
d tendo (*I stretch*)　　**i** surgo (*I rise*)
e trado (*I betray*)　　**j** discedo (*I depart*)

34 Translate the following future perfect tenses into English. Remember to check which verb they come from.

e.g. **traxerint** → *they will have dragged*

a duxeris　　**f** ambulaverimus
b manseritis　　**g** cepero
c vocavero　　**h** venerint
d monuerint　　**i** posueris
e feceritis　　**j** discesserimus

35 Translate the following into Latin. The verbs you should use are in brackets.

e.g. *we shall have seen* → **viderimus**

a she will have felt (**sentio**)

b it will have changed (**muto**)

c they will have watched (**specto**)

d I shall have owed (**debeo**)

e he will have wept (**fleo**)

f you (pl.) will have made (**facio**)

g we shall have lived (**vivo**)

h you (s.) will have sought (**peto**)

i they will have assembled (**convenio**)

j I shall have turned (**verto**)

36 Translate the following into English. This exercise contains a mixture of perfect and future perfect tenses. Remember to check the verbs in your dictionary.

e.g. **advenero sed discessit** → *I shall have arrived but he has left*

a timui et timueris

b mansitis sed effugerint

c laboraverimus et dormiveritis

d dedero et acceperit

e discesserint sed non advenistis

f cucurreris sed ambulavero

g narravit et audiverint

h imperavit et paruerint

i rogavisti et responderit

j coxit et cenavero

37 Translate the following into Latin. Notice that *non* not comes before the verb

e.g. *we have not been* → **non fuimus**

a I shall be

b it is not

c we used to be

d they were being

e you (pl.) will be

f you (s.) had been

g she will have been

h I was

i I have been

j we have been

38 Translate the following into English.

e.g. **fuistis** → *you* (pl.) *have been*

a erant

b fuerint

c fuerunt

d erit

e sunt

f sumus

g eramus

h fueram

i estis

j erunt

39 What tense do these parts of the verb come from?
e.g. **fuerat** → pluperfect

a eratis   **f** fuisti
b est   **g** fuerant
c fuerunt   **h** fueris
d erunt   **i** erit
e sumus   **j** eramus

Points to remember

1 Present tense endings are -o, -s, -t, -mus, -tis, -nt.

2 Future tense endings for the first and second conjugations are -bo, -bis, -bit, -bimus, -bitis, -bunt.

3 Future tense endings for the third and fourth conjugations are -am, -es, -et, -emus, -etis, -ent.

4 Imperfect tense endings are -bam, -bas, -bat, -bamus, -batis, -bant.

5 Perfect tense endings are -i, -isti, -it, -imus, -istis, -erunt.

6 Pluperfect tense endings are -eram, -eras, -erat, -eramus, -eratis, -erant.

7 Future Perfect tense endings are -ero, -eris, -erit, -erimus, -eritis, -erint.

8 Some verbs in the third declension, like **capio** (*I take*) and **facio** (*I make*), have the letter i at the end of their stems, like fourth conjugation verbs.

9 The formation of the present, future and imperfect tenses are based on the first principal part of a verb.

10 The formation of the perfect, pluperfect and future perfect tenses are based on the third principal part of the verb.

3

Nouns

First declension

A The **first declension** has mostly **feminine** nouns but the names of some male roles are **masculine,** e.g. **agricola agricolae** → *farmer*, **poeta, poetae** → *poet* and **scriba scribae** → *scribe*.

B The **case endings** for the **first declension** which are added to the present stem are as follows. Notice the ending -ae in the genitive singular which characterizes this declension.

Singular		Plural	
nominative	**-a**	nominative	**-ae**
vocative	**-a**	vocative	**-ae**
accusative	**-am**	accusative	**-ās**
genitive	**-ae**	genitive	**-ārum**
dative	**-ae**	dative	**-īs**
ablative	**-ā**	ablative	**-īs**

Notice that some cases end in the same way so we need to know the context in which a word is used to know which case is which. Notice also that the ablative singular ends in a long **a.**

▶ The model for a regular first declension noun is **puella -ae** f. → *girl*.

nom.	**puella**	*girl* (subject)
voc.	**puella**	*o girl* (when addressing her)
acc.	**puellam**	*girl* (object)
gen.	**puellae**	*of a girl*
dat.	**puellae**	*to or for a girl*
abl.	**puella**	*by, with or from a girl*

nom.	**puellae**	*girls* (subject)
voc.	**puellae**	*o girls* (when addressing them)
acc.	**puellas**	*girls* (object)
gen.	**puellarum**	*of girls*
dat.	**puellis**	*to or for girls*
abl.	**puellis**	*by, with or from girls*

C The nouns **filia** (*daughter*) and **dea** (*goddess*) have as their dative and ablative plural endings **filiābus** and **deābus**, to avoid confusion with **filiīs** and **deīs**, the dative and ablative plurals of the nouns **filius** (*son*) and **deus** (*god*) from the second declension.

Second declension

Basic forms.

D Most nouns of the **second declension** are either **masculine**, like **taurus** → *bull*, **filius** → *son*, **puer** → *boy* and **ager** → *field* or neuter, like **templum** → *temple*. The very few **feminine** words in it decline like **taurus**, e.g. **humus** → *ground* or **pinus** → *pine tree*. There are three unusual neuter nouns which decline like **taurus: pelagus** → *sea*, **virus** → *venom* and **vulgus** → *crowd* (sometimes masculine).

E The standard **case endings** for the **second declension** are as follows. Note the long **-i** in the ending of the genitive singular which characterizes this declension.

	Singular	Plural
nominative	**-us, -ius** or **-er** (m.) **-um** (n.)	**-ī** (m.) **-a** (n.)
vocative	**-e, -i** or **-er** (m.) **-um** (n.)	**-ī** (m.) **-a** (n.)
accusative	**-um**	**-ōs** (m.) **-a** (n.)
genitive	**-ī**	**-ōrum**
dative	**-ō**	**-īs**
ablative	**-ō**	**-īs**

▶ Most **masculine** nouns of this declension decline like **taurus -i** (*bull*).

Notice that the vocative singular is different from the nominative in nouns like this (see Unit 4A4).

	Singular	Plural
nom.	**taurus**	**tauri**
voc.	**taure**	**tauri**
acc.	**taurum**	**tauros**
gen.	**tauri**	**taurorum**
dat.	**tauro**	**tauris**
abl.	**tauro**	**tauris**

▶ All **neuter** nouns in the **second declension** decline like **templum -i** (*temple*).

Notice that, as with all neuter nouns, the nominative, vocative and accusative cases have the same endings in the singular and the same endings in the plural.

	Singular	Plural
nom. and voc.	**templum**	**templa**
acc.	**templum**	**templa**
gen.	**templi**	**templorum**
dat.	**templo**	**templis**
abl.	**templo**	**templis**

F Forms in -er and -ius.

▶ Words in this declension which go like **puer pueri** m. → *boy* and **ager agri** m. → *field* end in -er in the nominative and vocative singular but otherwise the endings are the same as those for **taurus**. Notice that the **stem** of **ager** (**agr-**) does not contain the letter **e** which was in the nominative and vocative. Words like **ager** (e.g. **magister magistri** m. → *teacher*) do not have the letter **e** in their stem but words like **puer pueri** *always* do.

	Singular	*Plural*
nom. and voc.	**ager**	**agri**
acc.	**agrum**	**agros**
gen.	**agri**	**agrorum**
dat	**agro**	**agris**
abl.	**agro**	**agris**

▶ The declension of **filius -ii** m. → *son* is slightly different from that of **taurus**.

	Singular	*Plural*
nom.	**filius**	**filii**
voc.	**fili**	**filii**
acc.	**filium**	**filios**
gen.	**filii** (or **fili**)	**filiorum**
dat.	**filio**	**filiis**
abl.	**filio**	**filiis**

Notice that the **vocative singular** ends in -i and that the genitive singular can end in -i or -ii. The word **genius** → *spirit* and proper names ending in -ius, like **Valerius**, decline like **filius**. Neuter nouns ending in -ium have a genitive singular ending -i or -ii.

G The declension of **vir viri** m. → *man* or *hero*, is slightly different from **puer**.

	Singular	Plural
nom. and voc.	**vir**	**viri**
acc.	**virum**	**viros**
gen.	**viri**	**virorum** (or **virum**)
dat.	**viro**	**viris**
abl.	**viro**	**viris**

H The declension of **deus dei** m. → *god* is different from **taurus** (nominative and vocative are the same).

	Singular	Plural
nom. and voc.	**deus**	**dei** or **di**
acc.	**deum**	**deos**
gen.	**dei**	**deorum** or **deum**
dat.	**deo**	**deis** or **dis**
abl.	**deo**	**deis** or **dis**

Romans usually called on deities by name, like Mars or Venus.

I A genitive plural in **-um** rather than **-orum** is sometimes found, especially in words for coins, sums, weights and measures like **talentum** → *talent* and **nummus** → *coin*. This can also happen with **socius** → *ally*, **faber** → *craftsman*, **liberi** → *children* and **superi** → *the gods*.

Third declension

Increasing nouns.
J Knowing the **stem** (Unit 1R) of a noun is important for understanding the **third declension** because the nominatives often

look quite different from the genitives. Take care to check the genitive when you look words up in a dictionary. There are two categories:

▶ Nouns with more syllables in the genitive singular than in the nominative are called **increasing nouns**. These have a genitive plural ending in **-um** and are sometimes called nouns with consonant stems.

▶ Nouns with the same number of syllables in the genitive singular as in the nominative are sometimes called **non-increasing nouns**. These have a genitive plural ending in **-ium** and are also called nouns with vowel stems.

K The structure and **case endings** of **increasing** nouns follow. Notice the ending **-is** in the genitive singular which characterizes this declension. The nominatives have various endings.

	Singular	*Plural*
nom.	various	**stem+-ēs** (m. and f.) **-a** (n.)
voc.	various	**stem+-ēs** (m. and f.) **-a** (n.)
acc.	**stem+-em** (m. and f.) various (n.)	**stem+-ēs** (m. and f.) **-a** (n.)
gen.	**stem+-is**	**stem+-um**
dat.	**stem+-ī**	**stem+ -ibus**
abl.	**stem+-e**	**stem+ -ibus**

▶ A good example of the **masculine** and **feminine** nouns of this type is **leo leonis** (m.) → *lion*:

	Singular	*Plural*
nom. and voc.	**leo**	**leones**
acc.	**leonem**	**leones**
gen.	**leonis**	**leonum**
dat.	**leoni**	**leonibus**
abl.	**leone**	**leonibus**

▶ A good model for the **neuter** nouns is **corpus corporis** → *body*:

	Singular	Plural
nom. and voc.	**corpus**	**corpora**
acc.	**corpus**	**corpora**
gen.	**corporis**	**corporum**
dat.	**corpori**	**corporibus**
abl.	**corpore**	**corporibus**

L Exceptions

▶ There are some nouns which increase the number of syllables in the genitive singular but are technically non-increasing nouns with vowel stems. These decline like **urbs urbis** f. → *city* with a genitive plural ending in **-ium** (see **N**).

▶ There are also some nouns with consonant stems which are non-increasing and have a genitive plural ending in **-um**. Most of these are the 'family' words: **pater patris** m. → *father*, **mater matris** f. → *mother*, **frater fratris** m. → *brother*, **iuvenis iuvenis** m. → *young man* and **canis canis** m. or f. → *dog*. These decline like **senex** (see **X**)

Non-increasing nouns.

M The structure and standard **case endings** of **non-increasing** nouns are as follows. Note the genitive singular ending **-is** which characterizes the declension.

	Singular	Plural
nom.	**stem** + **-is** or **-ēs** (m. and f.) **-e, -l** or **-r** (n.)	**stem** + **-ēs** (m. and f.) **-ia** (n.)
voc.	**stem** + **-is** or **-ēs** (m. and f.) **-e, -l** or **-r** (n.)	**stem** + **-ēs** (m. and f.) **-ia** (n.)
acc.	**stem** + **-em** or **-im** (m. and f.) **-e, -l** or **-r** (n.)	**stem** + **-ēs** or **-īs** (m. and f.) **-ia** (n.)
gen.	**stem** + **-is**	**stem** + **-ium**
dat.	**stem** + **-ī**	**stem** + **-ibus**
abl.	**stem** + **-ī** or **-e**	**stem** + **-ibus**

There are some nouns of this type with nominatives in -er, e.g. **venter ventris** m. → *stomach*.

▶ An example of the **masculine** and **feminine** nouns of this type is **civis, civis** m. → *citizen*.

	Singular	Plural
nom. and voc.	**civis**	**cives**
acc.	**civem**	**cives** or **civis**
gen.	**civis**	**civium**
dat.	**civi**	**civibus**
abl.	**civi** or **cive**	**civibus**

Nouns which have the accusative ending -**im** are not common. Examples are **vis** f. → *force*, **sitis** f. → *thirst*, **turris** f. → *tower*, **puppis** f. → *stern deck*, **securis** f. → *axe* and **Tiberis** m. → *the river Tiber*.

▶ In the **neuter** nominative singulars the last vowel of the stem (-**i**) is dropped (**animal animalis** → *animal*) or changes to an -**e** (**cubile cubilis** → *couch*).

	Singular	Plural
nom. and voc.	**cubile**	**cubilia**
acc.	**cubile**	**cubilia**
gen.	**cubilis**	**cubilium**
dat. and abl.	**cubili**	**cubilibus**

In the ablative singular **rete** → *net* ends in -**e**, while **mare** → *sea* ends in either -**i** or -**e**.

N Some nouns which have more syllables in the genitive than in the nominative still decline like **non-increasing** nouns with a genitive plural ending in -**ium**. They are mostly nouns of one syllable ending in a double consonant like **urbs urbis** f. → *city* (see L).

Other examples: **mons montis** m. → *mountain*, **arx arcis** f. → *citadel*, **ars artis** f. → *art*, **nox noctis** f. → *night*, **dens dentis** m. → *tooth*.

	Singular	Plural
nom. and voc.	**urbs**	**urbes**
acc.	**urbem**	**urbes**
gen.	**urbis**	**urbium**
dat.	**urbi**	**urbibus**
abl.	**urbe**	**urbibus**

Fourth declension

O The nouns of the **fourth declension** are mostly masculine, like **gradus** → *step*. Common feminine nouns are **manus** → *hand*, **porticus** → *colonnade*, **tribus** → *tribe* and **Idus** → *Ides* (see Unit 17C). Common neuter nouns are **genu** → *knee*, **cornu** → *horn* and **veru** → *a spit*.

P The following are the **case endings** for **fourth declension** nouns. Notice the genitive ending **-us** (with a long **u**) which is characteristic of this declension.

	Singular		Plural	
nom.	**-us** (m. and f.)	**-u** (n.)	**-ūs** (m. and f.)	**-ua** (n.)
voc.	**-us** (m. and f.)	**-u** (n.)	**-ūs** (m. and f.)	**-ua** (n.)
acc.	**-um** (m. and f.)	**-u** (n.)	**-ūs** (m. and f.)	**-ua** (n.)
gen.	**-ūs**		**-uum**	
dat.	**-uī** (m. and f.)	**-ū** (n.)	**-ibus**	
abl.	**-ū**		**-ibus**	

▶ The **masculine** and **feminine** nouns of this declension decline like **gradus** m. → *step*.

	Singular	Plural
nom. and voc.	**gradus**	**gradus**
acc.	**gradum**	**gradus**
gen.	**gradus**	**graduum**
dat.	**gradui**	**gradibus**
abl.	**gradu**	**gradibus**

▶ The very few **neuter** nouns in the fourth declension decline like **genu** → *knee*.

	Singular	Plural
nom. and voc.	**genu**	**genua**
acc.	**genu**	**genua**
gen.	**genus**	**genuum**
dat. and abl.	**genu**	**genibus**

Q In some words the dative and ablative plural ends in the more ancient form **-ubus**, rather than **-ibus**. This is always found in **arcus** m. → *bow* (arc**ubus**), tribus f. → *tribe* (trib**ubus**) and occasionally in **partus** m. → *offspring* (part**ubus**), artus m. → *limb, joint* (art**ubus**) and some other words.

Fifth declension

R All **fifth declension** nouns are feminine except for **dies** m. → *day* and its compound **meridies** m. → *midday*. However, even **dies** can be feminine if the day referred to is an appointed day. There are no neuters. Some nouns in this declension do not have plural forms.

S The **case endings** for the **fifth declension** are as follows. Notice the genitive singular ending in **-ei** which is characteristic of this declension.

	Singular	Plural
nom.	-ēs	-ēs
voc.	-ēs	-ēs
acc.	-em	-ēs
gen.	-eī	-ērum
dat.	-eī	-ēbus
abl.	-ē	-ēbus

▶ The declension of **dies** m. → *day* looks like this.

	Singular	Plural
nom.	dies	dies
voc.	dies	dies
acc.	diem	dies
gen.	diei	dierum
dat.	diei	diebus
abl.	die	diebus

▶ The word **res rei** f. → *thing* has a huge number of meanings. It basically means *thing* but it can also mean *issue, matter, story, object, affair, business, fact, the universe* and so on.

When it combines with the feminine adjective **publica** → *public* it means *state* or *republic* and both parts of the word decline.

	Singular	Plural
nom.	respublica	respublicae
voc.	respublica	respublicae
acc.	rempublicam	respublicas
gen.	reipublicae	rerumpublicarum
dat.	reipublicae	rebuspublicis
abl.	republica	rebuspublicis

Greek nouns

As Greek literature had a great influence on the Roman world
we find many Greek nouns used in Latin, mostly proper names.
These took on Latin forms and, often, Latin endings. However,
you will meet some which retain their Greek endings. Some nouns
are found with both Latin and Greek forms in their endings.
They may appear confusing at first because of the large variety of
forms but the general pattern is easy to get used to.

T **First declension** Greek nouns are of three types and most are
proper names. The **plurals** are the same as the normal first
declension nouns (see B).

▶ Examples are Aeneas m. (a Trojan hero) Anchises m. (Aeneas'
  father) and Circe f. (a goddess).

nom.	**Aenēās**	**Anchisēs**	**Circē** (or **-a**)
voc.	**Aenēā**	**Anchisē** (or **-ā**)	**Circē** (or **-a**)
acc.	**Aenēān**	**Anchisēn** (or **-an**)	**Circēn** (or **-am**)
gen.	**Aenēae**	**Anchisae**	**Circēs** (or **-ae**)
dat.	**Aenēae**	**Anchisae**	**Circae**
abl.	**Aenēā**	**Anchisē** (or **-ā**)	**Circē** (or **-ā**)

▶ **Patronymics** are names which mean 'son of' and end in **-ides**,
  like **Atr*ides*** → *son of Atreus* (Agamemnon) or **Pel*ides*** → *son
  of Peleus* (Achilles). These are declined like Anchises and their
  genitive plural ends in **-um.**

U **Second declension** Greek nouns are mostly proper names of two
types. Examples are **Delos** f. (the Aegean island where Apollo
and Artemis were born) and **Pelion** n. (a Greek mountain).

nom.	**Delos**	**Pelion**	gen.	**Delī**	**Pelī**
voc.	**Delos**	**Pelion**	dat.	**Delō**	**Peliō**
acc.	**Delon** (or **-um**)	**Pelion**	abl.	**Delō**	**Peliō**

V Third declension Greek nouns

	Singular	Plural
nom.	**cratēr**	**cratēres**
voc.	**cratēr**	**cratēres**
acc.	**cratēra** (or **-em**)	**cratēras** (or **-es**)
gen.	**cratēros** (or **-is**)	**cratērum**
dat.	**cratērī**	**cratēribus**
abl.	**cratēre**	**cratēribus**

▶ The declension of **crater crateris** (m.) *mixing bowl* gives the basic structure.

▶ There is a great variety of endings in the nominative of third declension Greek nouns, e.g. **heros herois** m. → *hero*, **Socrates Socratis** m. → *Socrates* (a philosopher), **Orpheus Orphei** m. → *Orpheus* (a poet), **Dido Didonis** f. → *Dido* (queen of Carthage) and **Paris Paridis** m. → *Paris* (a Trojan prince). Individual entries in a good dictionary will give you any unusual case endings.

▶ The third declension names in **-eus, -es** or **-is** can also form their vocative by dropping the **-s**, e.g. **Pari** (as well as **Paris**). They can also end their accusatives with **-n** or **-m**, e.g. **Socraten** or **Socratem; Parin** or **Parim** (as well as **Parida** or **Paridem**).

Irregular nouns

W **domus domus** f. → *house* has endings from the second and fourth declensions. The special locative forms (Unit 4F4) of **domus** are **domum** → *homeward*, **domi** → *at home* and **domo** → *from home*.

	Singular	Plural
nom.	domus	domūs
voc.	domus	domūs
acc.	domum	domūs or domōs
gen.	domūs	domuum or domōrum
dat.	domuī or domō	domibus
abl.	domō	domibus

X Important **third declension** irregular nouns are:

▶ **vis** f. → *violence, force*. This noun is **defective**. In other words it does not have all its cases. In the plural it means *strength*. Be careful not to confuse it with **vir** → *man* (see Unit G).

	Singular	Plural
nom.	vis	virēs
voc.	—	virēs
acc.	vim	virēs
gen	—	virium
dat.	—	viribus
abl.	vī	viribus

▶ **senex senis** m. → *old man* is a non-increasing noun but has a genitive ending in -**um**.

	Singular	Plural
nom.	senex	senēs
voc.	senex	senēs
acc.	senem	senēs
gen.	senis	senum
dat.	senī	senibus
abl.	sene	senibus

▶ **bos bovis** m. → *ox.*

	Singular	Plural
nom.	**bōs**	**bovēs**
voc.	**bōs**	**bovēs**
acc.	**bovem**	**bovēs**
gen.	**bovis**	**boum**
dat.	**bovī**	**bōbus** or **būbus**
abl.	**bove**	**bōbus** or **būbus**

▶ Jupiter, king of the gods.

nom.	**Iuppiter**
voc.	**Iuppiter**
acc.	**Iovem**
gen.	**Iovis**
dat.	**Iovi**
abl.	**Iove**

1 Write out the genitive singular, gender and meaning of the following first declension nouns.

e.g. **ianua** → **ianuae**, feminine, *door*

a charta	**f** area
b insula	**g** incola
c nauta	**h** via
d agricola	**i** nebula
e ancilla	**j** mensa

2 Write out the full declensions, singular and plural, of the following nouns.

e.g. **ara** (*altar*)

	Singular	Plural		
nom. →	**ara**	**arae**	**a** ripa (*river bank*)	**d** matrona (*lady*)
voc. →	**ara**	**arae**	**b** regina (*queen*)	**e** taberna (*shop*)
acc. →	**aram**	**aras**	**c** carina (*keel*)	**f** porta (*gate*)

gen.	→ arae	ararum	**g** clementia (*mercy*)
dat.	→ arae	aris	**h** dea (*goddess*)
abl.	→ ara	aris	

i cauda (*tail*)
j femina (*woman*)

3 Write out the following cases of these nouns.
e.g. the genitive plural of **ora** (*shore*) → **orarum**

a the accusative plural of **sagitta** (*arrow*)
b the genitive plural of **rosa** (*rose*)
c the accusative singular of **vacca** (*cow*)
d the dative singular of **sapientia** (*wisdom*)
e the ablative plural of **hasta** (*spear*)
f the dative plural of **sella** (*seat*)
g the genitive singular of **ballista** (*war catapult*)
h the ablative plural of **ala** (*wing*)
i the ablative singular of **iustitia** (*justice*)
j the vocative plural of **fera** (*wild beast*)

4 What case and number are these first declension nouns?
If there is more than one possible answer give them all.
Get used to using the abbreviations for case and number.
e.g. **ranae** (*frog*) → 1. gen. sing. 2. dat. sing. 3. nom. pl. 4. voc. pl.

a pennam (*feather*)
b casis (*cottage*)
c formicas (*ant*)
d togae (*toga*)
e capellis (*nanny goat*)
f linguas (*tongue*)
g arca (*box*)
h Italiam (*Italy*)
i fortunarum (*luck, fortune*)
j curae (*concern*)

5 Write out the genitive singular, gender and meaning of the following second declension nouns. They all decline like **taurus** or **templum**.
e.g. **dominus** → **domini**, masculine, *master*

a discipulus
b frumentum
c ventus
d maritus
e colus
f annus
g somnus
h eventum
i bellum
j umerus

6 Write out the full declensions, singular and plural, of the following nouns.

e.g. **equus** (*horse*)

	Singular	Plural
nom. →	**equus**	**equi**
voc. →	**eque**	**equi**
acc. →	**equum**	**equos**
gen. →	**equi**	**equorum**
dat. →	**equo**	**equis**
abl. →	**equo**	**equis**

a oculus (*eye*)
b legatus (*delegate*)
c lapillus (*pebble*)
d rostrum (*beak, prow*)
e praefectus (*prefect*)
f ludus (*play, school*)
g stilus (*pen*)
h pullus (chicken)
i animus (*mind*)
j iocus (*joke*)

7 Write out the following cases of these nouns.

e.g. the accusative plural of **cuniculus** (*rabbit*) → **cuniculos**

a the genitive singular of **digitus** (*finger, toe*)
b the dative plural of **officium** (*duty*)
c the vocative singular of **camelus** (*camel*)
d the ablative singular of **somnium** (*dream*)
e the accusative singular of **campus** (*plain*)
f the nominative plural of **odium** (*hatred*)
g the genitive plural of **initium** (*beginning*)
h the ablative plural of **medicus** (*doctor*)
i the accusative plural of **funambulus** (*tightrope walker*)
j the dative singular of **ferrum** (*iron, sword*)

8 What case and number are these second declension nouns? If there is more than one possible answer give them all.

e.g. **dona** (*gift*) → 1. nom. pl. 2. voc. pl. 3. acc. pl.

a tribuni (*tribune*)
b rivulis (*brook*)
c gladium (*sword*)
d tela (*weapon*)
e unguento (*ointment, perfume*)
f vinum (*wine*)
g cumulorum (*heap*)
h psittaco (*parrot*)
i ovi (*egg*)
j servi (*slave*)

9 Write out the genitive singular, gender and meaning of the following second declension nouns.

e.g. alabaster → alabastri, masculine, *perfume box*

a	Auster	**e**	administer	**i**	furcifer
b	Hister	**f**	aquilifer	**j**	laniger
c	caper	**g**	culter		
d	cancer	**h**	aper		

10 Write out the full declensions, singular and plural where appropriate, of the following nouns. Remember to check the genitive.

e.g. **gener** (*son-in-law*)

	Singular	Plural
nom.	→ **gener**	**generi**
voc.	→ **gener**	**generi**
acc.	→ **generum**	**generos**
gen.	→ **generi**	**generorum**
dat.	→ **genero**	**generis**
abl.	→ **genero**	**generis**

a arbiter (*umpire*)
b Lucifer (*the morning star, the planet Venus*) (singular only)
c ingenium (*nature, disposition*)
d Cornelius (*Cornelius*)
e Alexander (*Alexander*) (singular only)
f socer (*father-in-law*)
g liber (*book*)
h socius (*ally*)
i armiger (*armour bearer*)
j studium (*zeal, study*)

11 Write out the following cases of these nouns.
e.g. the dative plural of **aper** (*boar*) → **apris**

a the genitive plural of **liberi** (*children*)
b the dative singular of **trifurcifer** (*hardened criminal*)
c the accusative singular of **minister** (*attendant*)
d the ablative plural of **puer** (*boy*)
e the dative plural of **oleaster** (*wild olive*)

f the nominative plural of **fiber** (*beaver*)
g the vocative singular of **Tiberius** (*Tiberius*)
h the genitive singular of **faber** (*craftsman*)
i the accusative plural of **magister** (*teacher*)
j the ablative singular of **semivir** (*half-man*)

12 What case and number are these second declension nouns? If there is more than one possible answer give them all.

e.g. **deum** (*god*) → 1. acc. sing. 2. alternative gen. pl.

a libros (*book*)
b socer (*father-in-law*)
c magistro (*teacher*)
d pueri (*boy*)
e Iuli (*Julius*)
f fabrum (*craftsman*)
g ministri (*attendant*)
h socii (*ally*)
i liberis (*children*)
j ingenia (*nature, disposition*)

13 Write out the genitive singular, gender and meaning of the following third declension nouns.

e.g. **imperator** → **imperatoris**, masculine, *general*

a tempus
b consul
c caput
d miles
e coniunx
f iudex
g tempestas
h clamor
i opus
j dolor

14 When you meet third declension increasing nouns in your reading they will often not be in the nominative case and you will need to be able to look the noun up in a dictionary from knowing only the word you have in front of you. You should look for a noun which starts with the same few letters and check the genitive singular. If the stem of the genitive is the same as the stem of the word you are checking then that is your noun.

Use your dictionary to find out which nouns the following cases come from and write down the nominative singular and meaning. This will take some patience but do not give up because you will be practising a very important skill.

e.g. **lapidibus** → **lapis** (*stone*)

a amorum	**e** nomina	**i** aequoribus
b pariete	**f** salem	**j** homines
c aetates	**g** virtutum	
d custodis	**h** pecudi	

15 Write out the full declensions, singular and plural, of these nouns.

e.g. **rex** (*king*)

	Singular	Plural		
nom. →	**rex**	**reges**	**a** flos (*flower*)	**f** anser (*goose*)
voc. →	**rex**	**reges**	**b** dignitas (*worthiness*)	**g** laus (*praise*)
acc. →	**regem**	**reges**	**c** pes (*foot*)	**h** virgo (*maiden*)
gen. →	**regis**	**regum**	**d** aestas (*summer*)	**i** sol (*sun*)
dat. →	**regi**	**regibus**	**e** princeps (*chief*)	**j** carmen (*song*)
abl. →	**rege**	**regibus**		

16 What case and number are these third declension nouns? If there is more than one possible answer give them all.

e.g. **legionibus** (*legion*) → 1. dat. pl. 2. abl. pl.

a segetem (*crop*)	**f** corda (*heart*)
b libertate (*freedom*)	**g** quietis (*rest*)
c cineri (*cinder*)	**h** obsides (*hostage*)
d honorum (*honour*)	**i** nepotibus (*grandson*)
e ebur (*ivory*)	**j** litora (*shore*)

17 Write out the genitive singular, gender and meaning of the following third declension nouns.

e.g. **nubes** → **nubis**, feminine, *cloud*

a clades	**e** vectigal	**i** clavis
b ignis	**f** sedile	**j** iubar
c imber	**g** avis	
d amnis	**h** valles	

When you meet third declension non-increasing nouns in your reading they will not often be in the nominative case. As with increasing nouns, it is important to be able to find the nominative singular of the noun you are looking at. This is generally easier to do with non-increasing nouns because their nominative endings are more predictable (see exercise 14 above).

18 Use your dictionary to find which nouns the following cases belong to, then write down the nominative singular and meaning.

e.g. **cubilia** → **cubile** (*couch*)

a arietibus   **e** oves   **i** orbi
b ense   **f** crinis   **j** conclavia
c cutem   **g** axium
d securibus   **h** fronde

19 Write out the full declensions, singular and plural, of these nouns.

e.g. **rudis** (*practice sword*)

		Singular	Plural
nom.	→	**rudis**	**rudes**
voc.	→	**rudis**	**rudes**
acc.	→	**rudem**	**rudes** or **rudis**
gen.	→	**rudis**	**rudium**
dat.	→	**rudi**	**rudibus**
abl.	→	**rudi** or **rude**	**rudibus**

a puppis (*stern deck*)
b moles (*mass, bulk*)

20 What case and number are these third declension nouns? If there is more than one possible answer give them all.

e.g. **calcar** (*spur*) → 1. nom. sing. 2. voc. sing. 3. acc. sing.

a fami (*hunger*)   **d** bellis (*daisy*)   **h** stirpe (*stem*)
b nectaris (*nectar*)   **e** lintrem (*boat*)   **i** ancilia (*shield*)
c tribunal (*platform, judgement seat*)   **f** vermis (*worm*)   **j** vulpibus (*fox*)
    g artium (*art*)

21 Write out the full declensions, singular and plural, of these fourth declension nouns.

e.g. **veru** (*a spit*)

	Singular	Plural
nom. →	veru	verua
voc. →	veru	verua
acc. →	veru	verua
gen. →	verus	veruum
dat. →	veru	veribus
abl. →	veru	veribus

a saltus (*leap, mountain pass*)
b portus (*harbour*)
c cornu (*horn*)
d tribus (*tribe*)
e porticus (*colonnade*)
f ictus (*stroke, blow*)
g gemitus (*groan*)
h exitus (*exit*)
i impetus (*attack*)
j manus (*hand*)

22 What case and number are these fourth declension nouns? If there is more than one possible answer give them all.

e.g. **genibus** (*knee*) → 1. dat. pl. 2. abl. pl.

a artuum (*limb*)
b abitum (*departure*)
c magistratibus (*magistrate*)
d tonitru (*thunder*)
e versus (*verse*)
f arcui (*bow*)
g partubus (*offspring*)
h luctu (*lamentation*)
i monitus (*warning*)
j orsuum (*beginning*)

23 You will need to avoid confusion between the fourth and second declensions. Look up these nouns, check their genitives and say what declension they belong to.

e.g. **sonitus** (*sound*) → fourth declension

a coniectus (*heap, mass*)
b mundus (*world, universe*)
c quercus (*oak*)
d nodus (*knot*)
e mercatus (*trade*)
f questus (*complaint*)
g modulus (*measure*)
h ramus (*branch*)
i reditus (*return*)
j morsus (*bite*)

24 Write out the following cases of these nouns.

e.g. the ablative singular of **gradus** (*step*) → **gradu**

   a the genitive singular of **census** (*census*)
   b the dative plural of **circumiectus** (*enclosure*)
   c the accusative plural of **currus** (*chariot*)
   d the nominative plural of **electus** (*choice*)
   e the genitive plural of **anus** (*old woman*)
   f the dative singular of **usus** (*use*)
   g the ablative plural of **fructus** (*fruit, income*)
   h the accusative singular of **cursus** (*passage, course*)
   i the ablative singular of **domitus** (*taming*)
   j the vocative plural of **rictus** (*gaping jaws*)

25 Write out the genitive singular and meaning of the following fifth declension nouns.

e.g. **facies** → **faciei**, *face*

   a progenies   **f** congeries
   b pauperies   **g** temperies
   c caesaries   **h** materies
   d tristities   **i** macies
   e permities   **j** planities

26 Write out the full declensions, singular and plural, of the following fifth declension nouns.

e.g. **facies** (*face, appearance*)

		Singular	Plural
nom.	→	**facies**	**facies**
voc.	→	**facies**	**facies**
acc.	→	**faciem**	**facies**
gen.	→	**faciei**	**facierum**
dat.	→	**faciei**	**faciebus**
abl.	→	**facie**	**faciebus**

   a glacies (*ice*) (sing.)   **c** acies (*glance, battle line*)
   b canities (*grey hair, old age*) (sing.)   **d** effigies (*likeness, statue*)

e superficies (*surface*)　　　　**h** spes (*hope*)
f fides (*pledge, trust*)　　　　**i** species (*form, appearance*)
g meridies (*noon*)　　　　　　**j** diluvies (*flood*)

27 Which case and number are these fifth declension nouns? If there is more than one possible answer give them all.

e.g. **rei** (*thing*) → 1. gen. sing. 2. dat. sing.

a seriem (*row, series*)
b dierum (*day*)
c faciebus (*face, appearance*)
d meridiei (*midday*)
e sanie (*venom*)
f vastities (*ruin*)
g scabiem (*roughness, itch*)
h eluvie (*overflow, discharge*)
i rabiem (*madness*)
j carie (*dry rot*)

28 Write out the full declensions of the following first declension Greek nouns, in the singular only for proper names.

e.g. **campe** (*evasion*)

		Singular	Plural
nom.	→	campe	campae
voc.	→	campe	campae
acc.	→	campen	campas
gen.	→	campes	camparum
dat.	→	campae	campis
abl.	→	campe	campis

a Hylas (a friend of Hercules)
b Daphne (a nymph loved by Apollo)
c Atrides (son of Atreus) (include the plural)
d Hecate (goddess of witchcraft)
e harpe (*scimitar*)
f Boreas (the North Wind)
g crambe (*cabbage*)
h Cybele (an oriental goddess)
i Cyrene (a city in North Africa)
j Hebe (a nymph)

29 Write out the full declensions of the following second and third declension Greek nouns, in the singular only for proper names. Remember to check the genitive to see which declension they come from and to find their stems.

e.g. **Socrates** (*Socrates*)

Singular

nom.	→	**Socrates**
voc.	→	**Socrates** or **Socrate**
acc.	→	**Socraten** or **Socratem**
gen.	→	**Socratis**
dat.	→	**Socrati**
abl.	→	**Socrate**

  a lampas (*torch*)
  b lynx (*lynx*)
  c Babylon (a city)
  d Agamemnon (high king of Greece)
  e Pericles (an Athenian statesman)

  f Rhodos (Rhodes, an Aegean island)
  g Paris (a Trojan prince)
  h Orpheus (a poet)
  i Chios (an Aegean island)
  j heros (*hero*)

30 What case and number are the following Greek nouns? If there is more than one possible answer give them all.

e.g. **Panos** (the god Pan) → gen. sing.

  a chryso (*gold*)
  b Xerxen (Xerxes, king of Persia)
  c Platonis (Plato, a philosopher)
  d Naxi (Naxos, an Aegean island)
  e Didonem (Dido, queen of Carthage)

  f dorcadas (*gazelle*)
  g Tydeu (a hero, father of Diomede)
  h xiphiae (*swordfish*)
  i Typhoea (Typhoeus, a monster under Mt Etna)
  j Zancles (Messana, a town)

31 Write out the genitive singular, gender and meaning of the following Greek nouns. If you can, try to identify the proper names as well.

e.g. **Mithradates** → **Mithradatis**, masculine, Mithradates (a king of Pontus)

<table>
<tr><td>**a** poema</td><td>**e** Sophocles</td><td>**i** Theseus</td></tr>
<tr><td>**b** Euripides</td><td>**f** Eurydice</td><td>**j** Lemnos</td></tr>
<tr><td>**c** Phlegethon</td><td>**g** psephisma</td><td></td></tr>
<tr><td>**d** Tros</td><td>**h** Dione</td><td></td></tr>
</table>

32 Say what case and number the following nouns are and whether they come from *vis* → strength or *vir* → man. If there is more than one possible answer give them all.

e.g. **viro** → 1. dat. sing. 2. abl. sing. from **vir**

a vim	**f** virorum
b viris	**g** vi
c viros	**h** viri
d virum	**i** virium
e viribus	**j** vires

33 Write out the declensions of the following words which decline like *senex*. Remember to check the genitive.

e.g. **apis** (*bee*)

	Singular	Plural
nom. →	apis	apes
voc. →	apis	apes
acc. →	apem	apes
gen. →	apis	apum
dat. →	api	apibus
abl. →	ape	apibus

a frater (*brother*)	**f** sedes (*seat*)
b iuvenis (*young man*)	**g** accipiter (*hawk*)
c mater (*mother*)	**h** mensis (*month*)
d canis (*dog*)	**i** volucris (*bird*)
e pater (*father*)	**j** vates (*prophet*)

Points to remember

1 The declension of a noun is shown by its genitive singular ending which appears after the nominative in dictionary entries. These are -**ae** (first), -**ī** (second), -**is** (third), -**ūs** (fourth) and -**eī** (fifth).

2 The gender of nouns denoting male or female occupations is obvious. E.g. **mater** (*mother*) is feminine and **pater** (*father*) is masculine. Otherwise nouns can be of any gender. E.g. **fluvius** (masculine) and **flumen** (neuter) both mean *river*. As a general rule abstract nouns are feminine.

3 There are no neuter nouns in the first declension but plenty of masculine nouns and names. E.g. **nauta** (*sailor*), **scriba** (*scribe*), **agricola** (*farmer*), **poeta** (*poet*) and **Sulla** (the Roman dictator).

4 A second declension noun to watch out for is **vir** (*man* or *hero*) because it doesn't look exactly like the others in the declension. Be particularly careful not to confuse it with **vis** (*force*) from the third declension.

5 The increasing nouns in the third declension have one more syllable in the nominative singular than in the genitive singular.

6 The non-increasing nouns in the third declension have the same number of syllables in the nominative and genitive singular.

7 The masculine and feminine nouns of the fourth declension are not common and are easy to confuse with the masculine nouns of the second declension because their nominatives are the same. Watch out for this.

8 The nouns of the fifth declension are few in number and all feminine except for **dies** (*day*).

9 In the compound word **respublica** (*republic*), the nouns **res** and **publica** decline separately in their own declensions (fifth and first respectively).

10 Greek nouns used in Latin (mostly names) sometimes retain their original case endings. Note especially the third declension genitive singular ending -**os**.

4

Cases

A Nominative and vocative

1 Nominatives and vocatives are alike except in the singular of the second declension (see Unit 3E).

2 The subject

▶ The nominative case is the name of a noun and is used when that noun is the **subject** of a sentence. If the verb of a sentence is active (see Unit 1H), the subject is the person or thing performing the action of the verb.

e.g. *mus* elephantum terret → *the mouse frightens the elephant*. The mouse is doing the frightening so it is the subject.

▶ If the verb of the sentence is passive (see 1H and Unit 8), the subject is the person or thing experiencing the action of the verb.

e.g. *mus* ab elephanto terretur → *the mouse is frightened by the elephant*. The mouse is now experiencing the fright so it is the **subject**.

▶ In English we usually start our sentences with the subject but in Latin the subject can come anywhere in a sentence or clause (see Introduction).

e.g. *legiones* Gallos supervaerunt → *the legions have overcome the Gauls*

Caesaerem *Brutus* necavit → *Brutus killed Caesar*

plaustrum trahunt *boves* → *the oxen drag the plough*

3 The complement

The nominative is also used when one noun is the complement of another. In other words, the subject of the sentence is referred to by another noun.

e.g. **Caesar electus est *imperator*** → *Caesar has been chosen as general*. The noun **imperator** (*general*) refers to the subject (Caesar) and so is the **complement** and is in the nominative.

4 The vocative case

The **vocative case** is used when addressing someone or something.

e.g. **ave Caesar!** → *hail Caesar!*

salvete filii → *hello sons*

salve sol → *hello sun*

Examples of second declension vocatives are:

▶ **et tu Brute?** → *you too Brutus?* (Julius Caesar's dying words in Latin)
▶ **salve Valeri** → *hello Valerius*
▶ **o fili** → *o son*

5 Technically, the nominative case is known as the *casus rectus* but you will probably never meet this term. However, you will probably meet the term *oblique cases* which is another way of referring to all cases apart from the nominative.

B Accusative

Nouns in the accusative belong to one of the following categories.

1 The direct object

▶ The direct object, usually just called the object, is the noun which experiences or suffers the action of the verb when the verb is active (see Unit 1H) and transitive (see Unit 1M). When the verb is passive there is no object. The object is in the accusative case.

e.g. **mus *elephantum* terret** → *the mouse frightens the elephant*. The elephant suffers the fright so it is the object.

▶ In English we usually put the object after the verb but in Latin the object can come anywhere in a sentence or clause (see Introduction).

   e.g. *anserem* vulpes spectat → *the fox is watching the goose*
   corvus *caseum* gustat → *the crow is tasting the cheese*
   senator salutavit *amicum* → the senator greeted his *friend*

▶ Some verbs, usually of making, calling and teaching, take two accusatives, one of the person and another of the thing,

   e.g. *puerum Latinam* doceo → *I am teaching the boy Latin.*
   Tarquinium regem fecerunt → *they made Tarquin king.*

2 Extent of time or space

▶ For the accusative expressing duration of time ses G1.

▶ To express age, e.g. puer *decem annos* natus → *a ten-year-old boy* (i.e. born *for ten years*).

▶ To express extent of space, e.g. *tria mila* ambulabamus → *we walked for three miles*, draco *multa milia* aberat → *the dragon was many miles away*, rupes est *centum pedes* alta → *the crag is a hundred feet high*.

3 Direction towards

The accusative can mean motion towards, e.g. **Romam** → *to Rome*. (For more details and the **locative case**, see F.)

4 The accusative is used after certain **prepositions**, e.g. **ad curiam** → *to the senate house*. (See Unit 6 for a detailed account of prepositions.)

5 Internal accusative

This is also called the accusative of respect and the adverbial accusative. It is not used as the object of a verb, often refers to part of the body and is usually poetic, e.g. **saucius** *artus* → *wounded in (respect of) his limbs*.

6 Accusative of exclamation

This expresses amazement, disbelief, outrage or distress, often with an adjective, e.g. **o fortunatam Romam** → o *fortunate Rome* and **me miserum!** → *o wretched me!*

C Genitive

A good general rule is that the genitive is used for nouns which in English have the word 'of' before them. It has a wide variety of uses in Latin. Do not be put off by the official names. All the uses are straightforward.

1 Possessive genitive

▶ This is used as in English to express possession, e.g. **liber** *puellae* → *the girl's book* (i.e. the book *of the girl*) or **equus** *regis* → *the king's horse*.

▶ As in English this can be used to express association as well as ownership. This is sometimes called the subjective genitive, e.g. **libri** *Ovidii* → *the works of Ovid* (i.e. *books written by Ovid*), **coniuratio** *Catilinae* → *the conspiracy of Catiline* or **amor** *matris* → *the love* of *a mother* (i.e. the love felt *by* a mother).

2 Attributive genitive

This is used as in English to describe the content or material of which something consists, e.g. **acervus** *frumenti* → *a pile of corn* or **vincula** *ferri* → *shackles of iron*.

3 Appositional genitive or genitive of definition

This is used with another noun which it defines further, e.g. **ars** *scribendi* → *the art of writing* (for the verbal noun **scribendi** see gerund Unit 10E), **hoc nomen** *regis* → *this title* (*of*) *king* or **ipsum verbum** *veneni* → *the very word* (*of*) *poison*.

4 Genitive of characteristic

This is used where in English the characteristic, nature or duty of something is expressed, e.g. **est** *custodis* **curare portas** → *it is (the duty) of a guard* to look after the gates; **est** *viri pii* **deos colere** → *it is (the nature) of a pious man to worship the gods*.

5 Genitive of quality, description

This is used as in English with an adjective or number to express a quality of person or thing, as well as size, number and age, e.g. **vir** *egregiae virtutis* → *a man of outstanding valour*; **fossa** *viginti* *pedum* → *a ditch of twenty feet*; natio *quinque tribuum* → *a nation of five tribes*; puer *annorum septem* → *a boy of seven years*.

6 Objective genitive

This is used with nouns and adjectives (especially those ending in **-ax**) which contain a strong verbal sense, e.g. **odium *belli*** → *a hatred of war* and **amor *matris*** → *the love of a mother* (i.e. felt *for* a mother), **laudem tuam *nostri* amamus** → *we like your praise of us* (see also Unit 7A for the genitive pronoun **nostri**) and **mens *ingenii* capax** → *a mind capable of genius*.

7 Partitive genitive or genitive of the whole

▶ This is used when a part of a larger amount or number is referred to.

e.g. **pars *villae*** → *part of the estate*
partem *thesauri* celavit → *he hid part of the treasure*
multi *militum* → *many of the soldiers*
complures *nostrum* → *several of us* (see also Unit 7A on the genitive pronoun **nostrum**)

▶ The **partitive genitive** is often found with the following neuter pronouns and adjectives of quantity in a way not used in English. We generally leave out the 'of'.

e.g. **plus *vini*** → *more (of) wine* (see also Unit 5L on **plus** → *more*)

aliquid *novi* → *some (of) news*

quid *novi*? → *what (of) news?*

multum *sanguinis* → *much (of) blood*

satis *clamorum* → *enough (of) shouting*

nimis *violentiae* → *too much (of) violence*

parum *cibi* → *not enough (of) food*

tantum *doloris* → *so much (of) grief*

nihil *virium* → *no strength (nothing of strength)*

quantum *aquae*? → *how much (of) water?*

minus *papyri* → *less (of) paper*

hoc *temporis* → *at this (point in/of) time*

quicquam *panis* → *any (of) bread*

▶ The partitive genitive **gentium** (*of nations*) and **terrarum** (*of countries*) is used in questions like **ubi *gentium* sum?** → *where in the world am I?* (*where of the nations?* in Latin).

8 After verbs and adjectives

Some verbs and adjectives are followed by a genitive, as in English. A dictionary entry will tell you whether this happens for a particular verb or adjective. (For **impersonal verbs** which take the genitive see Unit 12D). It generally occurs after:

▶ Verbs and adjectives of condemning, accusing, acquitting or convicting, e.g. *maiestatis* **convictus est** → *he was convicted of treason*.

▶ Verbs and adjectives of want or fullness, e.g. **plenus** *aquae* → *full of water* and *armorum* **indiget** → *he is in need of weapons*. The deponent verb **potior** → *take possession* of (see Unit 8) is of this type.

▶ Verbs and adjectives of remembering, forgetting or reminding, e.g. *periculi* **memor** → *mindful of the danger* or *verborum* **oblitus sum** → *I forgot the words*.

▶ Verbs of valuing, buying and selling. The genitive is usually an adjective or pronoun and is called the **genitive of value**. The commonest examples are **magni, parvi, plurimi, minimi, tanti, quanti, pluris** and **minoris**, e.g. divitias *parvi* aestimat → *he values riches (of) little*, canem *magni pretii* emit → he bought the dog *for a great price* (*of a great price* in Latin), felem *minoris* emit → *he bought the cat for less* (*of less* in Latin).

D Dative case

The dative case has a wide variety of uses. It is generally used for nouns which in English have 'to' or 'for' before them.

1 Dative of indirect object

▶ In Latin (as in English), when transitive verbs of giving, sending, saying, telling, promising or showing etc. take a direct object in the accusative (see B1), the person (or thing) to whom the object is given, shown or sent etc. is the indirect object. In Latin the indirect object is in the dative, e.g. epistulam *imperatori* misisti → *you sent a letter to the emperor*. In English we do not always need the 'to', e.g. dic *mihi* causas → *tell me the reasons*.

► Some verbs which are transitive in English are intransitive in Latin and so, instead of taking a direct object in the accusative, they take the dative. The most common are the verbs below. Most of them contain the idea of being favourable to someone (or the opposite).

credo -ere credidi creditum → *believe*

desum deesse defui → *fail in one's duty, be lacking*

faveo -ere favi fautum → *support*

fido -ere fisus sum (semi-deponent: see Unit 8N) → *trust* (and its compounds like **diffido** → *mistrust*)

ignosco -ere ignovi ignotum → *forgive*

impero -are -avi -atum → *order*

indulgeo -ere indulsi → *indulge*

intersum interesse interfui → *be among*

invideo -ere invidi invisum → *envy*

irascor irasci iratus sum → *be angry with* (**deponent**: see Unit 8J)

minor -ari -atus sum → *threaten* (**deponent**)

noceo -ere -ui -itum → *harm*

nubo -ere nupsi nuptum → *marry a man* (only with a woman as the subject)

obsum obesse obfui → *be a hindrance to* (cf. **obviam ire** + dative → meet)

parco -ere peperci parsum → *spare*

pareo -ere -ui -itum → *obey*

placeo -ere -ui -itum → *please*

praesum praeesse praefui → *be in command of*

prosum proesse profui → *be of benefit to*

resisto -ere restiti → *resist*

servio -ire -ivi -itum → *serve, be a slave to*

studeo -ere -ui → *study, be keen on*

suadeo -ere suasi suasum → *advise* (and the compound **persuadeo** → *persuade*)

subvenio -ire subveni subventum → *come to help*

supersum superesse superfui → *survive*

For **impersonal verbs** with the dative, see Unit 12C.

▶ It can be used in the same way with adjectives which express likeness, help, proximity, trust etc, e.g. fidelis *amico* erat → *he was faithful **to his friend***; filia simillima *matri* est → *the daughter is very like **her mother***; Marcus par *fratri* est → *Marcus is like **his brother***.

Some of these adjectives can also take the genitive (see C8).

2 Dative of advantage and disadvantage

The person or thing for whose advantage or disadvantage something is done is in the **dative**, e.g. hoc *nobis* facimus → *we are doing this **for ourselves*** (for hoc see Unit 7E), Brutus *Caesari* vitam abstulit → *Brutus stole the life **from Caesar***.

3 Dative of reference and ethic dative

▶ The **dative of reference** indicates the person who is interested or involved in the action. It is often best translated by phrases such as *in the eyes of x*, *in x's judgement* or *as far as x is concerned* etc., e.g. Caesar *Cassio* regnare cupit → ***in Cassio's eyes** Caesar wants to be a king*.

▶ The so-called ethic dative of a personal pronoun (Unit 7A) is used to mark interest or call attention in familiar conversation, e.g. haec *vobis* mox fecit → *he soon did this, **mind you***.

4 The **dative of possession** is used with the verb *to be* to indicate ownership, e.g. **sunt *mihi* quinque equi** → *I have five horses* (literally: *there are five horses **for me***).

5 The **dative of agent** refers to the person or thing by whose agency something must be done and is used with the **gerundive** (see Unit 10J), **e.g. laborandum *est mihi*** → *I must work* (**literally:** *work must be done **by me***).

6 The **dative of purpose** expresses the intended purpose for which something is done, e.g. **Caesar locum *proelio* delegit** → *Caesar chose a site **for the battle***.

7 Predicative dative

▶ The predicative dative is not easily translatable into English. It is a specialized use of the dative, always accompanied by a dative of reference (or dative of advantage or dative of disadvantage). The verb most usually found in these expressions is *to be*, although other verbs do occur. The best way to translate it is to treat it as 'a source of', e.g. **Britanni** *auxilio* **erant Gallis** → *the Britons were a source of help to the Gauls* (literally: *the Britons were for a help to the Gauls*). The Gauls (**Gallis**) are in the dative of advantage.

▶ Other common examples apart from **auxilio esse** are:
beneficio esse → *to be a benefit to*
bono esse → *to be a source of good to*, e.g. **cui** *bono*? → *for whom is it good?* (who benefits?)

curae esse → *to be a source of concern to*	**decori esse** → *to be a source of glory to*
dedecori esse → *to be a disgrace to*	**exemplo esse** → *to be an example to*
honori esse → *to be an honour to*	**laudi esse** → *to be a credit to*
odio esse → *to be a source of hatred to*	**oneri esse** → *to be a burden to*
periculo esse → *to be a danger to*	**saluti esse** → *to be a salvation to*
subsidio esse → *to be a support to*	**usui esse** → *to be of use to*

E Ablative case

The ablative case is the one with the widest range of meanings in Latin. Broadly speaking, it corresponds to nouns in English which have 'by', 'with' or 'from' before them.

1 The **ablative of separation** is used with the adverb **procul** (*far away*) and verbs and adjectives which express the idea of keeping away from something, lacking something or being free of something.

e.g. **agricola leones gregibus abegit** → *the farmer drove the lions away from his flocks*

procul negotio, ad villam ambulat → *far from business, he is walking to the estate*

procul patria fugit → *he fled far from his fatherland*

2 The **ablative of origin** is used to indicate descent or origin, e.g. **Aeneas *dea* natus est** → *Aeneas was born of (from) a goddess.*

3 The **ablative of comparison** is used to show the point of comparison after comparative adjectives and adverbs instead of **quam** → *than* + nominative or accusative (see Unit 5M), e.g. **cameleopardus *elephanto* altior est** → *the giraffe is taller than the elephant.*

4 The **ablative of association** is used with verbs and adjectives with the sense of plenty etc., e.g. **insula *materia* abundat** → *the island abounds with timber.*

5 The **ablative of respect** is used like the accusative of respect (see B5) and means 'in respect of'. It is normally translated with the word 'in' before it. The adjective **dignus** → *worthy* regularly takes this kind of ablative.

e.g. **Philoctetes *pede* vulneratus est** → *Philoctetes has been wounded in the foot*

miles nautam *viribus* superat → *the soldier surpasses the sailor in strength*

Augustus certe *laude* dignus erat → *Augustus was certainly worthy of praise*

6 The **ablative of quality** or **description** is used with an adjective to describe something, e.g. ***praestanti forma* femina** → *a woman of outstanding beauty.*

7 The **ablative of manner** or **of attendant circumstances** expresses the way or the circumstances in which something happens or is done.

e.g. **draco lento *gradu* appropinquavit** → *the dragon approached with slow step*

***silentio* ambulabat** → *he was walking in silence*

per vias *clamoribus* ambulabat → *he was walking through the streets amid the shouting*

8 For the **ablative absolute** construction see Unit 13.

9 For the **ablative after prepositions** see Unit 6B.

10 For the **ablative of time when and time within which** see G2–3.

11 For the **ablative with impersonal verbs** see Unit 12F.

12 The **ablative of the agent** is used after **passive** verbs with the preposition **ab/a** to indicate the person (**agent**) by whom something is done (Unit 8E), e.g. **Caesar *a Bruto* necatus est** → *Caesar was slain **by Brutus**.*

13 The **ablative of instrument** or **means**
   ▷ This is used after **verbs** without a preposition and indicates the thing (instrument) by or with which something is done, e.g. **Brutus Caesarem *pugione* necavit** → *Brutus killed Caesar **with a dagger**.*
   ▷ It is also used after certain verbs (mostly **deponent**: see Unit 8M) which are transitive in English but **intransitive** in Latin. The most common are:
       abutor abuti abusus sum → *use up, exhaust*
       fruor frui fructus sum → *enjoy*
       fungor fungi functus sum → *perform*
       utor uti usus sum → *use*
       vescor vesci → *feed on*

14 The **ablative of cause** is used with adjectives and verbs (especially when describing a mental state) to express the reason for or cause of something, e.g. **servi domino parent *formidine* poenae** → *the slaves obey their master **through fear** of punishment.*

15 The **ablative of measure** of difference is used to express a degree of difference with comparatives and superlatives. The most common are:

hoc → *by this much*	**eo** → *by that much*
quo → *by which*	**nihilo** → *by nothing*
nimio → *by too much*	**dimidio** → *by half*
quanto → *by how much*	**tanto** → *by so much*
paulo → *by a little*	**multo** → *by much*
aliquanto → *by a little*	

e.g. **elephantus *multo* maior quam mus est** → *the elephant is **(by) much** bigger than the mouse.*

16 The **ablative of price** is used with verbs and adjectives of buying and selling, e.g. **equum *tribus talentis* emit** → *he bought the horse **for three talents**.*

NB **magno** → *at a great price*, **parvo** → *at a small price*, **vili** → *at a cheap price* and **minimo** → *very cheaply*.

17 The **ablative of place** (see also the **locative case** at F) is more common in verse and is used to indicate the place where something happens, e.g. *summo monte* **castra posuerunt** → *they pitched camp* **on the top of the mountain**; *terra marique* **monstrum petivit** → *he searched for the monster on land and sea*. (For the ending **-que** → *and,* see Unit 6E).

F Locative case

The **locative** is the remnant of a case which once existed independently in Latin. It is used to express location and is *never* accompanied by a preposition.

1 The names of cities, towns and small islands have a **locative** form. The locative endings for the different declensions follow. You will see that they look like the genitives or ablatives of the same noun. Remember that in Latin some place names exist in the plural. We do not find place names in the fourth and fifth declensions.

1st declension singular	**Roma** → *Rome*	**Romae** → *at Rome*
1st declension plural	**Athenae** → *Athens*	**Athenis** → *at Athens*
2nd declension singular	**Corinthus** → *Corinth*	**Corinthi** → *at Corinth*
2nd declension plural	**Philippi** → *Philippi*	**Philippis** → *at Philippi*
3rd declension singular	**Carthago** → *Carthage*	**Carthagini** → *at Carthage*
3rd declension plural	**Gades** → *Cadiz*	**Gadibus** → *at Cadiz*

2 Direction towards a place is expressed in the **accusative**, e.g. *Romam* **iter facimus** → *we are making a journey* **to Rome**.

3 Direction away from a place is expressed by the **ablative**, e.g. *Roma* **discessit** → *he departed* **from Rome**.

4 The nouns **domus -us** f. → *house*, **rus ruris** n, → *countryside*, **bellum -i** n. → *war*, **humus -i** f. → *ground* and **militia -ae** f. → *military service* also have special locative forms:

domi → *at home*	**rus** → *to the countryside*
domum → *homewards*	**ruri** → *in the countryside*
domo → *from home*	**humi** → *on the ground*
belli → *at war*	**militiae** → *on military service*

G Expressions of time

▶ The **accusative** is used to express *how long* something takes to happen, e.g. ***multos annos* terram errabat** → *he wandered the land for many years*. Notice that the accusative **terram** is the direct object of the verb, e.g. ***totam noctem* vigilabant** → *they stayed awake for the whole night*.

▶ The **ablative** is used to express the time **when** something happens, e.g. ***tertio die* ad oppidum pervenerunt** → *they arrived at the town on the third day*; ***hieme* ursi in speluncis dormiunt** → *in winter the bears sleep in caves*; ***vesperi* cantamus** → *in the evening we sing*.

▶ The **ablative** is also used to express time **within which** something happens, e.g. ***paucis diebus* pueri advenient** → *the boys will arrive in (within) a few days*.

1 Identify only the subjects in the following English sentences.

e.g. *Five red foxes ran through the farmyard* → foxes

a This box is not to be opened.

b Do the pirates have a flag?

c We have been released.

d It is finished.

e Where are the onions and cabbages?

f Marius was a great general.

g Diamonds are a girl's best friend.

h How heavy are those ostriches?

i Are you going out?

j The dish ran away with the spoon.

2 Translate the following sentences into English. The nominatives are used for the subjects. Remember that there is no word for 'the' in Latin so you will have to supply it if it helps the sense.

e.g. **canes saliebant** → *the dogs were leaping*

a pedites ambulaverunt sed legatus equitavit.

b grues avolaverant.

c non ridet imperator.

d lepus non vicit.

e gladiatores sumus.
f Cassius dormit.
g miles et nauta bibebant.
h pontifex dixit et plebs parebit.
i magister docebat sed discipuli non audiebant.
j Hercules diu laborabat

3 Translate the following sentences in which the nominative is used both for the subject and the complement.

e.g. **senatores erant proditores** → *the senators were traitors*

a Merlinus erat magus.
b pauper erit princeps.
c canis est pestis.
d Pheidias erat artifex.
e templa sunt aedificia.
f raptores captivi sunt.
g oratores sunt mendaces.
h Romani erant victores.
i praetoriani erunt percussores.
j Brutus fuerat consul.

4 Translate these sentences which have a mixture of nominatives and vocatives.

e.g. **non manebimus, pueri** → *we shall not wait, boys*

a domine, hospites discedunt.
b salvete agricolae!
c Valeria, Tite, iuvenis cadit.
d centurio, captivi effugerunt.
e hostes adveniunt o milites!
f Valeri, Iulius et Tiberius currunt.
g ave fili.
h pater, ver appropinquat.
i ubi es, Marce?
j Fortuna, dea es.

5 Identify the objects in the following sentences.

e.g. *we all like figs* → figs

a Asterix is chasing his dog.
b How many boxes have you filled?
c Wars cause misery.
d The wind helps boats.
e The otters are watching their mother.
f Why do flies eat dung?
g When will Hadrian visit the wall?
h I cannot see the signal.
i We are awaiting our orders.
j The doctor has cured the disease.

6 Translate the following sentences into English.

e.g. **ranae muscas capiebant** → *the frogs were catching flies*

a venatores clamores audiverunt.

b magistri pueros docebant.

c druides taurum sacrificaverunt.

d domine, servi panem portant.

e nuces sciuri celabant.

f fabri murum aedificant.

g milites Claudium imperatorem fecerunt.

h actorem puellae plauserunt.

i avarus nummos amat.

j navis scopulum percussit.

7 Translate the following simple sentences into Latin.

e.g. *the priests were leading the procession* → **sacerdotes pompam ducebant**

a The senator is calling the allies.

b The river has flooded the fields.

c Hercules attacked the hydra.

d The boys love Amelia.

e The Gauls fear the Romans.

f The guards have closed the gates.

g The dogs are watching the shepherd.

h The farmer has freed the birds.

i They are hiding the gold.

j Cats do not like water.

8 Translate these sentences which contain accusatives of respect, accusatives of extent and accusatives of exclamation. The adjectives are easy to find in a dictionary.

e.g. **deus oculos nitidus est** → *the god is shining in his eyes* (i.e. *his eyes are shining*)

a o incredibilem foeditatem.

b corpus valeo.

c viginti gradus ambulavit.

d o mirabilem fortitudinem.

e miles sex pedes altus est.

f saucius eram manus.

g lacus erat centum pedes altus.

h equus crurem claudicat.

i o gloriam inconstantem.

j nudus erat artus.

9 Translate the following sentences into English. There is a mixture of types of genitive in them.

e.g. **tecta urbis video** → *I see the roofs of the city*

a puer versus Vergilii recitat.
b disco artem equitandi.
c ianuam domus numquam aperio.
d pastor filiam regis amat.
e voces liberorum audivistis.
f capillos capitis senis tonsor numerat.
g catervam militum timemus.
h est medici aegrotos sanare.
i minae hostium liberos terrebant.
j acervi stercoris viam claudunt.
k sonitus tonitrus ancillae audiverunt.
l cives virum honestatis probant.
m Hannibal visum oculi amisit.
n aquae fluminis leniter fluebant.
o corona gemmarum fulsit.
p est ducis urbem curare.
q elephanti massas saxorum portant.
r vulnera militum non videmus.
s exploratores culmina montium aspectabant.
t linguam Romanorum discebant.

10 Translate the following sentences into Latin. Different types of genitive are included among them.

e.g. *The birds' voices delighted the listeners* → **voces avium auditores delectaverunt**

a The burdens press the donkeys' backs.
b Cassius is a man capable of cruelty.
c The men of the town will not fight.
d The slaves are washing the master's togas.
e We love the waves of the sea.
f The love of war destroys humanity.
g They did not see the light of the fire.
h I do not like the dog's breath.
i The wisdom of the queen has saved the ship.
j I have a weight of silver.
k It is a sailor's job to navigate.
l The prize of valour is glory.

m You (s.) will like the poet's house.
n Love of money is the root of evil.
o We have found the pile of eggs.
p The love of a mother sustains children.
q The Romans did not like the title king.
r We are seeking the wizard's treasure.
s Brutus' mother was sleeping.
t I know a man of a hundred years.

11 Translate the following sentences into English. There is a mixture of types of genitive in them.

e.g. **tantum felicitatis vidisti** → *you have seen so much happiness*

a agricola memor belli est.
b cives dignitatem magni aestimant.
c fossores aliquid auri invenerunt.
d ubi terrarum eramus?
e quanti pretii domum emisti?
f pauperes calceorum indigebant.
g fur honestatem parvi aestimat.
h multum veneni senator devoraverat.
i satis onerum portat.
j ascendatores parum funium habuerunt.
k minus proelii imperator vidit.
l puellae aliquid panis portabant.
m tantum casei vulpes cepit.
n partem muri delevimus.
o quicquam pecuniae habes?
p liberi nimis aquae biberunt.
q multi gladiatorum pugnabant.
r complures captivorum aegrotant.
s pars pompae constitit.
t naves magni pretii emerunt.

12 Translate the following sentences into Latin. There is a mixture of types of genitive in them.

e.g. *Caesar had too much glory* → **Caesar nimis gloriae habebat**

a We desire enough houses.
b The horses are dragging too much wood.
c Do you (s.) have any news?
d The lake is full of fish.
e The crow has taken some grain.
f He is mindful of the danger.

g Peace makes much wealth.

h Many of the children were playing.

i I have seen too much weeping.

j We are in need of water.

k At this point in time the guards are sleeping.

l He bought the farm for a small price.

m The shepherd is guarding part of the flock.

n Part of the battle line was approaching.

o The boy is carrying more fruit.

p We have not enough salt.

q How much of the story do they know?

r We saved part of the tree.

s The general values cowards little.

t Several of us disagreed.

13 Translate the following sentences into English.

e.g. **agricolae plaustrum demonstravimus** → *we have shown the farmer the wagon*

a liberis fabulam narras.

b auxilium sociis misimus.

c divisor suffragatoribus non persuadebit.

d dona matronis promisi.

e poetae civibus recitabant.

f oratori senatores non crediderunt.

g pauperes divitibus non invident.

h sorores fratribus subveniebant.

i Caesar inimicis pepercit.

j Arminius Germanis praeerat.

k candidato non favemus.

l praestigiatores hospitibus placuerunt.

m cives sacerdotibus fidunt.

n Romanis barbari diu resistebant.

o Vitellia par matri erat.

p custodes captivis deerant.

q servis domini imperaverunt.

r Sulla inimicis nocuit.

s militibus non serviemus.

t magister discipulis libros dedit.

14 Translate the following sentences into Latin.

e.g. *I shall send corn to the colonists* → **frumentum colonis mittam**

a You (s.) used to trust the queen.

b The hunters were studying the stag's footprints.

c The runners mistrust the ice.

d The women will be among the spectators.

e You (pl.) have not persuaded the allies.

f I envy the victors.

g The cowards will not come to help the boys.

h The master indulges the slaves.

i The sheep are a hindrance to the carts.

j The orders do not please the soldiers.

k He is supporting his mother.

l The foxes will not harm the chickens.

m The lady sent the rings to her daughters.

n The priests gave sacrifices to the gods.

o The judge will not forgive the assassin.

p Portia has married Brutus.

q The young men believed the messenger.

r Cats do not trust dogs.

s The dam will resist the waves.

t The witnesses are telling the judge the truth.

15 Translate the following into English. They contain datives of advantage and disadvantage.

e.g. **servi stolas matronis laverunt** → *the slaves washed the dresses for the ladies*

a pueri carbonem fabris colligebant.

b pacem posteritati faciemus.

c Romani thermas aedificaverunt incolis.

d elephanti stipites traxerunt silvicolis.

e pater equos filiabus emit.

f insidias paravistis hostibus.

g panem portat uxori.

h Brutus Caesarem reipublicae necavit.

i hostes agros agricolis vastaverunt.

j puella mala sorori carpsit.

16 Translate the following sentences into English.

e.g. **est magnus murus Seribus** → *the Chinese have a great wall*

a nomen peregrino fuit Ulysses.

b sunt elephanti Carthaginiensibus.

c gemmas aviae dono misi.

d civibus erat dux fortis.

e pueri locum pugnae delegerunt.

f artifices pulchritudini aedificium petiverunt.

g est nix culminibus montium.

h exploratores locum castris invenerunt.

i sunt Graecis centum naves.

j operarii stadium certamini verrebant

17 Translate the following sentences into English.

e.g. **Hector erat decori Troianis** → *Hector was a source of glory to the Trojans*

a naves erant beneficio Carthaginiensibus.

b Brutus honori erat Romanis.

c captivi sunt oneri militibus.

d Milo erat odio Clodio.

e Cloelia est exemplo puellis.

f maritus erit subsidio uxori.

g pedicae periculo sunt ursis.

h flumen saluti fuit viatoribus.

i filius curae erat matri.

j Catilina dedecori erat senatoribus.

18 Translate the following sentences into Latin. Use a mixture of types of dative.

e.g. *we have been an example to the children* → **exemplo liberis fuimus**

a We are carrying the chickens for a joke.

b The chieftains were a burden to the citizens.

c As far as the old man is concerned we are sleeping.

d The ovens are of use to the bakers.

e The Romans built an amphitheatre for spectacles.

f The charioteer has twenty horses.

g In the voters' judgement the candidate was not listening.

h The thieves took the gold from the miser.

i The rioters have clubs.

j You (s.) will remove the obstacles for the procession.

19 Translate the following sentences into English. They contain ablatives of separation.

e.g. **fugitivi procul proelio fugerunt** → *the fugitives fled far from the battle*

a cives servitudine liberabimus.

b raptores corporibus arma spoliaverunt.

c senatores proditore honores privaverunt.

d obsides cibo et aqua carent.

e pugil pugnat nudus vestimentis.

f milites hostes urbe arcent.

g philosophus vino semper abstinebat.

h puellae vespas crepundiis pellunt.

i reum crimine solvo.

j trabibus et clavis egemus.

20 Translate the following sentences into English. They contain ablatives of origin and association.

e.g. **pater filium equo donavit** → *the father presented his son with a horse*

a pecunia agricolas mercatores locupletaverunt.

b senatus cives pane praebuit.

c fluvius rivis natus est.

d ancillae urnas aqua implebunt.

e legati consules corona donaverunt.

f Romulus deo natus est.

g promus hospites vino implevit.

h olim metallum argento abundabat.

i magus avaritiam regis auro explevit.

j Mars geminis feminam gravidavit.

21 Translate the following sentences into English. They contain ablatives of respect, quality, manner and circumstance.

e.g. **sonitibus tonitrus dormiebas** → *you slept through the noises of thunder*

a navem nauta tempestate gubernat.

b Caesar tergo saucius fuit.

c anseres non silentio volant.

d ursi homines celeritate oppugnaverunt.

e ignavi genibus tremuerunt.

f latrones fraude pecuniam comparabant.

g canis pede claudicabat.

h avarus avaritia poetam superat.

i Cassius est vir praestanti dignitate.

j liberi hilaritate ludebant.

22 Translate the following sentences into Latin. They contain a mixture of types of ablative.

e.g. *the scouts were in need of light* → **exploratores luce indigebant**

a We shall not drive the exiles from the land.

b Achilles was born of a goddess.

c The desert lacks water.

d In war fathers bury sons.

e The farm abounds in cattle.

f Horatius is worthy of honour.
g We cross the river in fear.
h You (pl.) have filled the vat with milk.
i The victors will refrain from violence.
j Marcus has hit Titus in the head.

23 **Translate the following sentences into English. They contain the ablative of means.**

e.g. **pistores panem farina faciebant** → *the bakers were making bread with flour*

a piscatores pisces retibus capiunt.
b discipuli stilis scribebant.
c senatores Catilinam contumeliis exprobraverunt.
d pueri aleis ludebant.
e boves virgis bubulci impellunt.
f hortum rosis topiarii ornaverunt.
g orator cives verbis agitabat.
h securibus libertatem defendemus.
i casas facibus incenderunt.
j victimam sacerdos cultro percussit.

24 **Translate the following sentences into English. They contain ablatives of cause and measure of difference.**

e.g. **servitudinis causa gemebant** → *they groaned by reason of their slavery*

a portam terrore tenebrarum non aperit.
b celeritate venti lente ambulabant.
c Cassius nihilo melior quam Brutus est.
d exspectatione latronum aurum celavi.
e liberi gaudio saliunt.
f serpens longior quam vermis viginti pedibus est.
g pacis amore arma deposuerunt.
h canes herbam amant multo minus quam asini.
i quanto maior est bufo quam rana?
j odio regum Romani Tarquinium expulerunt.

25 **Translate the following sentences into English. They contain ablatives of place and price.**

e.g. **arietem dumis invenit** → *he found the ram in the thorn bushes*

a villam emi centum talentis.
b navis aequore navigat.
c sicarius horto corpus celavit.
d libros Tarquinius auro emit.
e amici thermis conveniunt.
f equi viginti talentis constant.
g vaccam quinque fabis vendidit.
h legiones urbibus hibernabunt.
i luscinia cacumine arboris canebat.
j victoriam sanguine et ferro confecit.

26 Translate the following sentences into Latin. They contain different types of ablative.

e.g. *the workmen were building a bridge with stones* → **fabri pontem saxis aedificabant.**

a The philosopher conquered his enemies with kindness.
b Aeneas was the best man by a little.
c You (s.) have frightened the birds with a noise.
d The cavalrymen rode on the plain.
e I sold the maps for four talents.
f The gods approve the plan with omens.
g The mother feeds her children with honey.
h We shall buy the mine at a small price.
i The Romans attacked the Carthaginians by land and sea.
j Horatius fought through love of his fatherland.

27 Translate the following sentences into English.

e.g. **heri cenabam domi Caesaris** → *yesterday I was dining at Caesar's house*

a aula episcopi Antiochiae erat.
b domi Bruti coniurati convenerunt.
c Londinii manebo tres dies.
d Claudius Romae habitabat.
e Romani Veiis castra posuerunt.
f senex humi dormiebat.
g vulpes et lepores ruri ludunt.
h classem exspectamus Brundisii.
i finis terrae Gadibus est.
j Plato et Aristoteles Athenis docebant.

28 Translate the following sentences into English.

e.g. **Rhodon peregrinatores iter facient** → *the pilgrims will journey to Rhodes*

a cras rus ambulabimus.

b domum pueri terrore festinabant.

c Sicila mox discedemus.

d Athenis legati Spartam venerunt.

e Alexandria medicus effugit.

f Carthaginem mercatores navigaverunt.

g aestate liberos Massiliam semper mittimus.

h domo nuntius cucurrit.

i Romani non semper belli vicerunt.

j Tyrum et Sidonem naves rex misit.

29 Translate the following sentences into English.

e.g. **decem annos captivus erat** → *he was a prisoner for ten years*

a quattuor diebus cameli advenient.

b quinque annos fundum colebant.

c tertio anno patrimonium excepisti.

d hieme arbores frondes non habent.

e septem dies iuvenes pontem custodient.

f mane agricola agrum arat.

g novem mensibus parentes erimus.

h centum annis phoenix surget.

i vesperi caelum rubescit.

j anseres sex noctes clamabant.

30 Translate the following sentences into Latin.

e.g. *In the morning you (s.) will milk the cows* → **mane vaccas mulgebis**

a I have left the gift at home.

b The fishermen drifted for eight days.

c Within five days the pilgrims came to Delphi.

d You (pl.) will wait for father in Paris.

e In winter the philosopher lives at Athens.

f Tomorrow the singer will come from Corinth.

g We shall not depart from London in the evening.

h Wthin six months the craftsmen will have finished the house.

i The tortoise lived for a hundred years.

j The ships carried the grain to Ostia.

Points to remember

1 The nominative is used for the subject of a verb and its complement.

2 The vocative is used when addressing someone and only differs from the nominative in the masculine singular of the second declension.

3 The accusative is used principally for the objects of verbs but also after some prepositions and for expressing extent of time, motion towards something, exclamations and reference to parts of the body.

4 The genitive is used where in English we would use the word *of*.

5 The dative is used for the indirect object, after certain verbs and in a small number of specialized constructions.

6 The ablative is the case with the widest range of uses. Broadly speaking it represents ideas of abstraction (*from*), agency or instrument (*by* or *with*) and (especially in poetry) location and time (*in, on* or *at*).

7 The locative is used to denote location in a town or on a small island. It is also a specialized case still attached to a small number of nouns. E.g. **domus** (*house*) and **rus** (*the countryside*).

8 The variety of uses for each case means that you will often meet multiple examples of the same case performing different functions in the same sentence. Watch out for this, especially with the ablative.

9 For expressions of time, Latin uses the accusative for duration of time and the ablative for time when or within which.

10 Remember, if cases seem confusing, that they also survive in English, in some pronouns. E.g. the nominatives *I, he, she, we, who*, the accusatives *me, him, her, us, whom*, and the genitives *mine, his, hers, ours* and *whose*.

5

....

Adjectives and adverbs

_____

Adjectives: first and second declension

An adjective describes a noun. Adjectives in Latin are used as in English except that they need not be written before the noun, e.g. miles *gloriosus* → **the** *boastful* **soldier. An adjective can also stand in for a noun, e.g.** *boni* → **good (men).**

A When you look up a first and second declension adjective in the dictionary you will find the **nominative singular** of its **masculine, feminine** and **neuter** forms, e.g. **bonus bona bonum** → *good*. This is often abbreviated, e.g. **bonus -a -um**.

B An adjective **agrees** with the noun it is describing, i.e. it is in the same **number, gender** and **case** as that noun so that we can tell exactly which noun it is describing. It is important to know this because in Latin adjectives are not always written next to nouns.

C In **first** and **second declension** adjectives the **masculine** and **neuter** forms are **second declension** while the **feminine** forms are **first declension**.

	Singular			Plural		
	Masculine	Feminine	Neuter	Masculine	Feminine	Neuter
nom.	bon**us**	bon**a**	bon**um**	bon**i**	bon**ae**	bon**a**
voc.	bon**e**	bon**a**	bon**um**	bon**i**	bon**ae**	bon**a**

(Contd)

	Singular			Plural		
	Masculine	Feminine	Neuter	Masculine	Feminine	Neuter
acc.	bon**um**	bon**am**	bon**um**	bon**os**	bon**as**	bon**a**
gen.	bon**i**	bon**ae**	bon**i**	bon**orum**	bon**arum**	bon**orum**
dat.	bon**o**	bon**ae**	bon**o**	bon**is**	bon**is**	bon**is**
abl.	bon**o**	bon**a**	bon**o**	bon**is**	bon**is**	bon**is**

▶ The majority decline like **bonus -a -um** → *good*.
▶ Some adjectives in these declensions go like the nouns **puer** and
  ager in the masculine (see Unit 3F). Their declension differs from
  bonus only in the **nominative** and **vocative masculine singular**.
  They decline like **tener** → *tender*, which keeps an **e**, or **pulcher** →
  beautiful which loses an **e**. The adjective **dexter** → *on the right*
  can decline either like **tener** or **pulcher**, with either **dexteri** or
  dextri as its genitive masculine singular.

Insight
English adjectives ending in *ious* often end in **-iosus** in Latin,
e.g. **furiosus** *furious*.

	Masculine	Feminine	Neuter
nom.	ten**er**	tener**a**	tener**um**
voc.	ten**er**	tener**a**	tener**um**
acc.	tener**um**	tener**am**	tener**um** etc. like **bonus**
nom.	pulch**er**	pulch**ra**	pulch**rum**
voc.	pulch**er**	pulch**ra**	pulch**rum**
acc.	pulch**rum**	pulch**ram**	pulch**rum** etc. like **bonus**

▶ The adjectives **medius** → *middle*, **imus** → *bottom* or *lowest*,
  summus → *top* or *highest*, primus → *first* and **ultimus** →
  furthest are used in two ways. First, they follow a noun to
  express order in both time and space, e.g. **mons summus** →
  the highest mountain, **hora media** → *the middle hour*. Second,
  they precede a noun to refer to a part of it, e.g. **summus mons**
  → *the top* (part) *of the mountain*, **media hora** → *the middle*
  (part) *of the hour*.

Third declension

D Adjectives in the third declension decline like nouns of the third declension (Units 3K and 3M). Notice particularly that third declension adjectives end in **-i** in the ablative singular, unless they are standing in for a noun, e.g. compare **puer servatus est ab *ingenti* nauta** → *the boy was saved **by a huge** sailor* with **puer servatus est ab *ingente*** → *the boy was saved **by a huge** (man)*.

E Third declension adjectives which have **one ending** for all genders in the nominative singular decline like **ingens ingentis** → *huge,* as do **present participles** (see Unit 10B). Note that in dictionary entries these adjectives are given with their nominative and genitive singular.

	Singular Masc. & Fem.	Neuter	Plural Masc. & Fem.	Neuter
nom. and voc.	ingens	ingens	ingent**es**	ingent**ia**
acc.	ingent**em**	ingens	ingent**es** or **-is**	ingent**ia**
gen.	ingent**is**	ingent**is**	ingent**ium**	ingent**ium**
dat. and abl.	ingent**i**	ingent**i**	ingent**ibus**	ingent**ibus**

F Third declension adjectives which have **two endings** in the nominative singular, one for both masculine and feminine and another for the neuter, decline like **fortis -is -e** → *brave, strong.*

	Singular Masc. & Fem.	Neuter	Plural Masc. & Fem.	Neuter
nom. and voc.	fort**is**	fort**e**	fort**es**	fort**ia**
acc.	fort**em**	fort**e**	fort**es** or fort**is**	fort**ia**
gen.	fort**is**	fort**is**	fort**ium**	fort**ium**
dat. and abl.	fort**i**	fort**i**	fort**ibus**	fort**ibus**

G Third declension adjectives with **three endings** in the nominative singular, one for each gender, decline like **acer acris acre** → *keen.*

Singular	Masculine	Feminine	Neuter
nom. and voc.	ac**er**	acr**is**	acr**e**
acc.	acr**em**	acr**em**	acr**e**
gen.	acr**is**	acr**is**	acr**is** etc. like **fortis**

H Some third declension adjectives resemble nouns in their declension, e.g. **vetus veteris** → *old*.

| | Singular | | Plural | |
	Masc. & Fem.	Neuter	Masc. & Fem.	Neuter
nom. and voc.	vetus	vetus	veter**es**	veter**a**
acc.	veter**em**	vetus	veter**es**	veter**a**
gen.	veter**is**	veter**is**	veter**um**	veter**um**
dat.	veter**i**	veter**i**	veter**ibus**	veter**ibus**
abl.	veter**e**	veter**e**	veter**ibus**	veter**ibus**

Like **vetus**, and also often used as nouns, are **pauper -eris** → *poor* and **dives -itis** → *rich*, although **dives** has the contracted forms: sing. nom. **dis**, acc. **ditem**, gen. **ditis**, dat. and abl. **diti**, plural nom. and acc. **dites** (m. and f.), **ditia** (n.), gen. **ditium**, dat. and abl. **ditibus**.

Comparison of adjectives

I There are three degrees of comparison:

- ▶ **positive** e.g. **fortis -is -e** → *brave*
- ▶ **comparative** e.g. **fortior fortior fortius** → *braver*, *rather brave*, *too brave*
- ▶ **superlative** e.g. **fortissimus -a -um** → *bravest*, *very brave*, *most brave*

J The **comparative adjective** is formed by adding **-ior -ior -ius** to the positive stem, e.g. **durus** → *harsh*: **durior** → *harsher*. These are third declension and decline like **fortior** → *braver*.

	Singular		Plural	
	Masc. & Fem.	Neuter	Masc. & Fem.	Neuter
nom. and voc.	fortior	fortius	fortiores	fortiora
acc.	fortiorem	fortius	fortiores	fortiora
gen.	fortioris	fortioris	fortiorum	fortiorum
dat.	fortiori	fortiori	fortioribus	fortioribus
abl.	fortiore	fortiore	fortioribus	fortioribus

K Superlative adjectives are first and second declension and decline like **bonus -a -um** (see C).

▶ These are formed mostly by adding **-issimus -issima -issimum** to the **stem** of the positive form, e.g. **durus** → *harsh*: **durissimus** → *very harsh*.

▶ The superlatives of adjectives which end in **-er**, like **tener** → *tender*, **acer** → *keen* etc. end in **-errimus -errima -errimum**, e.g. **acer** → *keen*: **acerrimus** → *very keen*.

▶ The superlatives of six adjectives which end in **-ilis** (**facilis** → *easy*, **difficilis** → *difficult*, **similis** → *like*, **dissimilis** → *unlike*, **gracilis** → *slender, graceful* and **humilis** → *lowly*) all end in **-illimus -illima -illimum**, e.g. **facilis** → *easy*: **facillimus** → *very easy*.

▶ Adjectives ending in **-eus**, **-ius** or **-uus** use the adverbs **magis** → *more* and **maxime** → *most*, e.g. **dubius** → *doubtful*, **magis dubius** → *more doubtful* and **maxime dubius** → *most doubtful*. However, adjectives ending in **-uus** can be regular, e.g. **antiquior** → *older*, **antiquissimus** → *oldest*.

L Irregular forms of comparison

bonus → *good*	**melior** → *better*	**optimus** → *best, very good*
inferus → *lower*	**inferior** → *lower*	**infimus** (or **imus**) → *lowest*
magnus → *big*	**maior** → *bigger*	**maximus** → *biggest, very big*
malus → *bad*	**peior** → *worse*	**pessimus** → *worst, very bad*
multi → *many*	**plures** → *more*	**plurimi** → *most, very many*
multus → *much*	**plus** → *more*	**plurimus** → *most, very much*
nequam → *wicked*	**nequior** → *more wicked*	**nequissimus** → *very wicked*

| parvus → *small* | minor → *less, smaller* | minimus → *least, very small* |
| superus → *upper* | superior → *higher* | supremus (or summus) → *highest* |

Plus (*more*) is used in the singular only as a neuter noun. In the plural it is an adjective.

	Singular Neuter	Plural Masc. & Fem.	Neuter
nom., voc. and acc.	**plus**	**plures**	**plura**
gen.	**pluris**	**plurium**	**plurium**
dat.	**—**	**pluribus**	**pluribus**
abl.	**plure**	**pluribus**	**pluribus**

M In Latin comparisons are expressed in one of two ways.

▶ With **quam** → *than*, using the same case after **quam** as before it. This is how we express comparison in English, e.g. **Brutus altior *quam* Cassius est** → *Brutus is taller than Cassius*.

▶ With the ablative of comparison (see Unit 4E3). This is only used if the thing or person being compared is in the nominative or accusative, e.g. **nihil *libertate* melius est** → *nothing is better than freedom*.

N Comparatives are also used with the ablative of measure of difference (see Unit 4E15), e.g. **formica *nihilo maior* musca est** → *the ant is no bigger than the fly*.

O For comparatives in a purpose clause, see Unit 14E.

P The word **quam** is used with the superlative to mean *as ... as possible*, e.g. ***quam plurimas* urbes Romani ceperunt** → *the Romans took as many cities as possible*.

Adverbs

Adverbs describe the action of a verb as well as adjectives, phrases or even other adverbs.

Q Formation

Adverbs do not decline. Most are formed from the stems of the positive forms of **adjectives**.

▶ Those which come from first and second declension adjectives end in **-e** (or sometimes **-o**), e.g. **dur_e_** → *harshly*, from **durus**, **dign_e_** → *worthily*, from **dignus** and **tut_o_** → *safely*, from **tutus**.

> **Insight**
>
> Latin adverbs frequently end in **-e**, e.g. **lente** *slowly* from **lentus** *slow*.

▶ Those which come from third declension adjectives usually end in **-iter** or **-ter**, e.g. **fort_iter_** → *bravely*, from **fortis**, **pruden_ter_** → *prudently*, from **prudens**.
▶ Some adverbs are formed from the accusatives or ablatives of adjectives, e.g. **primum** or **primo** → *firstly*, **multum** → *much* and **paulum** → *little*, **facile** → *easily*.
▶ Some are formed from verbs, e.g. **stat_im_** → *at once*, from **sto** → *I stand*; **curs_im_** → *quickly*, from **curro** → *I run*.
▶ Some words used as adverbs are also used as prepositions, e.g. **ante** → *before*, **post** → *after*.

R Negatives

▶ The negative adverbs are **non** → *not*, **haud** → *not*, which is used with other adverbs, adjectives and some verbs of knowing or thinking and **ne** → *do not / let not*, which is used to make commands negative (see Unit 11Q) and to make subjunctives in a main clause negative (see Unit 9H). A common phrase is **ne ... quidem** → *not even*, e.g. **ne Brutus quidem** → *not even Brutus*.

▶ Note also that **neve** or **neu** are used for **et ne** and the following conjunctions are often used: **nec** → *nor*, **nec ... nec** → *neither ... nor*, and **neque ... neque** → *neither ... nor*.

S Comparison

▶ The regular **comparative adverb** is the **neuter accusative singular** of the corresponding comparative adjective (see J), e.g. fort*ius* → *more bravely*, from **fortis**; tut*ius* → *more safely*, from **tutus**.

▶ The regular **superlative adverb** ends in -issime, -errime or -illime, e.g. fort*issime* → *very bravely*, cel*errime* → *very quickly* and fac*illime* → *very easily*.

▶ When it follows **quam**, the superlative adverb means *as ... as possible*, e.g. **quam celerrime** → *as quickly as possible*, **quam facillime** → *as easily as possible*.

T Irregular and other forms

bene → *well*	melius → *better*	optime → *best*
diu → *for a long time*	diutius → *for a longer time*	diutissime → *for a very long time*
intus → *within*	interius → *further within*	intime → *furthest within*
magnopere → *greatly*	magis → *more greatly*	maxime → *very greatly*
male → *badly*	peius → *worse*	pessime → *worst*
multum → *much*	plus → *more* (in quantity)	plurimum → *most*
nequiter → *wickedly*	nequius → *more wickedly*	nequissime → *most wickedly*
nuper → *recently*	(no comparative)	nuperrime → *most recently*
paulum → *little*	minus → *less*	minime → *least*
post → *after*	posterius → *later on*	postremo → *finally*
(prae → *before*)	prius → *earlier*	primum, primo → *earliest*
prope → *near*	propius → *nearer*	proxime → *very near*
saepe → *often*	saepius → *more often*	saepissime → *very often*
(no positive)	potius → *rather*	potissimum → *especially*

1 What number, gender and case are the following phrases? If there is more than one possible answer give them all.

e.g. **puellis pulchris** → 1. dat. f. pl. 2. abl. f. pl.

a manum teneram
b tempestates magnae
c virginum pulchrarum
d deabus benignis
e agricolas bonos
f diei festi
g leonibus magnis
h hominem scelestum
i maria alta
j clamore claro

2 Translate the following into English.

e.g. -**ad summum montem ascendemus** → *we shall climb to the top of the mountain*

a pulchras gemmas in arca lignea inveni.
b scelera scelesta boni non probant.
c heri quinque equos albos emi.
d noctem atram liberi timent.
e ursi villosi in densis silvis hibernant.
f nubes opacas supra mare nautae viderunt.
g profugi miseri per terras errabant.
h dextras manus Gallorum Caesar abscidit.
i ad saxa rubra iuvenes pugnabunt.
j navis parva in imo mari iacet.

3 Translate the following into Latin using first and second declension adjectives.

e.g. *the little ship sails on the blue sea* → **navis parva in mari caeruleo navigat**

a The mischievous ghost lived in the bottom of the well.
b The great and the good are sometimes cowardly.
c The angry voters do not like the candidate's dirty toga.
d The brown bears are walking next to a beautiful river.
e The wily magician wrote in a secret book.
f The haughty king neglected the wretched peasants.
g Dread goddesses will punish the wicked.
h The ancient tree stood on the top of the hill.

i The tender chicks are sleeping in the high nest.

j Tomorrow the tired women will arrive at the first gate.

4 Write the word for *good* **which agrees in number, gender and case with the following nouns. If there is more than one possible answer give them all.**

e.g. agricolae → **boni** or **bono**

a	rebus	**f**	urbi
b	regis	**g**	imperatore
c	capitum	**h**	manuum
d	cives	**i**	mare
e	domine	**j**	legionem

5 Translate the following sentences into English. The adjectives decline like *ingens.*

e.g. **canem ingentem habeo** → *I have a huge dog*

a iuvenes audaces trans flumen nataverunt.

b togam viri felicis pueri tangebant.

c pugiles viribus paribus pugnaverunt.

d moenia ingentia circum urbem aedificaverunt.

e speluncae ferarum ferocium in montibus sunt.

f senex cum adulescente per vias ambulabat.

g prudentem maritum feminae probant.

h magistratus impotentes erant.

i cives regi atroci resistebant.

j mentem ingenii capacem philosophus habet.

6 Translate the following sentences into English. The adjectives go like *fortis.*

e.g. **per ianuam humilem insignis venit** → *the famous man came through the lowly door*

a clamores fortium audio.

b fabulas tristes fidicen cantabat.

c oratori insigni cives parent.

d iter facile fortibus est.

e saporem mellis dulcis amo.
f liberis omnibus pater dona dedit.
g Athenienses communem thesaurum habebant.
h pompae grandes per vias procedebant.
i onera gravia trans pontem aselli portant.
j in loco incolumi gemmas celavi.

7 Translate the following sentences into English. The adjectives go like *acer* or *vetus*.

e.g. **fabulas veteres liberi amant** → *the children love old stories*

a sonitum equorum acrium audio.
b vetera templa Augustus renovavit.
c cum monstris volucribus Iason pugnavit.
d aquas salubres ad fontem bibimus.
e cursus non semper celeribus est.
f actorem celebrem in theatro plaudimus.
g pauper ad portas divitis sedebat.
h peregrinatores ad delubrum sospites advenerunt.
i alacribus gradibus nuntii festinaverunt.
j elephanti omnium memores sunt.

8 Translate the following sentences into Latin using third declension adjectives.

e.g. *we were sitting in a packed inn* → **in taberna frequenti sedebamus**

a The swift runner greeted the sad citizens.
b I shall send a letter to the cruel tyrant.
c Marcus is the son of a poor man.
d The house is on a green hill.
e Pericles persuaded everyone.
f Young men respect the old.
g Lions like the taste of bold children.
h The Gauls closed the road with huge rocks.
i You (pl.) will not overcome the brave.
j We seek a swift horse.

9 Translate the following sentences into English.

e.g. **mare altius quam lacus est** → *the sea is deeper than the lake*

a est ovum avis maioris.
b fabulam peiorem numquam vidi.
c puella filium divitioris amat.
d nihil durius quam adamas est.
e iter longius via quam mari est.
f Alpes multo altiores quam colles Romani sunt.
g Romani hostibus fortioribus quam Graecis resistebant.
h clamores equitum plurium audivimus.
i aedificia meliora Romani habent quam Galli.
j ovis paulo minor quam caper est.

10 Translate the following sentences into English.

e.g. **glacies gelidior aqua est** → *ice is colder than water*

a Socrates sapientissimus hominum erat.
b verba proditoris maxime dubia erant.
c monstrum dentes acutissimos habet.
d sanguis densior aqua est.
e grues gracillimi super tecta volabant.
f stilus gladio fortior est.
g horti magis idonei agris sunt.
h puella quam plurimas rosas matri colligebat.
i plurimi civium aurum quaesiverunt.
j elephanti multo gravidiores tauris sunt.

11 Translate the following sentences into English.

e.g. **boves lente in agro ambulant** → *the oxen are walking slowly in the field*

a puellae in lacum ultro desiluerunt.
b avarus liberos parum alebat.
c machinam fabri male refecerunt.
d senex iuvenes sapienter erudiebat.
e crimen vehementer reus abiuravit.
f Marcus facile altissimus erat.
g Ciceronem magnopere laudavisti.

h fere mille naves Graeci habebant.
i haud bene negotium agebant.
j Iuliettam Romeo valde amabat.

12 Translate the following sentences into English.
e.g. **statim ad patrem cucurrit** → *he ran to his father immediately*

a civibus semper fideles erimus.
b domine, hospites mox advenient.
c nusquam feminam pulchriorem vidi.
d alibi hostes oppugnabimus.
e cenam non multo ante paraverat.
f haud diu in cubiculo mansi.
g Cicero Catilinam iterum vituperavit.
h cras Caesarem fortasse videbis.
i identidem filium advocavit.
j pacem legati profecto petent.

13 Translate the following sentences into English.
e.g. **responsum regi minime placuit** → *the reply pleased the king very little*

a sicarii senatorem nequissime necaverunt.
b poeta versus postremo perfecerat.
c sacerdotes e templo tutissime fugerunt.
d quam celerrime ad custodes festinavi.
e facilius ambulo quam curro.
f Varus bellum peius quam Caesar gessit.
g nuntium diutius exspectavimus.
h Cyclops minus callidus erat quam Ulysses.
i equites ad urbem pervenerunt celerius quam pedites.
j ancilla multo melius saltat quam cantat.

Points to remember

1 Positive adjectives which combine elements of the first and second declensions decline like **bonus-a-um** (*good*), **miser**

misera miserum (*wretched*) and **pulcher pulchra pulchrum**
(*beautiful*).

2 Positive third declension adjectives have a very wide variety
of nominatives, just like the nouns. Sometimes they only have
one nominative ending, like **ingens** (*huge*) and **audax** (*bold*).

3 Comparative adjectives decline like **fortior fortius** (*braver*).

4 Superlative adjectives decline line **bonus-a-um** (*good*) and have
the endings -issimus-a-um, errimus-a-um and -illimus-a-um.

5 Adjectives ending in -eus, -ius or -uus keep the same formation
but use the adverbs **magis** (*more*) *and* **maxime** (*most*).
E.g. **magis dubius** (*more doubtful*).

6 Adjectives can be used as nouns. E.g. **boni** (*good men*), **bona**
(*goods*).

7 The commonest endings of adverbs are -e (**digne** *worthily*), -ter
(**fortiter** *bravely*), -um (**multum** *much*) or -im (**cursim** *quickly*).

8 Comparative adverbs are formed from the neuter accusative
singular of the comparative adjectives (e.g. **fortius** *more
bravely*) and superlative adverbs are formed from the stems of
the superlative adjectives (e.g. **celerrime** *very quickly*).

9 Comparison is expressed either with **quam** (*than*) followed
by the same case after it as before it, or with the ablative of
comparison.

10 **quam** is used with the superlative adverb to mean *as...as
possible*. E.g. **quam celerrime** (*as quickly as possible*).

6

Prepositions, conjunctions and numerals

Prepositions

A preposition is a word which denotes the relationship (usually spatial) between one noun and another. In Latin most prepositions are followed by (govern) either the accusative case or the ablative case, except in, sub, super and subter which can take either, depending on whether there is movement involved (accusative) or not (ablative).

A Prepositions governing (followed by) the accusative case are:

ad → *to, at*
adversus / adversum →
  opposite, towards, against
ante → *before*
apud → *among, near, at the*
  house of
circum → *around*
circa / circiter → *about*
cis / citra → *on this side of*
clam → *unknown to*
contra → *against*
erga → *towards*
extra → *outside*
in → *into, onto, against*

infra → *below*
inter → *amongst, between*
intra → *within*
iuxta → *next to*
ob → *in the way of, on*
  account of
penes → *in the power of*
per → *through*
pone → *behind*
post → *after, behind*
praeter → *beside, except, past*
prope → *near*
propter → *on account of, near*

secundum → *according to, next to, along*

sub → *up to*

subter → *close up to*

super → *over*

supra → *above*

trans → *across*

ultra → *beyond*

versus / versum → *towards*

B Prepositions governing (followed by) the ablative case are:

a (ab before a vowel or h) → *by, from*

absque → *without*

coram → *in the presence of*

cum → *with, in the company of*

de → *from, down from, concerning*

e (ex before a vowel or h) → *out of, from*

in → *in or on*

palam → *in the sight of*

prae → *before, in front of*

pro → *before, on behalf of, for*

sine → *without*

sub → *under*

subter → *underneath*

super → *upon*

tenus → *as far as, reaching*

C In the case of **gratia** → *sake* and **causa** → *reason*, the ablative of the noun has almost come to be used as a preposition which takes the genitive.

    e.g. **ars *gratia* artis** → **art for the sake of art**

          exempli *gratia* → **for the sake of example** (abbreviated to e.g.)

          honoris *causa* → **by reason of** honour

D Many Latin words have prepositions as prefixes, i.e. the preposition is added to the start of the word. These are called **compound** words. The meaning of the preposition alters the sense of the word accordingly, e.g. *praesideo* → I sit **in front of** (hence *president*).

Conjunctions

Insight

Conjunctions are words like *and*, or *because* that link clauses.

Conjunctions (*coniungo*) are used to join linguistic units together. They may join words, phrases, clauses or entire sentences. Notice that some are used in a number of different ways.

E **Coordinative conjunctions** connect either two or more nouns in the same case or two or more simple sentences.

▶ **Connective: et, -que** (ending), **atque, ac** → *and*; **neque, nec** → *nor*; **et, etiam, quoque, item** → *also*.
▶ **Separative: aut, vel, -ve** (ending) → *either*, or; **sive, seu** → *whether, or*.
▶ **Adversative: sed, ast, at** → but; **autem** → *but, however*; **atqui** → *but yet*; **ceterum, verum, vero** → *moreover*, but; **at enim** → *but it will be said*; **tamen** → *however, nevertheless*; **attamen, verumtamen** → *but nevertheless*.
▶ **Causal: nam, namque, enim, etenim** → *for* and **enimvero** → *for indeed*.
▶ **Conclusive: ergo, itaque, igitur** → *therefore*; **quare, quamobrem, quapropter, quocirca** → *wherefore*.
▶ **Interrogative** (see also Unit 7U and V): **num** → *surely not?*; **nonne** → *surely?* **-ne** (an ending which turns a statement into a question); **utrum ... an** → *whether ... or*; **annon, necne** → *or not?*

F **Subordinative conjunctions** are used to introduce a clause which is grammatically subordinate to another (see Unit 1T).

▶ **Consecutive: ut** → *so that, with the result that*; **ut non** → *so that not*; **quin** → *but that*.
▶ **Final: ut** → *so that, in order that*; **ne, ut ne** → *lest*; **neve, neu** → *and lest*; **quo** → *whereby, in order that*; **quominus** → *whereby not, in order that not*.
▶ **Causal: quod, quia** → *because*; **cum, quoniam, quandoquidem** → *since*; **quippe** → *seeing that*; **siquidem** → *inasmuch as*.
▶ **Temporal: cum, ut** → *when, since*; **quando, ubi** → *when*; **dum, donec, quoad** → *while, as long as, until*; **quatenus** → *how long*; **antequam, priusquam** → *before*; **postquam** → *after*; **simul ac** → *as soon as*; **quotiens** → *as often as*.

► **Conditional: si** → *if*; **sin** → *but if*; **sive, seu** → *whether, or if*; **nisi, ni** → *unless*; **si non** → *if not*; **si modo** → *if only*; **modo, tantum** → *only*; **modo, dummodo** → *provided that*.

► **Concessive: etsi, etiamsi** → *even if, although*; **tametsi** → *although*; **quamquam, utut** → *however, although*; **quamvis** → *although, however much*; **cum** → *whereas*; **ut, licet** → *granting that*.

► **Comparative: ut, uti, velut, veluti, sicut, sicuti ceu** → *as*; **quomodo, quemadmodum** → *as, how*; **quam** → *as*; **utpote** → *as being*; **quasi, ut si** → *as if*; **ceu, tamquam** → *as though*.

G The following pairings of conjunctions are commonly found:

adeo ... ut → *so far ... that*	**neque ... neque, nec ... nec**, and **neve ... neve** → *neither ... nor*
aut ... aut and **vel ... vel** → *either ... or*	**sic ... ut** → *so ... as*
et ... et, -que ... -que and **-que ... et** → *both ... and*	**sive ... sive** and **seu ... seu** → *whether ... or*
ita ... ut → *so ... that*	**tam ... quam** → *so (as) ... as*
	ut ... ita → *as ... so*

H Position

Some conjunctions never appear as the first word in their phrase, clause or sentence, notably **enim** → *for*, **autem** → *however*, **igitur** → *therefore* and **vero** → *but*. When translating you should usually put them first in the clause or phrase in English, unless sense dictates otherwise, e.g. **pater autem ianuam clausit.** → *However, father closed the door.*

Numerals

I There are four types of numerals, each answering a question: **cardinal** (*how many*), **ordinal** (*in what order*), **distributive** (*how many each* or *at a time*) and **numeral adverbs** (*how often*).

J Selected numbers from 1 to 2000. Note that there is no zero in Latin.

Numeral	Cardinal	Ordinal	Numeral	Cardinal	Ordinal
1 I	unus -a um	primus -a -um	29 XXIX	undetriginta	undetricensimus
2 II	duo -ae -o	secundus	30 XXX	triginta	tricensimus
3 III	tres tria	tertius	40 XL	quadraginta	quadragensimus
4 IV	quattuor	quartus	50 L	quinquaginta	quinquagensimus
5 V	quinque	quintus	60 LX	sexaginta	sexagensimus
6 VI	sex	sextus	70 LXX	septuaginta	septuagensimus
7 VII	septem	septimus	80 LXXX	octoginta	octogensimus
8 VIII	octo	octavus	90 XC	nonaginta	nonagensimus
9 IX	novem	nonus	99 XCIX	undecentum	undecentensimus
10 X	decem	decimus	100 C	centum	centensimus
11 XI	undecim	undecimus	101 CI	centum et unus	centensimus primus
12 XII	duodecim	duodecimus	200 CC	ducenti -ae -a	ducentensimus
13 XIII	tredecim	tertius decimus	300 CCC	trecenti	trecentensimus
14 XIV	quattuordecim	quartus decimus	400 CCCC	quadringenti	quadringentensimus
15 XV	quindecim	quintus decimus	500 D	quingenti	quingentensimus
16 XVI	sedecim	sextus decimus	600 DC	sescenti	sescentensimus
17 XVII	septendecim	septimus decimus	700 DCC	septingenti	septingentensimus
18 XVIII	duodeviginti*	duodevicensimus	800 DCCC	octingenti	octingentensimus
19 XIX	undeviginti*	undevicensimus	900 CM	nongenti	nongentensimus
20 XX	viginti	vicensimus	1000 M	mille	millensimus
21 XXI	unus et viginti	unus et vicensimus	2000 MM	duo milia	bismillensimus

* or **octodecim** → *eighteen* and **novendecim** → *nineteen*

K The **cardinal numbers** *one*, *two* and *three* decline. Note the endings **-ius** in the genitive singular and **-i** in the dative singular. These endings are also found in some pronouns (see Unit 7).

▶ One

> **Insight**
> The Latin cardinal numbers **unus, duo, tres** (*one, two, three*) change for gender and case: **cum duabus amicis** *with two (female) friends*; **cum duobus amicis** *with two (male) friends*.

Singular	Masc.	Fem.	Neuter	Plural	Masc.	Fem.	Neuter
nom. and voc.	unus	una	unum		uni	unae	una
acc.	unum	unam	unum		unos	unas	una
gen.	unius	unius	unius		unorum	unarum	unorum
dat.	uni	uni	uni		unis	unis	unis
abl.	uno	una	uno		unis	unis	unis

▶ Two

	Masc.	Fem.	Neuter
nom. and voc.	duo	duae	duo
acc.	duos	duas	duo
gen.	duorum	duarum	duorum
dat.	duobus	duabus	duobus
abl.	duobus	duabus	duobus

▶ Three

Masc. and Fem.	Neuter
tres	tria
tres	tria
trium	trium
tribus	tribus
tribus	tribus

L Cardinal numbers from 4 to 100 do not decline. Hundreds from 200 to 900 decline like the plural of bonus (see Unit 5C). The singular **mille** → *1000* is an adjective which does not decline but its plural **milia** is a noun which goes like **cubilia** (see Unit 3M) and is followed by a genitive, **e.g. multa milia passuum** → *many thousands of paces* (i.e. many miles).

M In compound numbers between 20 and 99 either the smaller number with **et** comes first or the larger number without **et**. Usually **unus** comes first but in numbers above 100 the larger comes first, whether with **et** or without it. Thousands are expressed either by putting cardinal numbers before **milia** (as in the preceding list) or by putting numeral adverbs like **bis** before **mille.**

N Ordinal and distributive numbers decline like **bonus** (see Unit 5C).

▶ **Distributive** numbers are **singuli** → *one each, one at a time*, **bini** → *two each, two at a time*, **terni** → *three each, three at a time*, **quaterni** → *four each, four at a time*, **quini** → *five each, five at a time*, **seni** → *six each, six at a time* etc.
▶ Distributive numbers are used instead of cardinals with nouns which are plural in form but singular in meaning (e.g. **terna castra** → *three camps*), except that the plural of **unus** is used with such words instead of **singuli,** e.g. **una castra** → *one camp.*
▶ Distributive numerals are also used in the multiplication of numbers, e.g. **bis terna sunt sex** → *twice three are six.*

O Numeral adverbs are **semel** → *once*, **bis** → *twice*, **ter** → *thrice*, **quater** → *four times*, **quinquiens** (or **-es**) → *five times*, etc.

P When answering the question '**times how much?**', the 'multiplicative' adjectives are used, e.g. **simplex -icis** → *single, times one*, **duplex -icis** → *double, twofold*, **triplex -icis** → *triple, threefold*, **quadruplex -icis** → *times four, fourfold*, **decemplex -icis** → *times ten, tenfold* etc.

Q Titles like **triumvir** → *member of a board of three*, **duumvir** → *member of a board of two* and **decemvir** → *member of a board of ten*, refer to positions of authority in Rome and the empire. They are usually not translated but left in their Latin nominative form. They are declined like **vir** (see Unit 3G. In the plurals **duoviri** and **tresviri**, both parts of the word decline, e.g. **duorumvirorum** → *of the duoviri*.

1 Translate the following sentences into English. The prepositions take the accusative.

e.g. **Hannibal ad portas est** → *Hannibal is at the gates*

  a pueri ob capros sedent.
  b cervae ad silvas cucurrerunt.
  c apud Marcum praestigiatores hospitibus placent.
  d murum circum hortum senex aedificaverat.
  e corvi super cacumina arborum volant.
  f equi trans flumen natabant.
  g servus poculum pone sedem celavit.
  h Cicero orationes in Marcum Antonium scripsit.
  i valles inter montes iacebat.
  j duces citra urbem convenerunt.

2 Translate the following sentences into English. The prepositions take the ablative.

e.g. **monstrum sub ponte latebat** → *the ogre was hiding under the bridge*

  a palam civibus Horatius Etruscis resistebat.
  b orator prae multitudine stetit.
  c iudex pro reo dixit.
  d sine comitibus ambulo.
  e Catilinam Cicero coram senatoribus incusavit.
  f avarus aurum sub pavimento sepelivit.
  g de fundo controversiam habuimus.
  h aqua e fonte fluebat.
  i pueri cum puellis in area ludebant.
  j delphinus in portu natabat.

3 Translate the following sentences into English. They contain a mixture of prepositions.

e.g. **trans mare amoris causa natavit** → *he swam across the sea because of love*

a panem super mensa pistor posuit.
b Galli tenus urbe agros vastaverunt.
c cameli ante meridiem non bibunt.
d gemmas iuxta coronam ponunt.
e puero osculum dedit palam parentibus.
f ad tabernam propter pluviam currimus.
g crocodilus subter ripa latet.
h potestatem gratia pecuniarum petis.
i aestate liberi extra cubicula dormient.
j thesaurum in speluncis petimus.

4 Translate the following into Latin.

e.g. *I watched the man through the door* → **virum per ianuam spectabam**

a You (s.) will write the poem for honour's sake.
b She rode between the cottages.
c Unknown to the guards, they opened the gates.
d Tomorrow we shall depart from the woods.
e I am working on behalf of the merchants.
f The animals were asleep except for the geese.
g We are walking close up to the river bank.
h The statues are standing in front of the temple.
i The islands lie beyond the sea.
j After noon we sleep in the sun.

5 Translate the following sentences into English.

e.g. **aut Caesar aut nullus ero** → *I shall either be a Caesar or a nobody*

a panem circensesque civibus imperator praebuit.
b cogito ergo sum.
c non modo pontes sed etiam aquaeductus aedificabant.

d Milo extra portas stat nam custos est.

e actores male recitaverant; spectatores tamen plauserunt.

f neque aurum neque argentum inveni.

g omnes tacebant nam dominus aegrotabat.

h et Brutus et Cassius Caesarem oppugnaverunt.

i nonne templum visitabis?

j laborem perfecimus itaque domum ambulamus.

6 Translate the following sentences into English.

e.g. **cenam non edebam quod ova non amo** → *I did not eat dinner because I do not like eggs*

a quotiens canes latrant, corvi avolant.

b simul ac tuba sonuit, hostes impetum fecerunt.

c ut caelum tepescet, ita maria dilatabunt.

d liberi dum ludunt discunt.

e postquam mater discessit pueri clamabant.

f quoniam ludos edidit Caesarem laudamus.

g etiamsi mons altus est, ascendemus.

h quia hostes ubique sunt idcirco Romani semper pugnant.

i sive manebis sive discedes, civibus semper fidelis ero.

j Titus decidit quod celerius currebat.

7 Translate the following into English. Put the Roman numerals into Arabic numerals.

e.g. **DCCCLXXXVIII** → *888*

a duobus diebus aedificium perfecerimus.

b MCMLXVI

c rex septem et triginta annos regnabat.

d princeps ternos equos fratribus dedit.

e animalia bina in navem intrabant.

f nonagensimo anno Graeci foedus renovaverunt.

g viginti milia militum exploratores viderunt.

h cives decemviros valde timebant.

Points to remember

1 Prepositions generally denote spatial relationships between one noun and another. They can refer to temporal relationships.

2 Most prepositions are followed by either the accusative or ablative case. Some take both and alter their meaning accordingly. Note especially that **in** plus accusative means *into* or *on to*, whereas **in** plus ablative means *in* or *on*.

3 The ablatives of the words **gratia** (*sake*) and **causa** (*reason*) became tantamount to prepositions taking the genitive. E.g. **ars gratia artis** (*art for art's sake*).

4 Many Latin words are compounds with prepositions used at the front of the word as a prefix. E.g. **praesideo** (*I sit in front of*).

5 Compound words formed with prepositions which end in a consonant sometimes alter or lose that final consonant, often doubling the following one. E.g. **traicio** (*I throw across*) from **trans iacio**, **colligo** (*I gather*) from **cum lego** and **attingo** (*I touch upon*) from **ad tango**.

6 Conjunctions link clauses and sentences together and some never appear as the first word in their clause. E.g. **enim** (*for*) and **igitur** (*therefore*).

7 The numerals are I *1*, V *5*, X *10*, L *50*, C *100*, D *500* and M *1,000*. The Romans had no zero.

8 The cardinal numbers **unus-a-um** (*one*), **duo duae duo** (*two*) and **tres tria** (*three*) decline. Those from *4–100* do not.

9 Note especially the endings **-ius** and **-i** in the genitive and dative singular of **unus-a-um**. This word does not decline like **bonus-a-um** (*good*).

10 **mille** (*a thousand*) is a singular, indeclinable adjective but its plural **milia** (*thousands*) is a noun which is followed by the genitive. E.g. **mille passus** (*a thousand paces* or *a Roman mile*) and **multa milia passuum** (*many thousands of paces* or *many Roman miles*).

7

Pronouns and questions

Personal pronouns

> **Insight**
>
> Pronouns are words like '*it, him, us*'. They are used to replace nouns.

A **Personal pronouns** (*I*, *you*, etc.) are used only in place of nouns. They decline in Latin.

	1st person singular		2nd person singular	
nom. and voc.	ego	I	tu	you
acc.	me	me	te	you
gen.	mei	my, mine, of me	tui	of you, your, yours
dat.	mihi *or* mi	to, for me	tibi	to, for you
abl.	me	by, with, from me	te	by, with, from you

	Plural		Plural	
nom. and voc.	nos	we	vos	you
acc.	nos	us	vos	you

(Contd)

	Plural		*Plural*	
gen.	nostri	of us, our, ours	vestri	of you, your, yours
	or nostrum	of us	*or* vestrum	of you
dat.	nobis	to, for us	vobis	to, for you
abl.	nobis	by, with, from us	vobis	by, with, from you

▶ The genitives **nostri** and **vestri** are **objective genitives** (see Unit 4C6), e.g. **nostri memor** → *mindful of us*, while the genitives **nostrum** and **vestrum** are partitive genitives (see Unit 4C7), e.g. **multi vestrum** → *many of you*.

▶ For the **personal pronoun** of the 3rd person (*he, she, it* and *they*) Latin makes use of the pronouns **is, ea, id** → *he, she, it* or *that* (see D).

▶ The nominatives of personal pronouns are usually used only for emphasis in Latin because the endings of verbs already tell us who is performing the action.

▶ If **cum** → *with* is used with the ablative of personal pronouns it is always written after the word: **mecum** → *with me*, **tecum** → *with you*, **nobiscum** → *with us* and **vobiscum** → *with you*.

Reflexive pronouns

B Reflexive pronouns (*myself, yourself, himself* etc.) are used only in place of nouns. **NB** These must not be confused with the emphatic pronoun **ipse, ipsa, ipsum** (see I).

▶ The **reflexive pronouns** of the 1st and 2nd person (*myself, yourself, ourselves, yourselves*) are the same as the personal pronouns but without the nominative, e.g. **me** lavavi → *I washed myself*, **vos** fraudavistis → *you have cheated yourselves*.

▶ The reflexive pronoun of the 3rd person is the same in the singular and the plural:

acc.	se or sese	himself, herself, itself or themselves
gen.	sui	of himself, herself, itself or themselves
dat.	sibi	to or for himself, herself, itself or themselves
abl.	se	by, with or from himself, herself, itself or themselves

For example: **Brutus** *se* **necavit** → *Brutus killed **himself**.*

Possessive pronouns

C The **possessive** pronouns are used as adjectives and decline either like **bonus -a -um** or **pulcher -chra -chrum** (see Unit 5C).

meus mea meum → *my, mine*   **noster nostra nostrum** → *our, ours*
tuus tua tuum → *your, yours*   **vester vestra vestrum** → *your*
 (singular)   *yours* (plural)

suus sua suum → *his, hers, its* or *their own* (contrast **eius** and **eorum:** see D).

NB Of these only **meus** and **noster** have vocatives and the masculine vocative singular of **meus** is irregular: **mi**, e.g. **o** *mi* **fili** → *o my son.*

Demonstrative pronouns

D The **demonstrative pronoun is ea id** has two meanings. Either it is used as the 3rd personal pronoun (*he, she* and *it*) or it means 'that' (compare **ille illa illud** in F).

Singular	Masc.	Fem.	Neuter	Plural	Masc.	Fem.	Neuter
nom.	is	ea	id		ei	eae	ea
acc.	eum	eam	id		eos	eas	ea
gen.	eius	eius	eius		eorum	earum	eorum
dat.	ei	ei	ei		eis, iis	eis, iis	eis, iis
abl.	eo	ea	eo		eis, iis	eis, iis	eis, iis

The genitives **eius** and **eorum** are used to mean *his*, *hers*, *its* or *theirs* when referring to someone other than the subject, e.g. **fratrem *eius* agnovit** → *he recognized his (someone else's) brother*, but **fratrem *suum* agnovit** → *he recognized his (own) brother* (see C).

E The **demonstrative pronoun hic haec hoc** → *this*

Singular	Masc.	Fem.	Neuter	Plural	Masc.	Fem.	Neuter
nom.	hic	haec	hoc		hi	hae	haec
acc.	hunc	hanc	hoc		hos	has	haec
gen.	huius	huius	huius		horum	harum	horum
dat.	huic	huic	huic		his	his	his
abl.	hoc	hac	hoc		his	his	his

F The **demonstrative pronoun ille illa illud** → *that (over there)* can also be used to mean *he*, *she* or *it*. It is where the French articles **le** and **la** come from.

Singular	Masc.	Fem.	Neuter	Plural	Masc.	Fem.	Neuter
nom.	ille	illa	illud		illi	illae	illa
acc.	illum	illam	illud		illos	illas	illa
gen.	illius	illius	illius		illorum	illarum	illorum
dat.	illi	illi	illi		illis	illis	illis
abl.	illo	illa	illo		illis	illis	illis

G The **demonstrative pronoun iste ista istud** → *that*, declines like
ille and means '*that near you*' as opposed to '*that over there*'.
It is often disparaging in tone, e.g. *iste* amicus me vituperavit →
that friend *of yours has insulted me.*

Definitive pronoun

H The **definitive pronoun idem eadem idem** → *the same*, is like **is
ea id**, with **-dem** added.

Singular	Masc.	Fem.	Neuter	Plural Masc.	Fem.	Neuter
nom.	idem	eadem	idem	eidem	eaedem	eadem
acc.	eundem	eandem	idem	eosdem	easdem	eadem
gen.	eiusdem	eiusdem	eiusdem	eorundem	earundem	eorundem
dat.	eidem	eidem	eidem	eisdem *or* iisdem	eisdem *or* iisdem	eisdem *or* iisdem
abl.	eodem	eadem	eodem	eisdem *or* iisdem	eisdem *or* iisdem	eisdem *or* iisdem

---

Emphatic pronoun

I The **emphatic pronoun: ipse ipsa ipsum**

The **emphatic** (or **intensive**) **pronoun ipse ipsa ipsum** → *self*, draws
attention to something and is used as an adjective. It must not be
confused with the reflexive pronoun (see B) which is used as a noun
and is an essential part of the sentence structure whereas **ipse** is
not. It can be translated in a variety of ways into English provided
that there is some emphasis, e.g. **Marcus equum *ipsum* delegit** →
*Marcus chose **the very** horse*, or *Marcus chose the horse **itself**.*

Singular	Masc.	Fem.	Neuter	Plural	Masc.	Fem.	Neuter
nom.	ipse	ipsa	ipsum		ipsi	ipsae	ipsa
acc.	ipsum	ipsam	ipsum		ipsos	ipsas	ipsa
gen.	ipsius	ipsius	ipsius		ipsorum	ipsarum	ipsorum
dat.	ipsi	ipsi	ipsi		ipsis	ipsis	ipsis
abl.	ipso	ipsa	ipso		ipsis	ipsis	ipsis

Relative pronoun

J The **relative pronoun: qui quae quod** (see also Unit 13-AF).

Singular	Masc.	Fem.	Neuter	Plural	Masc.	Fem.	Neuter
nom.	qui	quae	quod		qui	quae	quae
acc.	quem	quam	quod		quos	quas	quae
gen.	cuius	cuius	cuius		quorum	quarum	quorum
dat.	cui	cui	cui		quibus	quibus	quibus
abl.	quo	qua	quo		quibus	quibus	quibus

NB The dative and ablative plurals of this word can also be **quīs**.

▶ The **relative pronoun qui quae quod** → *who*, *which*, is used to introduce **relative clauses**. These clauses give us some more information about a word in the main clause, e.g. in the sentence **canem** *quem avia mihi dedit* **amo** → *I like the dog which my grandmother gave to me*, the relative clause (in bold italics) tells us something about the dog and the relative pronoun **quem** → *which*, introduces the clause and relates to the word *dog* in the main clause.
▶ The word to which a relative pronoun relates is called the **antecedent** (**canem** → *dog* in the preceding example). In Latin, the relative pronoun always agrees in **number** and **gender** with the antecedent but its **case** always depends on its function in the clause, e.g. in the previous example the word **quem** → *which*

is accusative in Latin because it is the object of the clause 'which my grandmother gave to me'.

▶ In English, when the relative pronoun refers to a person it is one of the few words which decline (compare the personal pronouns in A): nom. **who**, acc. **whom** and gen. **whose**. In English, however, we sometimes use the word **that** or **what** instead of **who** or **which**, or even omit the relative pronoun altogether where the sense is obvious.

e.g. I know the man *whom* you   I know the man you
      mean.   mean.

    I know the man *that* you mean.

▶ In Latin, the antecedent can sometimes be omitted in the main clause if the sense is clear, e.g. **virum quem tu vidisti ego quoque vidi** → *I too have seen the man whom you saw*, can also be written **quem tu vidisti ego quoque vidi**. Furthermore, the antecedent can even be repeated in the relative clause, e.g **virum quem tu vidisiti ego virum quoque vidi.**

▶ The relative pronoun is far more common in Latin than in English. In addition to situations where we would use 'who' or 'which' in English, the Romans frequently used **qui quae quod** where we would use a demonstrative pronoun like 'this' or 'that', or even a personal pronoun, e.g. **quod consilium probo** → *I approve of that plan* (literally: *which plan I approve.*)

▶ For the use of **qui** in **final** (**purpose**) clauses, see Unit 14D.

Indefinite pronouns

K The **indefinite pronoun quidam quaedam quoddam** (or **quiddam**) → *a certain person*, *someone*, is quite close to the English indefinite article '*a*'. It looks similar to the relative pronoun (see J) with the ending **-dam**. Other compounds of **qui** or **quis** (see N) decline in a similar way, changing the -m of the acc. sing. and gen. pl. to **-n**, as in **idem eadem idem** (see H).

Sing.	Masc.	Fem.	Neuter	Plural	Masc.	Fem.	Neuter
nom.	quidam	quaedam	quoddam		quidam	quaedam	quaedam
acc.	quendam	quandam	quoddam		quosdam	quasdam	quaedam
gen.	cuiusdam	cuiusdam	cuiusdam		quorundam	quarundam	quorundam
dat.	cuidam	cuidam	cuidam		quibusdam	quibusdam	quibusdam
abl.	quodam	quadam	quodam		quibusdam	quibusdam	quibusdam

The dative and ablative plurals of this word can also be **quīsdam**.

L Another **indefinite pronoun** is **quis qua quid** (or **qui quae quod**) → *anyone, anything*. This declines in a similar way to the relative pronoun (see J) apart from the alternative forms of the nominative and accusative singulars; one used as a pronoun, the other as an adjective:

Sing.	Masc.	Fem.	Neut.	Plural	Masc.	Fem.	Neut.
nom.	quis	qua	quid *(pronoun)*		qui	quae	quae *(or qua)*
	or qui	quae	quod *(adjective)*				
acc.	quem	quam	quid *(or quod)*		quos	quas	quae *(or qua)*
gen.	cuius	cuius	cuius		quorum	quarum	quorum
dat.	cui	cui	cui		quibus	quibus	quibus
abl.	quo	qua	quo		quibus	quibus	quibus

Interrogative pronouns

M The **interrogative pronoun quis? quis? quid?** (or **qui? quae? quod?**) → *who? what?* is used to ask questions. It declines in almost exactly the same way as the relative pronoun (see J) apart from the alternative forms of the nominative and accusative singulars; one used as a pronoun, the other as an adjective:

N In these **compounds** of **quis** and **qui** the forms in brackets are used only as adjectives.

Sing.	Masc.	Fem.	Neut.
nom.	quis? or qui?	quis? quae?	quid? *(pronoun)* quod? *(adjective)*
acc.	quem?	quam?	quid? *(or* quod) etc. *as the relative pronoun*

Masculine	Feminine	Neuter	
quicumque	quaecumque	quodcumque	*whosoever, whatsoever*
quisquis	quisquis	quidquid (*or* quicquid)	*whosoever, whatsoever*
aliquis	aliqua	aliquid	*someone, something*
aliqui	aliqua	aliquod	*someone, something*
quisque	quaeque	quidque (*or* quodque)	*each*
quisquam	quisquam	quidquam (*or* quicquam)	*anyone at all*
quispiam	quaepiam	quippiam (*or* quodpiam)	*someone*
quivis	quaevis	quidvis (*or* quodvis)	*anyone you like*
quilibet	quaelibet	quidlibet (*or* quodlibet)	*anyone you like*
unusquisque	unaquaeque	unumquidque (*or* unumquodque)	*every single one*
ecquis?	ecqua?	equid (*or* equod)?	*is there anyone who?*
quisnam?	quaenam?	quidnam (*or* quodnam)?	*who, then?*

Pronouns used as adjectives

O The following pronouns (also called pronominal adjectives) decline like **unus una unum** → *one* (see 6K): **ullus -a -um** → *any*, **nullus -a -um** → *none*, **totus -a -um** → *whole* and **solus -a -um** → *sole, lone*.

Singular	Masc.	Fem.	Neuter	Plural	Masc.	Fem.	Neuter
nom.	solus	sola	solum		soli	solae	sola
acc.	solum	solam	solum		solos	solas	sola
gen.	solius	solius	solius		solorum	solarum	solorum
dat.	soli	soli	soli		solis	solis	solis
abl.	solo	sola	solo		solis	solis	solis

P The declension of the pronoun **alius alia aliud** → *other, another* is:

Singular	Masc.	Fem.	Neuter	Plural	Masc.	Fem.	Neuter
nom.	alius	alia	aliud		alii	aliae	alia
acc.	alium	aliam	aliud		alios	alias	alia
gen.	alius	alius	alius		aliorum	aliarum	aliorum
dat.	alii	alii	alii		aliis	aliis	aliis
abl.	alio	alia	alio		aliis	aliis	aliis

Q The declension of **alter altera alterum** → *one (or the other) of two* is:

Singular	Masc.	Fem.	Neuter	Plural	Masc.	Fem.	Neuter
nom.	alter	altera	alterum		alteri	alterae	altera
acc.	alterum	alteram	alterum		alteros	alteras	altera
gen.	alterius	alterius	alterius		alterorum	alterarum	alterorum
dat.	alteri	alteri	alteri		alteris	alteris	alteris
abl.	altero	altera	altero		alteris	alteris	alteris

R uter utra utrum → *which (of two)?* or *whichever (of two)* and neuter neutra neutrum → *neither*, decline like **alter** except that they keep the letter **e** only in the nominative masculine singular **uter** and **neuter**.

S nemo → *nobody* declines: nom. **nemo,** acc. **neminem,** gen. **nullius,** dat. **nemini,** abl. **nullo.**

T Of the other adjectival pronouns which decline, the following decline:

- ▶ like **bonus -a -um** (see Unit 5C): **tantus -a -um** → *so great,* **quantus -a -um** → *how great, how big,* **quantuscumque -acumque -umcumque** → *however great* and **aliquantus -a -um** → *some* (quantity), *considerable.*
- ▶ like **fortis -is -e** (see Unit 5F): **talis -is -e** → *of such a kind,* **qualis -is -e?** → *of what kind?*, **qualiscumque -iscumque -ecumque** → *of whatsoever kind.*
- ▶ like **uter utra utrum** (see R): **alteruter alterutra alterutrum** → *one or other (of two),* **utercumque utracumque utrumcumque** → *whichever of two.*

Direct questions

Direct questions are those asked directly of someone and ending in a question mark.

U Single direct questions

- ▶ In English, when we turn a statement into a question we change the position of the verb.
  e.g. statement: *This is a kangaroo.* question: *Is this a kangaroo?*
  In Latin, the syllable **-ne** is added to the first word.
  e.g. statement: **tu hoc fecisti** → *you did this.* question: **tune hoc fecisti?** → *did you do this?*

▶ When **nonne** introduces the question it implies that the questioner would like to hear the answer 'yes'. This requires something like 'surely?' in English.
   e.g. **nonne hoc fecisti?** → *surely you did this?* or *you did do this, didn't you?*

▶ When **num** introduces the question it implies that the questioner would like to hear the answer 'no'. This requires something like 'surely not?' in English.
   e.g. **num hoc fecisti?** → *surely you did not do this?* or *you did not do this, did you?*

▶ When **an** introduces a question it expresses the speaker's surprise.
   e.g. **an tu hoc fecisti?** → *did you really do this?*

▶ As in English, direct questions may be introduced by an interrogative (question) word, such as **quis? / qui?** (*who?*) or one of its compounds which decline (listed in N), or any of the following:

quo? → *to where (whither)?*	**ubi?** → *where?*	**unde?** → *from where (whence)?*
quando? → *when?*	**qualis?** → *what kind of?*	**quantus -a -um?** → *how great?*
quotiens? → *how often?*	**quot?** → *how many?*	**uter?** → *which (of two)?*
quomodo? → *how (in what way)?*	**cur?** → *why?*	**quam?** → *how (as in how long)?*
qua? → *by what way?*	**quare?** → *why?*	**quamobrem?** → *why?*
quamdiu? → *for how long?*		

   e.g. **quomodo hoc fecisti?** → *how did you do this?*

▶ Sometimes a single direct question is not introduced by a question word but is implied in the tone of voice. In Latin the question mark will tell you whether it is such a question.
   e.g. **tu hoc fecisti?** → *did you do this?*

V **Direct questions** which offer an alternative are introduced by **utrum ... an** (or **anne**). The negative is **annon**. Sometimes the word **utrum** is omitted.

e.g. **utrum vos exspectabimus annon?** → *shall we expect you or not?*

W The **subjunctive** is used for deliberative questions (Unit 9H).
e.g. **quid faciamus?** → *what are we to do?*

X **Rhetorical questions** are those which do not really expect an answer and take **the accusative and infinitive construction (Unit 15B–C).**
e.g. **cur hostibus auxilium misisse?** → *Why has he sent help to his enemies?*

Y The single answers *yes* and *no* do not exist in Latin. The closest are phrases like **ita** → *just so*, **ita vero** → *just so indeed*, **vero** or **sane** → *truly*, **etiam** → *even (so)*, **non ita** or **non vero** → *not so* and **minime** or **minime vero** → *least of all*.

1 Translate the following sentences into English.
e.g. **ego puerum laudo sed tu castigas** → *I praise the boy but you criticize him*

  a heri me Salvius visitavit.
  b vobiscum ad fundum ambulabimus.
  c te amo.
  d mihi pater fabulam narravit.
  e nostri odium Romanum notissimum est.
  f tibi aurum dabo.
  g iudices vobis ignoscent.
  h equites nobis lente appropinquabant.
  i complures vestrum adsunt.
  j nos manebimus sed vos discedetis.

2 Translate the following sentences into English.
e.g. **Sphinx se humum coniecit** → *the Sphinx hurled herself to the ground*

  a nos vertimus ad septentriones.
  b latrones se in speluncis celaverunt.

c pecuniae gratia vobis favetis.
d cur tibi non ignosces?
e prae civibus te dedecoravisti.
f donum mihi tenebo.
g nos numquam culpabimus.
h mane semper me rado.
i sibi domum aedificaverunt.
j Titus cultro se laesit.

3 Translate the following sentences into English.

e.g. **Caesar suos trans Rubiconem duxit** → *Caesar led his men across the Rubicon*

a vestimenta nova liberis vestris emi.
b fundum nostrum Romani vastaverunt.
c equus tuus maior quam meus est.
d anseres mei per noctem clamabant.
e cum suis fratribus pontem defendit.
f o mi fili, tandem te inveni.
g tua culpa fur domum intravit.
h consilia vestra non probo.
i sonitum vocis suae amat.
j nostri contra Gallos pugnabunt.

4 Translate the following sentences into Latin.

e.g. *Tomorrow we shall see your* (pl.) *island* → **cras insulam vestram videbimus**

a I have shown you (s.) my beautiful villa.
b We shall ride but you (pl.) will walk.
c Narcissus loved himself too much.
d The women came to the forum with us.
e Hercules, your glory is eternal.
f The gladiators have overcome our men.
g The prisoners will save themselves.
h The traitor will not save me.
i Father has made a raft for us.
j The sailors collected food for themselves.

5 Translate the following into English.

e.g. **id consilium optimum est** → *that plan is the best*

  a Portia eum valde amat.
  b eae puellae in horto ludunt.
  c eo tempore domi eramus.
  d eandem feminam amamus.
  e ei candidato non faveo.
  f heri idem monstrum vidi.
  g vestimenta eorum peto.
  h ea pictura eorundem puerorum est.
  i eos numquam vidi.
  j eam servavi sed eum deserui.

6 Translate the following into English.

e.g. **hic puer fortior quam Marcus est** → *this boy is stronger than Marcus*

  a haec verba incredibilia sunt.
  b vestigia huius ferae maxima sunt.
  c pro libertate hoc die pugnabimus.
  d hanc fabulam saepe audivi.
  e hos diu exspectavimus.
  f leones in hac spelunca habitant.
  g procul ab hoc loco curremus.
  h huic Cassius invidet.
  i sculptor effigies horum civium facit.
  j hunc fundum non ememus.

7 Translate the following into English.

e.g. **faciem illius agnosco** → *I recognize that man's face*

  a istud non probamus.
  b illi senatores Caesarem necaverunt.
  c per illam portam urbem intrabimus.
  d pro illo reo orator eloquenter causam oravit.
  e filium istius latronis non defendam.
  f pictores illas domus ornabant.

g duces gentium illarum Romanis favent.
h iuvenis illam intente spectat.
i illum heri in foro vidimus.
j iste canis me momordit.

8 Translate the following into Latin.

e.g. *these seats are too high* → **hae sellae altiores sunt**

a We shall see her soon.
b These are the same trees.
c That plough is heavier than this one.
d Nobody likes those clothes of yours.
e I have not heard it.
f This meal is excellent.
g I have washed this man's toga.
h We arrived at the temple on the same day.
i I like the sound of those bells.
j They have given him that letter.

9 Translate the following sentences into English.

e.g. **Brutus ipse epistolam legit** → *Brutus read the letter himself*

a quis custodiet ipsos custodes?
b ea ipsa stolam elegit.
c hoc ferro ipso Dido se necavit.
d hi captivi sunt liberi regis ipsius.
e eandem umbram ipsam heri iterum vidi.
f meo avunculo ipso pecuniam dedi.
g cenam ipse coxi.
h milites praetoriani ipsi imperatorem necaverunt.
i scelus ipsum auctorem patefecit.
j deam ipsam in templo vidi.

10 Translate the following sentences into English.

e.g. **sumus quae edimus** → *we are what we eat*

a quos tu amas ego quoque amo.
b illi sunt quibus numquam favebo.

c cena quam paraveras erat pessima.
d is qui audet vincet.
e sunt optiones duae quarum neutra bona est.
f Titus est iudex prae quo stabimus.
g ille est dux cui semper parebimus.
h hic est senator cuius filium Vitellia amat.
i aurum quod inveni gravissmum est.
j qui gladium e saxo extraxerit ille regnabit.

11 Translate the following sentences into Latin.

e.g. *the king crowned the queen himself* → **rex ipse reginam coronavit**

a I have found the very gold which the miser himself hid.
b We shall catch the thieves who robbed you (s.).
c They will build the house you (s.) desire.
d I do not like what I have seen.
e The monster itself is not unfriendly.
f She herself has avoided the dangers that we feared.
g We do not trust a man whose father was a traitor.
h The women will save the city itself.
i You (pl.) will catch those very thieves.
j Not everything that glistens is gold.

12 Translate the following sentences into English.

e.g. **quendam in horto heri vidi** → *I saw someone in the garden yesterday*

a equus cuiusdam super saepem saluit.
b viator quidam quendam in via vidit.
c candidato cuidam quem non nominabo favi.
d subter arbore quadam thesaurum celaverunt.
e quaedam verba infausta haruspex susurravit.
f venenis quibusdam senatorem sicarius interfecit.
g cervos quosdam venatores aspexerunt.
h quoddam consilium periculosum cepimus.
i profugi quodam die ab urbe clam discedent.
j nomina quorundam coniuratorum numquam sciemus.

13 Translate the following sentences into English.

e.g. quis nobis semitam monstrabit? → *who will show us the way?*

  a quid novi audivisti?
  b quemque virum de auro rogavi.
  c quisnam illud monstrum liberavit?
  d Romani unumquemque vicanorum necaverunt.
  e quae signa arcana habent magi?
  f quidquid pecuniae comparavi, tibi dabo.
  g num avarus quidquam filio suo legavit?
  h ecqua Antonium amabit?
  i quos testes ad basilicam citabis?
  j cuius est hic fundus?

14 Translate the following into Latin.

e.g. *each man was carrying an axe* → securim quisque portabat

  a Who is that woman?
  b Titus will come to Rome with some friends.
  c I have heard a certain story from the old man.
  d Melissa told me something about the master.
  e Each man has seen the temple.
  f Whose (s.) gift have you (s.) taken?
  g Whom (pl.) will the ambassador choose?
  h Have you (s.) seen anyone at all today?
  i With whom (pl.) was the queen walking?
  j Some women will not support you (s.).

15 Translate the following sentences into English.

e.g. soli pro portis stabamus → *we were standing alone before the gates*

  a utrum consulem Carthaginienses interfecerunt?
  b ullis modis montes ascendemus.
  c Cloelia sola hostibus resistebat.
  d fratrem alterum alteri antepono.
  e aliud consilium capiemus.
  f nullas naves in portu vidimus.

g Cicero laudem totius senatus accepit.
h neutra puella actorem agnovit.
i neminem Hercules timebat.
j Clodia maritum alius feminae amat.

16 Translate the following sentences into English.

e.g. **tempestatem tantam numquam vidimus** → *we have never seen such a great storm*

a custodes alterutrum captivorum necaverunt.
b talibus verbis orator civibus persuasit.
c qualia sunt haec dona?
d quantus est elephantus?
e utrocumque consuli qui mercedes dabit favebo.
f aliquantam pecuniam a patre comparavi.
g talis iuvenis numquam miles erit.
h cum qualibus comitibus iter facies?
i tantas fabulas Petronius semper dat.
j aliquanto condimento coquus cenam condivit.

17 Translate the following sentences into Latin.

e.g. *we have seen the peoples of the whole world* → **populos totius mundi vidimus**

a What kind of husband will Cloelia marry?
b How great is the power of the gods?
c Nobody believed Cassandra.
d The one consul has seriously offended the other.
e I alone shall support Lepidus.
f Tomorrow we shall see the temples of another city.
g Which of the (two) sisters do you (s.) love?
h Desperate men will adopt any plans.
i We have not often seen such treasures.
j They have seen neither brother today.

18 Translate the following questions into English.

e.g. **visne fabulam spectare?** → *do you want to watch the play?*

a an Caesar necatus est?
b canemne meam vidisti?
c an ille pecuniam abstulit?
d num Titus cras veniet?
e nonne felem aluisti Septime?
f illumne gladiatorem antea vidistis?
g an Cassius illud dixit?
h puerine in harena ludunt?
i num isto candidato favetis?
j nonne flores pulchrae sunt?

19 **Translate the following questions into English.**
e.g. **quo vadis domine?** → *where are you going, master?*

a quando princeps meus adveniet?
b quomodo Caesar Rhenum transiit?
c cur eam non amas?
d qua fur in atrium venit?
e ubi sunt sellae, ancillae?
f quamdiu in cubiculo iacebas Quinte?
g quomodo urbem antiquam invenisti?
h quam durus est hic gladius?
i quot oves sunt in agris?
j unde Claudius illam togam comparavit?

20 **Translate the following questions into English.**
e.g. **utrum domi manebis an mecum ambulabis?** → *will you stay at home or walk with me?*

a clipeum perfecisti faber?
b utrum Tiberium an Quintum amas?
c quotiens haec verba dicit?
d cenam parabis annon?
e utrum undeviginti anne viginti annos natus es?
f quare servus ianuam claudit?
g utrum Vesuvium visitavisti annon?
h quamobrem Romani Gallos oppugnant?

i nuces an uvas mavis?

j utrum Tullius equitabit an Iulius?

21 Translate the following questions into Latin.

e.g. *you are not waiting for the emperor, are you?* → **num imperatorem exspectas?**

a Why are the soldiers destroying the bridge?

b You (s.) did hide the gold, didn't you?

c Where are the merchant's gems?

d Is Marcus at home?

e Shall we visit the Colosseum or the Circus Maximus?

f How many elephants did Hannibal have?

g Did the dog really bite you (s.)?

h Surely he has not sold the farm?

i Will Aemilia come to Rome or not?

j Where are the wells in this village?

Points to remember

1 Pronouns are words used as substitutes for nouns. E.g. **ille dixit** *(that man spoke)* instead of **imperator dixit** *(the general spoke)*.

2 Note the distinctive genitive and dative singular endings in **-ius** and **-i** respectively which are characteristic of so many pronouns and distinguish them clearly from nouns.

3 Be careful to avoid confusing **ille-a-ud** *(that far from both of us)* with **iste-a-ud** *(that near you)*.

4 The relative pronoun **qui quae quod** was the Romans' favourite word. It is used so often in Latin that we sometimes have to translate is not as who but as *this* or *that*.

5 Remember that **is ea id** can mean *he, she, it* or *that*.

6 To turn a Latin statement into a question, add the ending -ne to the first word.

7 The subjunctive mood is used for deliberative questions. Otherwise the indicative mood is used.

8 A question which would like to hear the answer 'yes' is introduced by **nonne** *(surely)* and one which would like to hear the answer 'no' is introduced by **num** *(surely...not)*.

9 A question which offers an alternative contains **utrum** *(whether)* ... **an** *(or)* or ...**anonn** *(or not)*.

10 The closest Latin comes to using 'yes' and 'no' in answers is **ita vero** and **mimine vero** respectively.

8

....

Passive and deponent verbs

Present, future and imperfect passive tenses

A The two **voices** of a verb reflect whether the subject is
performing the action (**active voice**) or **experiencing** the action
(**passive voice**).
e.g. The dog **has stolen** the biscuit (active).
The dog **has been stolen** by the pirate (passive).

B In English we form the **passive voice** by using the appropriate
tense of the verb *to be* with the **past participle**. In the example
has been is the appropriate tense of 'to be' (perfect) and **stolen** is
the past participle.

C The form of the **passive voice** for **present, future** and **imperfect**
tenses of all the four conjugations is straightforward. The
following table compares the endings:

	Active ending	*Passive ending*
1st person singular (I)	**-o / -m**	**-or / -r**
2nd person singular (you)	**-s**	**-ris / -eris** (*or* **-re**)
3rd person singular (he/she/it)	**-t**	**-tur**
1st person plural (we)	**-mus**	**-mur**
2nd person plural (you)	**-tis**	**-mini**
3rd person plural (they)	**-nt**	**-ntur**

D Examples of the passive form of each of the three tenses from the four conjugations are:

- ▶ present first conj.: portor portaris portatur portamur portamini portantur
- ▶ future first conj.: portabor portaberis portabitur portabimur portabimini portabuntur
- ▶ imperfect first conj.: portabar portabaris portabatur portabamur portabamini portabantur
- ▶ present second conj.: habeor haberis habetur habemur habemini habentur
- ▶ future second conj.: habebor habeberis habebitur habebimur habebimini habebuntur
- ▶ imperfect second conj.: habebar habebaris habebatur habebamur habebamini habebantur
- ▶ present third conj.: agor ageris agitur agimur agimini aguntur
- ▶ future third conj.: agar ageris agetur agemur agemini agentur
- ▶ imperfect third conj.: agebar agebaris agebatur agebamur agebamini agebantur
- ▶ present fourth conj.: audior audiris auditur audimur audimini audiuntur
- ▶ future fourth conj.: audiar audieris audietur audiemur audiemini audientur
- ▶ imperfect fourth conj.: audiebar audiebaris audiebatur audiebamur audiebamini audiebantur

E Agent and instrument
- ▶ When a passive verb is used we need to know the **agent** (person) or **instrument** (thing) **by whom** or **by which** the action is performed. In the example in A the pirate is the **agent** because it was he who did the stealing.
- ▶ In Latin the **agent** is expressed using **a / ab** → *by*, plus the **ablative of agent** (see Unit 4E12), e.g. **canis** *a matrona* **portatur** → *the dog is being carried by the lady*.
- ▶ In Latin the instrument is expressed using the plain **ablative of instrument** (see Unit 4E13), e.g. **agri** *flumine* **inundantur** → *the fields are being flooded by the river*.

Perfect, future perfect and pluperfect passive tenses

These tenses are formed in the same way for verbs of all four conjugations.

F Perfect passive

▶ The **perfect passive tense** is formed by using the **perfect passive participle** (see Unit 10C) and the present tense of *to be* (**sum es est** etc.).

    e.g. portatus sum → I have been carried

        portatus es → you (s.) have been carried

        portatus est → he has been carried

        portati sumus → we have been carried

        portati estis → you (pl.) have been carried

        portati sunt → they have been carried

▶ The participle declines and so changes **number** and **gender** depending on the number and gender of the subject. So, if the subject is feminine we find e.g. **portata est** → *she has been carried*, while if the subject is neuter we find e.g. **portatum est** → *it has been carried*.

G Future perfect passive

▶ The **future perfect passive** is formed with the **perfect passive participle** (see Unit 10C) and the future tense of *to be* (**ero eris erit** etc.).

    e.g. portatus ero → I shall have been carried

        portatus eris → you (s.) will have been carried

        portatus erit → he will have been carried

        portati erimus → we shall have been carried

        portati eritis → you (pl.) will have been carried

        portati erunt → they will have been carried

▶ The participle declines, just as for the perfect passive, e.g. **portata erit** → *she will have been carried*, **portatum erit** → *it will have been carried*.

H Pluperfect passive

▶ The **pluperfect passive** is formed with the **perfect passive participle** (see Unit 10C) and the imperfect tense of *to be* (**eram eras erat** etc.).

e.g. portatus eram → I had been carried
portatus eras → you (s.) had been carried
portatus erat → he had been carried
portati eramus → we had been carried
portati eratis → you (pl.) had been carried
portati erant → they had been carried

▶ The participle declines, just as for the perfect passive, e.g.
portat_a_ erat → *she had been carried*, **portat_um_ erat** → *it had been carried*.

I For the **agent** and **instrument** after these verbs, see E.

_____

Deponent verbs

J Deponent verbs are **passive in form** but **active in meaning**.
There is no equivalent to this phenomenon in English. Just as
for normal active verbs, you can tell which conjugation they
belong to by examining their **present infinitive** ending (the second
principal part: see Unit 1K). In dictionaries only their first three
principal parts **are given.**

▶ Deponent verbs of the first conjugation are characterized by
a present infinitive ending -ari, e.g. **conor con_ari_ conatus
sum** → *try*.

▶ Deponent verbs of the second conjugation are characterized by
a present infinitive ending -eri, e.g **confiteor confit_eri_ confessus
sum** → *confess, acknowledge*.

▶ Deponent verbs of the third conjugation are characterized by
a present infinitive ending -i, e.g. **loquor loqui locutus sum** →
speak.

▶ Deponent verbs of the fourth conjugation are characterized by
a present infinitive ending -iri, e.g. **mentior ment_iri_ mentitus
sum** → *tell lies*.

K Although the indicative, subjunctive and imperative moods
and perfect participles of deponent verbs are passive in form
and active in meaning, their **present and future participles,**

future infinitives, supines and gerunds are active in form and meaning, as in normal verbs. The gerundives of deponent verbs are passive in form and meaning.

L Sample forms for the first conjugation verb **conor -ari -atus sum** → *try* are:

	Indicative	Subjunctive	Imperative	Infinitive	Participle
present	conor	coner	conare	conari	conans
future	conabor	—	—	conaturus esse	conaturus
imperfect	conabar	conarer	—	—	—
perfect	conatus sum	conatus sim	—	conatus esse	conatus
future perfect	conatus ero	—	—	—	—
pluperfect	conatus eram	conatus essem	—	—	—

Gerund: conandum   Gerundive: conandus -a -um   Supine: conatum

M Some important deponent verbs are followed by the ablative:
e.g. **utor uti usus sum** → *use, employ, enjoy*
   abutor abuti abusus sum → *use up, exhaust*
   fruor frui fructus sum → *enjoy, have the use of*
   fungor fungi functus sum → *perform, discharge*
   vescor vesci (no perfect) → *feed on, enjoy*
   potior potiri potitus sum → *take possession of*

Semi-deponent verbs

N Semi-deponent verbs are those which have an **active** present, imperfect and future, but a **passive** perfect, pluperfect and future perfect. There are not many but they are common:

Second conjugation: **audeo audere ausus sum** → *dare*; **gaudeo gaudere gavisus sum** → *rejoice*; **soleo solere solitus sum** → *be accustomed to*.

Third conjugation: **fido fidere fisus sum** → *trust* (+ dative); **confido** → *trust*; **diffido** → *mistrust*.

1 Write out the following passive tenses of the verbs below.

e.g. the present passive of **amo** → amor, amaris, amatur, amamur, amamini, amantur

a the future passive of **duco**
b the present passive of **facio**
c the imperfect passive of **rego**
d the present passive of **servo**
e the future passive of **capio**
f the imperfect passive of **doceo**
g the present passive of **custodio**
h the future passive of **iubeo**
i the imperfect passive of **dico**
j the present passive of **moneo**

2 Translate the following verbs into English.

e.g. **liberabimur** → *we shall be freed*

a persuaderis
b trahar
c secabimur
d amaberis
e sentiebatur
f rapientur
g dantur
h arcessimur
i movebamini
j delebaris

3 Translate the following sentences into English.

e.g. **precibus non movebimur** → *we shall not be moved by prayers*

a dumis aries tenebatur.
b ab Artemidoro Caesar monebitur.
c dona a nepotibus tibi dabuntur.
d cena a coquo coquebatur.
e imperator ab hostibus capietur.
f montibus impedimur.
g agmen a Tiberio ducetur.
h Aeneas sagitta vulneratur.
i a consulibus laudabamur.
j grana ab agricolis sparguntur.

4 Translate the following sentences into Latin.

e.g. *you (s.) are loved by a worthy man* → **a viro digno amaris**

  a I shall be heard by all.
  b You (pl.) will be taught by the best teachers.
  c The orator is believed by many.
  d The story was being narrated by the old man.
  e They are being watched by the dogs.
  f The doors were being closed by the slaves.
  g The girl will be bitten by a snake.
  h The ship was being broken by the waves and rocks.
  i It will be announced tomorrow.
  j The book was being written by a very clever scribe.

5 Write out the passive tenses of the following verbs.

e.g. the perfect passive of **amo** → **amatus sum, amatus es, amatus
     est, amati sumus, amati estis, amati sunt**

  a the perfect passive of **habeo**
  b the future perfect passive of **ago**
  c the pluperfect passive of **audio**
  d the future perfect passive of **capio**
  e the pluperfect passive of **duco**
  f the perfect passive of **moneo**
  g the perfect passive of **custodio**
  h the pluperfect passive of **facio**
  i the perfect passive of **laudo**
  j the perfect passive of **exspecto**

6 Translate the following verbs into English.

e.g. **visa est** → *she has been seen*

  a factum erat
  b laudata est
  c perfectum erit
  d prodita est
  e scriptum erat
  f ignota erit

g servata erat

h notatum est

i punita est

j aedificatum erit

7 Translate the following sentences into English.

e.g. **naves a nautis ornatae erant** → *the ships had been decorated by the sailors*

a dona a rege data erant.

b asini oneribus oppressi sunt.

c epistulae a legatis missae erunt.

d seges tempestatibus corrupta erat.

e cras urbs capta erit.

f reges a civibus expulsi sunt.

g gemmae a furibus surreptae erant.

h nodus notissimus ab Alexandro intercisus est.

i agna aquila erepta est.

j consilia a proditoribus patefacta erunt.

8 Translate the following sentences into Latin.

e.g. *the prisoners had been bound by the guards* → **captivi a custodibus vincti erant**

a The lamps will have been lit by the servant.

b The farms had been sold by the bailiff.

c Mother has been eaten by crocodiles.

d The beautiful roses had been plucked by the girl.

e The hare will have been beaten by the tortoise.

f We have been cheated by the merchants.

g The ghost had never been seen by the boys.

h The fields had been laid waste by the soldiers.

i This land was ruled by a wizard.

j The citizens will have been provoked by the barbarians.

9 Translate the following sentences into English.

e.g. **Romani imperio maximo potiti erant** → *the Romans had acquired a very great empire*

a philosophi de natura sapientiae rebantur.
b nolite morari liberi.
c athletas hortemur cives!
d nihil peius quam mortem patiemur.
e rex anno sexagensimo suo mortuus est.
f mane domo proficiscemur.
g fabri pontem experiuntur.
h equi per flumen trepide gressi sunt.
i puellae laete pompam secutae sunt.
j Galli per portas Romae ingressi erant.

10 Translate the following sentences into English.

e.g. **saxa de monte paulatim labebantur** → *rocks were gradually slipping down the mountain*

a hamadryades de arboribus ortae sunt.
b cras Romani Graecos aggredientur.
c gaudeamus igitur, iuvenes dum sumus!
d puella quattuordecim annos nata est.
e ille artifex modo marmore optimo utebatur.
f mercator domum locupletem nanctus est.
g servi horto domini benigni fruebantur.
h hieme agricola faeno abusus erat.
i post cladem imperator valde irascebatur.
j consules officio optime fungentur.

11 Translate the following sentences into English.

e.g. **numquam mortuorum obliviscemur** → *we shall never be forgetful of the dead*

a sol mox coorietur.
b vaccae herbis vescuntur.
c femina Caesari contradicere ausa est.
d noli umquam mentiri mi fili.
e percussores senem adorti sunt.
f olim puellae ad fontem mane convenire solitae erant.
g avarus mihi numquam fisus est.
h omnes pueri taurum verentur.

i custodes de captivis non loquentur.

j cur iuvenes minaris o iudex?

12 Translate the following sentences into Latin. Use deponent verbs.

e.g. *the citizens encourage me* → cives me hortantur

a Why has the magistrate lied about the money?
b Have you (s.) obtained the books?
c Do not fear the dark, my son.
d I have not forgotten the animals.
e Let us hunt the huge stag.
f Tomorrow we shall talk about the plan.
g The enemy are advancing slowly across the plain.
h You (pl.) are not accustomed to work carefully.
i The citizens have always trusted the orator.
j The captives will not come out from the gaol.

Points to remember

1 The personal endings of the present passive are -or, -ris, -tur, -mur, -mini, -ntur.

2 The personal endings of the future passive of the first and second conjugations are -bor, -beris, -bitur, -bimur, -bimini, -buntur.

3 The personal endings of the future passive of the third and fourth conjugations are -ar, -eris, -etur, -emur, -emini, -entur.

4 The personal endings of the imperfect passive are -bar, -baris, -batur, -bamur, -bamini, -bantur.

5 The perfect passive uses the perfect participle and the present indicative tense of **esse** (*to be*) as an auxiliary verb.

6 The pluperfect passive uses the perfect participle and the imperfect indicative tense of **esse** (*to be*) as an auxiliary verb.

7 The future perfect passive uses the perfect participle and the future indicative tense of **esse** (*to be*) as an auxiliary verb.

8 The agent after a passive verb is expressed by **a** (or **ab**) plus the ablative. The instrument after a passive verb is expressed by the plain ablative.

9 Deponent verbs are passive in form and active in meaning. They occur in all conjugations and include many common verbs like **loquor** (*I speak*) and **utor** (*I use*).

10 Semi-deponent verbs have active present, future and imperfect tenses, but deponent perfect, pluperfect and future perfect tenses. The ones you are likeliest to meet are **gaudeo** (*I rejoice*) **audeo** (*I dare*), **soleo** (*I am accustomed*) and **fido** (*I trust*).

9

Subjunctive verbs

A The **subjunctive mood** is used to denote an action that is desired, willed, anticipated, conditional or prospective. As a result it is normally found in subordinate clauses rather than as a main verb (see Unit 1U). The meaning and usage of the subjunctive are explained in H and I and under the relevant constructions. The mood has no regular future or future perfect tenses. Instead the future participle (see Unit 10D) is used with the present or imperfect subjunctive of the verb 'to be' (see Unit 12P).

B The **present subjunctive** active is formed from the present stem. The letter -e- comes before the personal endings -m, -s, -t, -mus, -tis, -unt in the first conjugation while the letter -a- comes before them in the second, third and fourth conjugations.

▶ Present active tense

	First conjugation	*Second conjugation*	*Third conjugation*	*Fourth conjugation*
1st person singular	portem	habeam	agam	audiam
2nd person singular	portes	habeas	agas	audias
3rd person singular	portet	habeat	agat	audiat
1st person plural	portemus	habeamus	agamus	audiamus

	First conjugation	Second conjugation	Third conjugation	Fourth conjugation
2nd person plural	portetis	habeatis	agatis	audiatis
3rd person plural	portent	habeant	agant	audiant

▶ The present subjunctive passive is formed as normal (see Unit 8C):
▶ **Present passive tense**

	First conjugation	Second conjugation	Third conjugation	Fourth conjugation
1st person singular	porter	habear	agar	audiar
2nd person singular	porteris	habearis	agaris	audiaris
3rd person singular	portetur	habeatur	agatur	audiatur
1st person plural	portemur	habeamur	agamur	audiamur
2nd person plural	portemini	habeamini	agamini	audiamini
3rd person plural	portentur	habeantur	agantur	audiantur

C The **imperfect subjunctive** active is formed by taking the **present infinitive** (**second principal part**) and adding the personal endings -m, -s, -t, -mus, -tis, -unt:

▶ **Imperfect active tense**

	First conjugation	Second conjugation	Third conjugation	Fourth conjugation
1st person singular	portarem	haberem	agerem	audirem
2nd person singular	portares	haberes	ageres	audires

(Contd)

	First conjugation	*Second conjugation*	*Third conjugation*	*Fourth conjugation*
3rd person singular	portaret	haberet	ageret	audiret
1st person plural	portaremus	haberemus	ageremus	audiremus
2nd person plural	portaretis	haberetis	ageretis	audiretis
3rd person plural	portarent	haberent	agerent	audirent

▶ The imperfect subjunctive passive is formed as normal (see Unit 8C):

▶ **Imperfect passive tense**

	First conjugation	*Second conjugation*	*Third conjugation*	*Fourth conjugation*
1st person singular	portarer	haberer	agerer	audirer
2nd person singular	portareris	habereris	agereris	audireris
3rd person singular	portaretur	haberetur	ageretur	audiretur
1st person plural	portaremur	haberemur	ageremur	audiremur
2nd person plural	portaremini	haberemini	ageremini	audiremini
3rd person plural	portarentur	haberentur	agerentur	audirentur

NB There is an alternative ending -re for -ris for the 2nd person singular in the present and imperfect passive subjunctive.

D The **perfect subjunctive active** is formed by adding **-erim, -eris, -erit, -erimus, -eritis, -erint** to the **perfect stem**. Be careful not to confuse these with some of the endings of the indicative future perfect active (see Unit 2W). The forms for the different

conjugations, from **porto** → *carry*, **habeo** → *have*, **ago** → *do*
and **audio** → *hear* are as follows:

	First conjugation	Second conjugation	Third conjugation	Fourth conjugation
1st person singular	portaverim	habuerim	egerim	audiverim
2nd person singular	portaveris	habueris	egeris	audiveris
3rd person singular	portaverit	habuerit	egerit	audiverit
1st person plural	portaverimus	habuerimus	egerimus	audiverimus
2nd person plural	portaveritis	habueritis	egeritis	audiveritis
3rd person plural	portaverint	habuerint	egerint	audiverint

E The **perfect subjunctive passive** is formed by a combination of the **perfect passive participle** (see Unit 10C) and the **present subjunctive tense** of *to be* (see Unit 12P). Remember that the participle agrees in number, gender and case with the noun it describes.

	First conjugation	Second conjugation	Third conjugation	Fourth conjugation
1st person singular	portatus sim	habitus sim	actus sim	auditus sim
2nd person singular	portatus sis	habitus sis	actus sis	auditus sis
3rd person singular	portatus sit	habitus sit	actus sit	auditus sit
1st person plural	portati simus	habiti simus	acti simus	auditi simus
2nd person plural	portati sitis	habiti sitis	acti sitis	auditi sitis
3rd person plural	portati sint	habiti sint	acti sint	auditi sint

F The pluperfect subjunctive active is formed by adding -issem, -isses, -isset, -issemus, -issetis, -issent to the perfect stem.

	First conjugation	Second conjugation	Third conjugation	Fourth conjugation
1st person singular	portavissem	habuissem	egissem	audivissem
2nd person singular	portavisses	habuisses	egisses	audivisses
3rd person singular	portavisset	habuisset	egisset	audivisset
1st person plural	portavissemus	habuissemus	egissemus	audivissemus
2nd person plural	portavissetis	habuissetis	egissetis	audivissetis
3rd person plural	portavissent	habuissent	egissent	audivissent

G The **pluperfect subjunctive passive** is formed by a combination of the **perfect passive participle** (see Unit 10C) and the **imperfect subjunctive tense** of to be (see Unit 12P). Remember that the participle agrees in number, gender and case with the noun it describes.

	First conjugation	Second conjugation	Third conjugation	Fourth conjugation
1st person singular	portatus essem	habitus essem	actus essem	auditus essem
2nd person singular	portatus esses	habitus esses	actus esses	auditus esses
3rd person singular	portatus esset	habitus esset	actus esset	auditus esset
1st person plural	portati essemus	habiti essemus	acti essemus	auditi essemus

	First conjugation	Second conjugation	Third conjugation	Fourth conjugation
2nd person plural	portati essetis	habiti essetis	acti essetis	auditi essetis
3rd person plural	portati essent	habiti essent	acti essent	auditi essent

The perfect and pluperfect subjunctives cannot really be translated into English in isolation. They are used in various constructions.

Subjunctive: uses

The subjunctive mood expresses possibility. We do not often use it in English but it exists (e.g. if I were you). When translating subjunctives it is almost always necessary to use accompanying auxiliary verbs such as would, should or might.

H In **main clauses** (see Unit 1T) the subjunctive is not common but when it is found it expresses what is desired or regarded as possible and appears as one of the following types.

▶ The **jussive subjunctive** (negative: **ne**) in the 2nd and 3rd person is almost a command. Present and perfect tenses are used, e.g. *caveat* emptor → *let the buyer beware*; *ne transieris* flumen → *do not cross the river*; cura *ne* me *vexes* → *take care you do not annoy me*; *petas* aurum → *(please) seek the gold*.

▶ The **hortative subjunctive** (negative: **ne**) in the 1st person expresses encouragement. The present tense is used, e.g. meliora *sequamur* → *let us seek better things*.

▶ The **concessive subjunctive** (negative: **ne**) expresses a concession such as granted that or supposing that. Present or perfect tenses are used, e.g. *celet* pecuniam Titus → *supposing that Titus is hiding the money*.

▶ The **deliberative subjunctive** (negative: **non**) is used for questions in which what ought to be done is uncertain. Present and imperfect tenses are used, e.g. quid *faciam*? → *what am I to do?*, quid *agerem*? → *what should I have done?*

▶ The **optative subjunctive** (negative: **ne**) expresses wishes. The present and perfect express a wish for the future, the imperfect a wish that something were so now and the pluperfect a wish that something had been so in the past. They are often introduced by **utinam** → *would that / if only*, e.g. **di te** *servent* → *may the gods preserve you*; **utinam haec** *diceres* → *if only you were saying this (now)*; **utinam id** *fecissem* → *would that I had done it*.

▶ The **potential subjunctive** (negative: **non**) expresses something which has the potential to happen and may depend upon a condition, although that condition is not always present. The present and perfect tenses are used with reference to the present and future; the imperfect with reference to the past, e.g. **quis** *audeat* **hoc facere?** → *who would dare to do this?* **eum fortem** *esse putares* → *you would have thought him to be brave*. **velim** → *I would like*, **nolim** → *I would not like* and **malim** → *I would prefer*, are common examples of this subjunctive.

I In subordinate clauses (see Unit 1T) the subjunctive is more common and is found:

▶ In expressions of desire or will or condition which depend on another sentence, e.g. in **indirect commands** (see Unit 15OQ) **rogo te ut** *venias* → *I ask you to come*.

▶ As the **prospective subjunctive** to represent something as anticipated rather than as a fact, e.g. **manebimus dum periculum** *augeat*? → *shall we remain until the danger may increase?*

▶ With its meaning so weak that it reports actual facts, e.g. in **result clauses** (see Unit 14H) **totiens rogavit ut** *adsentirem* → *he asked me so many times that I consented*.

▶ In indirect speech the verbs of subordinate clauses are in the subjunctive even if they were indicative in direct speech, except that in **dum** (→ *until*) clauses in indirect speech the present indicative is kept.

The subjunctives in these exercises are in main clauses. The uses of the subjunctive in subordinate clauses is tested under each of the subordinate constructions.

**1 Write out the present subjunctives, active or passive,
of the following verbs.**

e.g. the present subjunctive passive of sedeo → sedear, sedearis,
sedeatur, sedeamur, sedeamini, sedeantur

  a the present subjunctive passive of **facio**
  b the present subjunctive active of **seco**
  c the present subjunctive active of **rego**
  d the present subjunctive passive of **teneo**
  e the present subjunctive active of **moveo**
  f the present subjunctive passive of **capio**
  g the present subjunctive passive of **aperio**
  h the present subjunctive active of **cedo**
  i the present subjunctive active of **amo**
  j the present subjunctive passive of **venio**

**2 Write out the imperfect subjunctives, active or passive,
of the following verbs.**

e.g. The imperfect subjunctive active of **moneo** → monerem,
moneres, moneret, moneremus, moneretis, monerent

  a the imperfect subjunctive passive of **trado**
  b the imperfect subjunctive active of **video**
  c the imperfect subjunctive passive of **rogo**
  d the imperfect subjunctive active of **verto**
  e the imperfect subjunctive active of **iacio**
  f the imperfect subjunctive passive of **sentio**
  g the imperfect subjunctive active of **iubeo**
  h the imperfect subjunctive passive of **duco**
  i the imperfect subjunctive passive of **sto**
  j the imperfect subjunctive active of **frango**

3 Write out the perfect subjunctives, active or passive, of the following verbs.

e.g. the perfect subjunctive active of gero → gesserim, gesseris, gesserit, gesserimus, gesseritis, gesserint

  a the perfect subjunctive passive of **rideo**
  b the perfect subjunctive active of **ludo**
  c the perfect subjunctive active of **parco**
  d the perfect subjunctive passive of **cupio**
  e the perfect subjunctive active of **dormio**
  f the perfect subjunctive passive of **pugno**
  g the perfect subjunctive passive of **mitto**
  h the perfect subjunctive active of **suadeo**
  i the perfect subjunctive passive of **paro**
  j the perfect subjunctive active of **reperio**

4 Write out the pluperfect subjunctives, active or passive, of the following verbs.

e.g. the pluperfect subjunctive active of ruo → ruissem, ruisses, ruisset, ruissemus, ruissetis, ruissent

  a the pluperfect subjunctive passive of **relinquo**
  b the pluperfect subjunctive active of **deleo**
  c the pluperfect subjunctive passive of **laboro**
  d the pluperfect subjunctive active of **custodio**
  e the pluperfect subjunctive active of **accipio**
  f the pluperfect subjunctive passive of **pello**
  g the pluperfect subjunctive active of **dico**
  h the pluperfect subjunctive passive of **doceo**
  i the pluperfect subjunctive active of **claudo**
  j the pluperfect subjunctive passive of **sepelio**

5 Translate the following into English. The subjunctives are jussive or hortative.

e.g. ne te mater inveniat → *do not let mother find you*

  a portae aperiantur o custodes.
  b omnia vincit amor et nos cedamus amori.

c cives, imperatorem victorem salutemus!
d ne canes excitaveris.
e quam laetissime vivamus!
f aprum venatores caveant.
g ne pugnetis in horto pueri.
h nunc diligenter laboremus.
i appropinquent legati.
j Ciceronem audiamus.

6 Translate the following into English. The subjunctives are concessive or deliberative.

e.g. **quotiens haec verba dicam?** → *how often should I say these words?*

a quo nunc veniamus?
b necaverit maritum Clodia.
c habitet monstrum in spelunca.
d quomodo tibi subvenirem?
e cur vobis faveamus?

f Caesarem timuerit Cassius.
g ubi villam aedificem?
h victa sit Britannia a Romanis.
i cur tot annos laborem?
j cui libros meos legem?

7 Translate the following into English. The subjunctives are optative or potential.

e.g. **absit omen** → *may the (bad) omen be gone*

a vivat rex!
b cras velim te visitare.
c floreat civitas!
d heri Brutum ridentem videres.
e nolim umbram in tenebris videre.

f cadent inimici!
g utinam flumen Caesar ne transiisset.
h quis Catilinam crederet?
i utinam Cato nunc viveret.
j malim equitare potius quam ambulare.

8 Translate the following sentences into Latin.

e.g. *let the contest be started* → **certamen excitetur**

a Who would love the miser?
b Let us not walk to the shore.

c May you (s.) always sing beautifully.

d Do not let the old man hurt the horse.

e What should I say to the senator?

f Would that you (s.) had not killed the goose.

g Why would you (s.) have hidden the book?

h Let the general himself lead us.

i Let us depart from the forum.

j Granted that Caesar likes Antonius.

Points to remember

1 The present active subjunctive is formed by adding the letter -e- before the endings of the first conjugation and -a- before the endings of the other conjugations. The present passive subjunctive is formed as normal.

2 The imperfect active subjunctive is formed by adding the personal endings -m, -s, -t, -mus, -tis, -nt to the present active infinitive. The imperfect passive subjunctive is formed as normal.

3 The perfect active subjunctive is formed by adding -erim, -eris, -erit, -erimus, -eritis, -erint to the perfect stem. The perfect passive subjunctive is formed from the perfect participle and the present subjunctive of the verb to be.

4 The pluperfect active subjunctive is formed by adding -issem, -isses, -isset, -issemus, -issetis, -issent to the perfect stem. The pluperfect passive subjunctive if formed from the perfect participle and the imperfect subjunctive of the verb *to be*.

5 The subjunctive is a mood used to express anticipated or conditional actions, as opposed to the indicative mood which makes statements which deal more with certainty.

6 In English we express the subjunctive using auxiliary verbs, such as *may*, *might* or *would*. E.g. *May I see? Would I were elsewhere!*

7 The subjunctive doesn't often occur in main clauses and when it does, expresses what is desired or regarded as possible. E.g. **vivat rex!** *Long live the king!*

8 The following types of subjunctive are found in main clauses: jussive, hortative, concessive, deliberative, optative and potential.

9 In subordinate clauses the subjunctive is much more common and although it usually expresses a desire, wish or condition, it can also be used where we in English would simply use an indicative.

10 To express a negative desire with the subjunctive, the word **ne** is used. E.g. **ne dicatur** *Let it not be said.*

10

Verbal nouns and adjectives

Participles

> **Insight**
> Participles are words derived from verbs, such as *undone*, *walking*.

A **Participles** are the parts of a verb which are used like adjectives or nouns either to denote a state or condition, or to denote a person or thing in that state or condition. They have three tenses:

- ▶ The **present** and the **future**, which are **active**, i.e. the person or thing referred to by the participle is **performing** the action, e.g. *walking* (**present**); *about to go* (**future**).
- ▶ The **perfect**, which is **passive**, i.e. the person or thing referred to by the participle is **experiencing** the action, e.g. **loosened**, *having been loosened*.

B The **present participle** is formed by adding -**ns** on to the **present stem** of first and second conjugation verbs and -**ens** to the final consonant of the present stem of third conjugation verbs and to the characteristic long ī of the present stem of fourth conjugation verbs. The resulting word declines like the third declension adjective **ingens** (see Unit 5E), e.g. **porta*ns*** portantis → *carrying*, **habe*ns*** habentis → *having*, **ag*ens*** agentis → *doing*, **capi*ens*** capientis → *taking* and **audi*ens*** audientis → *hearing*.

The **present participle** is used as in English as an adjective to describe someone or something performing an action **at that moment**. Because the present participle is an **active** form of the verb, it can take an object, e.g. **pueri onera *portantes* ad urbem currunt** → *the boys run to the city **carrying** loads*.

It is also used as a noun to refer to a person or thing doing something, e.g. **voces *clamantium* audivi** → *I heard the voices of the people shouting*.

C The **perfect participle** is formed from the **fourth principal part** of a verb. Either the **fourth principal part** will be the **supine** (see G) or it will be the **perfect participle** itself. If it is the **supine** then replace the final **-um** with **-us** and you have the **perfect participle**. It declines like the first and second declension adjective **bonus -a -um** (see Unit 5C), e.g. **portat*us* -a -um** → *carried, having been carried*; **habit*us* -a -um** → *had, having been had*; **act*us* -a -um** → *done, having been done*; **audit*us* -a -um** → *heard, having been heard*.

▶ The **perfect participle** is used as in English as an adjective to describe someone or something who or which has experienced the action of the verb **and may still be doing so**, e.g. **flumen inundatum aspectabamus** → *we were gazing at the **flooded river***.

It is also used as a noun to refer to something which has experienced the action of a verb, e.g. ***captos* per loca deserta ducebat** → *he led **the captured men** across the desert*.

D The **future participle** is formed by adding **-urus** to the stem of the **perfect participle** (above). The word declines like the first and second declension adjective **bonus -a -um** (see Unit 5C), e.g. **portat*urus* -a -um** → *about to carry*, **habit*urus* -a -um** → *about to have*, **act*urus* -a -um** → *about to do*, **audit*urus* -a -um** → *about to hear*.

▶ The **future participle** is used as an adjective to describe someone about to, on the point of doing or intending to do something. Because the future participle is an **active** form of the verb, it can take an object, e.g. **puer patrem *salutaturus* e horreo cucurrit** → *the boy ran out of the barn (intending) to greet his father.*

It is also used as a noun to refer to people who are about to do something, e.g. **ave Caesar! morituri te salutant** → *Hail Caesar! Those about to die salute you.*

The gerund

E The **gerund** is a **verbal noun** which exists only in the singular. It is active in meaning and therefore can sometimes take an object if it is from a transitive verb. It declines as a neuter second declension noun in **-um** (see Unit 3E) but without a nominative. It is formed by adding **-ndum** to the present stem of first and second conjugation verbs and **-endum** (or sometimes **-undum**) to the final consonant of the present stem of third conjugation verbs and to the characteristic long ī of the present stem of fourth conjugation verbs.

e.g. first conjugation **porta<u>ndum</u>** → *the* (act of) *carrying*
second conjugation **habe<u>ndum</u>** → *the* (act of) *having*
third conjugation: **age<u>ndum</u>** (or **agu<u>ndum</u>**) → *the* (act of) *doing*
fourth conjugation: **audie<u>ndum</u>** (or **audiu<u>ndum</u>**) → *the* (act of) *hearing.*

F The **gerund** is used:

▶ In the accusative after **ad** (to express purpose) and sometimes after **ob** or **inter**, e.g. **Titus *ad dormiendum* domum venit** → *Titus went home to sleep.*
▶ In the genitive after abstract nouns and adjectives which take the genitive, e.g. **amor *bibendi*** → *a love of drinking*; **cupida te videndi est** → *she is desirous of seeing you* (i.e. she wants to see you).

- In the dative (rarely) after some verbs, adjectives and nouns implying help, fitness or use, e.g. **par est** *currendo* → *he is equal to **running***.
- In the ablative, with or without a preposition to indicate cause or instrument (see Unit 4E13), e.g. **clarissime** *clamando* **eum servaverunt** → *they saved him **by shouting** very loudly*.

The supine

G The **supine** is a fourth declension verbal noun and is usually the **fourth principal part** (see Unit 1K4). It means the act of doing something and exists in two cases: accusative (ending in **-um**) and ablative (ending in **-u**).

H The supine is used:

- In the **accusative** after verbs of motion to express purpose, e.g. **ad fundum frumentum** *messum* **veniunt** → *they go to the farm **(in order) to harvest** the grain*.
- In the **accusative** to form the future passive infinitive (see Unit 11G).
- In the **ablative** after certain adjectives of perception like **facilis, mirabilis, crudelis, dulcis, miserabilis,** turpis, **terribilis** and after **fas** → *right* and **nefas** → *wrong*, where in English we would use a gerund or an infinitive, e.g. **mirabile visu** → *marvellous in the seeing* (or *wonderful to see*), **nefas dictu** → *wrong in the telling* (or *wrong to mention*) and **miserabile auditu** → *wretched in the hearing* (or *wretched to hear*).

....

Insight

The following common expressions use respectively a gerund and a supine: **modus operandi** *way of working* (**operandum**, from **operare**); **mirabile dictu** *wonderful to say* (**dictum**, from **dicere**).

....

The gerundive

I The **gerundive** is a **passive** verbal adjective which is formed by adding -**us** -**a** -**um** to the stem of the gerund (see E). The word declines in three genders like **bonus** -**a** -**um** (see Unit 5C) and must agree with whatever it refers to. It is a distinctly Latin form which is hard to parallel in English. It refers to someone or something which **ought to** experience the action of the verb.

e.g. first conjugation portand**us** -**a** -**um** → he/she/that which is to be carried

second conjugation habend**us** -**a**-**um** → he/she/that which is to be had or held

third conjugation agend**us** -**a** -**um** → he/she/that which is to be done

fourth conjugation audiend**us** -**a** -**um** → he/she/that which is to be heard

(Sometimes the third and fourth conjugation gerundives end in the older form -**undus** -**a** -**um**.) The gerundive's basic use is as an adjective with the sense of what could or should happen, best translated as 'capable of being' or 'worthy of being' etc.,

e.g. **femina** *laudanda* **est** → *The woman is worthy to be praised (of being praised)*.

Insight

The names 'Amanda' and 'Miranda' are derived from gerundives: '*she who is to be loved*' and '*she who is to be admired*'.

J The **gerundive** of obligation

▶ This is used as an adjective with a forceful sense of necessity, conveying the idea of something which ought to be done, must be done or should be done, rather than simply what could be done or is worth being done, e.g. **res** *agendae* → *things which must be done*; **agri** *arandi* → *fields which must be ploughed*.

▶ The gerundive of obligation is used with the dative of agent by whom the thing must be done (see Unit 4D5), e.g. **milites, oppida capienda sunt vobis** → *soldiers, you must capture the towns* (literally: *the towns are to be captured by you*).

If there is another dative in the sentence, the ablative of agent or instrument may be used, e.g. **redemptio a patre mihi** *danda* **erat** → *the ransom had to be given to me by the father*.

▶ If the verb is intransitive or is being used intransitively, the nominative neuter singular of the gerundive is used with the verb 'to be' in an impersonal passive construction, e.g. *laborandum* **est nobis** → *we must work* (literally: *it is to be worked by us*); **Romam nobis** *eundum* **est** → *we must go to Rome* (literally: *it is to be gone to Rome by us*).

▶ After the verbs do → *I give*, **curo** → *I arrange*, **trado** → *I entrust* and **mitto** → *I send*, the gerundive is used in agreement with the object to show that something is caused to be done, e.g. **theatrum consules** *faciendum* **curaverunt** → *the consuls caused a theatre to be built.*

K The gerundive of purpose

▶ This is used in the accusative after the preposition **ad** to express purpose, e.g. **ad foedus renovandum convenerunt** → *they met to renew the treaty* (literally: *for the treaty which had to be renewed*).

▶ The gerundive of purpose is sometimes found in the genitive followed either by **gratia** or **causa** → *for the sake of*, e.g. **Cicero revenit urbis servandae causa** → *Cicero returned for the sake of saving the city* (literally: *for the sake of the city which had to be saved*).

▶ The gerundive of purpose can also be used in the dative, e.g. **diem constituit liti audiendae** → *he established a day for the lawsuit to be heard* (literally: *for the lawsuit which had to be heard*).

1 Translate the following sentences into English.

e.g. dormientem hospitem caupo necavit → *the innkeeper slew the guest as he slept*

a agricolae frumentum in agris demetentes cantabant.
b animalia per flumen salientia crocodili oppugnabant.
c puerum ad portas currentem video.
d alas pueri volantis sol liquefecit.
e clamores diem festum celebrantium audivimus.
f trans flumen fremens caute vadebamus.
g civibus dubitantibus orator persuasit.
h matri convalescenti dona misi.
i feles murem in herba latentem spectabat.
j peregrinatores urbi appropinquantes salutavimus.

2 Translate the following sentences into English.

e.g. placentas incensas coquus celavit → *the cook hid the burnt cakes*

a rotam fractam fabri reficiebant.
b milites victi ad castra cucurrerunt.
c nuntium exspectatum tandem audivimus.
d ossa in ruinis templi deleti inveni.
e orator pro civibus fraudatis eloquenter dixit.
f exploratores, a custodibus visi, statim diffugerunt.
g meam puellam amatam saepe visito.
h effigiem deae ornatam sacerdotes portabant.
i nitorem lapidum expolitorum puer amat.
j verba in libro scripta pulcherrima erant.

3 Translate the following sentences into English.

e.g. hic iacet Arturus; rex quondam rexque futurus → *here lies Arthur; once and future king*

a puerum in lutum salturum castigavi.
b filius militi patrem necaturo obstitit.
c vas casurum cepi.

d tempestatem venturam timemus.
e pontem transituri, ex equis descenderunt.
f gladiatores pugnaturos acriter plauserunt.
g matronae ad forum ambulabant, stolas empturae.
h haec est lyra poetae canturi.
i prae oratore dicturo stabamus.
j voces adventurorum audio.

4 Write out the gerunds or supines of the following verbs.
e.g. the gerund of **facio** → **faciendum**

a the supine of **sedeo**
b the gerund of **effugio**
c the gerund of **excuso**
d the supine of **intexo**
e the gerund of **spero**
f the supine of **adduco**
g the gerund of **valeo**
h the supine of **sopio**
i the gerund of **perdomo**
j the supine of **statuo**

5 Translate the following sentences into English.
e.g. **milites ad pugnandum exercent** → *the soldiers are training to fight*

a nautae navem ad navigandum parabant.
b Quintilianus artem dicendi docebat.
c ludos edendo imperator cives delectabat.
d Fabius cunctando rem publicam servabat.
e fugitivi ob pugnando ad arcem non pervenerunt.
f Icarus timorem volandi non cepit.
g Claudius in triclinium ad cenandum intravit.
h princeps non est aptus regnando.
i fabri strenue laborando templum perfecerant.
j verba oratoris inter clamandum non audivimus.

6 Translate the following sentences into English.

e.g. caedes terribilis visu erat → *the slaughter was terrible to see*

a pueri in flumen natatum desiluerunt.
b fabula mirabilis dictu erat.
c puellae in agros lusum cucurrerunt.
d eques in templum vigilatum venit.
e rex minas auditu crudeles emisit.
f milites hibernatum ad oppidum iter fecerunt.
g res facilis actu erit.
h solus per silvam tacitum ambulavi.
i arcanum nefas est patefactu.
j arca difficilis apertu erat.

7 Translate the following sentences into Latin.

e.g. *the tribune hurried to intervene* → tribunus intercessum festinavit

a The slave won his freedom by saving his master.
b Our love of sailing is very great.
c The bird's song was sweet to hear.
d By hurrying quickly we arrived at the inn.
e It is right to tell.
f The Romans overcame the Gauls by fighting bravely.
g Julius delights his mother by singing.
h The monster's skin was foul to touch.
i The punishment of Mettius was terrible to see.
j Turnus rushed in to attack.

8 Translate the following sentences into English.

e.g. imperatori timendo miles appropinquat → *the soldier approaches the fearsome general*

a Cato candidatus eligendus erat.
b uxor mea vere amanda est.
c verba oratoris audienda sunt.
d Brutus vir laudandus apud Romanos erat.
e multas gemmas habendas congerebam.

f musca minima non videnda est.
g ludos spectandos consules ediderunt.
h equos quosdam emendos heri vidi.
i nodus ingens non solvendus erat.
j coquus optimus cenam edendam parabat.

9 Translate the following sentences into English. They contain gerundives of obligation.

e.g. **imperator vias faciendas curavit** → *the emperor caused roads to be built*

a argumentum quod erat demonstrandum praebui.
b nunc vobis tacendum est.
c Carthago delenda est.
d Tarpeiam puniendam cives de saxo deiecerunt.
e cavendum est tibi.
f parentes semper nobis honorandi sunt.
g Claudius aquaeductum faciendum curavit.
h hostes vobis non timendi sunt.
i nihil dixi de consilio celando.
j nunc est bibendum.

10 Translate the following sentences into English. They contain gerundives of purpose.

e.g. **ad aurum petendum in sepulcrum intraverunt** → *they entered the tomb to look for gold*

a ad magistratus eligendos cives in foro congregebant.
b rhetorem Graecum ad filium educandum comparavi.
c pueri in tecta ascenderunt pompae videndae causa.
d Plinius otium quaerebat librorum scribendorum gratia.
e venatores in montes ad feras capiendas iter fecerunt.
f athleta celerimme cucurrit ad praemium petendum.
g Sulla dictaturam deposuit legum servandarum causa.
h donum misimus matri delectandae.
i Spartacus rebellavit servorum liberandorum causa.
j artifex diligenter ad statuam pulchram faciendam laborabat.

Points to remember

1 Participles denote a state or condition. They are verbal adjectives which describe what something *is doing*, rather than what something looks like.

2 Present participles are always active (even in deponent verbs) and are declined like the adjective **ingens -entis** (*huge*).

3 Perfect particples are normally passive, but are active in deponent verbs. They are formed from the fourth principal part of a verb, end in **-us-a-um**, and decline like **bonus-a-um** (*good*).

4 Future participles are always active (even in deponent verbs), end in **-urus-a-um**, and decline like **bonus-a-um** (*good*).

5 Like adjectives and pronouns, participles can be used as nouns. E.g. **morituri te salutant** (*those about to die salute you*).

6 The gerund is a second declension neuter verbal noun ending in **-ndum**, active in meaning, existing only in the singular. It denotes the act of doing something.

7 The supine is a fourth declension verbal which is usually the fourth principal part of a verb. It exists only in the accusative and ablative singular and, like the gerund, denotes the act of doing something.

8 The gerundive is a passive verbal adjective ending in **-ndus-a-um** which declines like **bonus-a-um** (*good*) and has no equivalent in English. It denotes something which *ought* to experience the action of a verb. E.g. **miranda est Cloelia** (*Cloelia is worthy of admiration*).

9 The gerundive of obligation expresses a forceful sense of necessity. The dative of the person by whom the action should be performed is used. E.g. **effugiendum est nobis** (*We must escape*).

10 The gerundive of purpose is used in the accusative after **ad** to express intent. E.g. **ad pacem petendam advenit** (*He arrived to seek peace*).

11

Infinitives and imperatives

Insight

In Latin, as in English, there are several infinitives: 'to bite, to have bitten, to be bitten, to have been bitten'. As ever, these various English forms are conveyed by endings to the verb in Latin.

Infinitives: formation

A The infinitives are those parts of the verb which in English have the word **to** in front of them. They have active and passive voices and present, future and perfect tenses. They express a verbal idea generally, without being limited to a person or number (i.e. not finite).

B In Latin the **second principal part** of a verb is its **present active infinitive** (Units 1K2 and 2C). The **present active infinitives** end in **-re**.

e.g. first conjugation **-are**, e.g. port*are* → *to carry, to be carrying*
second conjugation **-ēre**, e.g. hab*ēre* → *to have* etc.
third conjugation **-ere**, e.g. ag*ere* → *to do* etc.
fourth conjugation **-ire**, e.g. aud*ire* → *to hear* etc.

C The **present passive infinitives** are similar to the present active but all end in **-i / -ri**.

e.g. first conjugation **-ari**, e.g. port*ari* → *to be carried*
second conjugation **-eri**, e.g. hab*eri* → *to be had*

third conjugation -i, e.g. ag*i* → *to be done*
fourth conjugation -iri, e.g. aud*iri* → *to be heard*

D The **perfect active infinitives** are formed by adding -isse to the **perfect stem** (found in the **third principal part** (see Units 1K3 and 2M).

e.g. first conjugation portav*isse* → *to have carried* (a syncopated form port*asse* is sometimes found)
second conjugation habu*isse* → *to have had*
third conjugation eg*isse* → *to have done*
fourth conjugation audiv*isse* → *to have heard* (a syncopated form aud*isse* is sometimes found)

E The **perfect passive infinitives** are formed using the **perfect passive participle** (see Unit 10C) and the present infinitive of the verb to be (**esse**).

e.g. first conjugation **portatus esse** → *to have been carried*
second conjugation **habitus esse** → *to have been had*
third conjugation **actus esse** → *to have been done*
fourth conjugation **auditus esse** → *to have been heard*

NB The participle must always agree in number, gender and case with the noun it describes.

F The **future active infinitives** are formed from the **future participle** (see Unit 10D) and the present infinitive of the verb to be (**esse**).

e.g. first conjugation **portaturus esse** → *to be about to carry, to be on the point of carrying*
second conjugation **habiturus esse** → *to be about to have* etc.
third conjugation **acturus esse** → *to be about to do* etc.
fourth conjugation **auditurus esse** → *to be about to hear* etc.

NB The participle must always agree in number, gender and case with the noun it describes.

G The **future passive infinitives** are formed from the **fourth principal part** (the supine: see Units 1K4 and 10G) and the present passive infinitive of to go (**iri**).

e.g. first conjugation **portatum iri** → *to be about to be carried, to be on the point of being carried*
second conjugation **habitum iri** → *to be about to be had* etc.
third conjugation **actum iri** → *to be about to be done* etc.
fourth conjugation **auditum iri** → *to be about to be heard* etc.

Infinitives: usage

H The **prolative infinitive** is used as in English; to carry on the construction:

▶ After verbs of possibility, habit or duty such as:
possum → *I am able* (irregular: see Unit 12R), **queo** →
I am able, **nequeo** → *I am unable*, **debeo** → *I ought*
and **soleo** → *I am accustomed* (semi-deponent: see
Unit 8N), e.g. **non possum** *intellegere* → *I am not able
to understand*.

▶ After verbs of wishing, intending or daring such as: **volo** →
I want, **nolo** → *I do not want*, **malo** → *I prefer* (irregular:
see Unit 12S–U), **cupio** → *I desire*, **opto** → *I choose*,
statuo → *I determine*, **constituo** → *I decide* and **audeo** →
I dare (semi-deponent: see Unit 8N), e.g. **malo** *equitare* →
I prefer to ride.

▶ After verbs of beginning, ceasing, trying, continuing, hurrying
and hesitating such as: **incipio** → *I begin*, **coepi** → *I begin*,
desino → *I cease from*, **desisto** → *I cease from*, **conor** → *I
try* (deponent verb: see Unit 8J and L), **pergo** → *I continue*,
persevero → *I persist*, **festino** → *I hurry*, **propero** → *I hasten*,
dubito → *I hesitate* and **timeo** → *I fear*, e.g. **desino** *pugnare* →
I cease to fight.

▶ After verbs of knowing how to, learning and teaching such as:
scio → *I know how to*, **disco** → *I learn* and **doceo** → *I teach*,
e.g. **disco** *equitare* → *I am learning to ride*.

▶ After passive verbs of saying and thinking, e.g. **Caesar dicitur
advenisse** → *Caesar is said to have arrived*.

I The **historic infinitive** is the **present infinitive** when it is used to make something which happened in the past seem more vivid, e.g. **pueri clamare, currere, cadere** → *the boys shouted, ran and fell.*

J The infinitive is also used after verbs of commanding:

▶ After **iubeo** → *I order* and **veto** → *I forbid* in indirect commands (see Unit 15P), e.g. **veto te currere** → *I forbid you to run.*
▶ After the irregular negative imperative **noli** *(s.),* **nolite** *(pl.)* → *do not, in* **direct commands** (see Q and T), e.g. **nolite** *pugnare* **pueri** → *do not fight, boys.*

K The infinitive is tantamount to a noun in constructions after **impersonal verbs** such as **placet** → *it pleases,* **licet** → *it is allowed* (see also Unit 12) and with impersonal phrases such as **difficile est** → *it is difficult,* **decorum est** → *it is seemly,* **iuvat** → *it helps* etc., e.g. **forsan et haec olim** *meminisse* **iuvabit** (Virgil) → *one day perhaps it will help* **to have** **remembered** *even these* (*troubles*).

L For the infinitive depending upon an accusative in an **indirect statement**, see Unit 15A–K.

Imperatives

M The **imperative mood** is used to give **direct commands** and **requests** in Latin as in English. It is a finite form of the verb existing in one tense (present), in the 2nd and 3rd persons, singular and plural and in both the active and passive voices. Imperatives do not always appear at the ends of clauses and sentences.

N The 2nd person imperative endings are formed as follows:

	Active Singular Plural	Passive Singular Plural
1st conjugation	porta portate → carry!	portare portamini → be carried!
2nd conjugation	habe habete → hold (have)!	habere habemini → be held!
3rd conjugation	age agite → do!	agere agimini → be done!
4th conjugation	audi audite → hear!	audire audimini → be heard!

▶ Common irregular imperatives are: **dic** → *say, tell!* from **dico**; **duc** → *lead!* from **duco**; **fer** *(s.)*, **ferte** (pl.) → *carry!, bring!*, from **fero** (see Unit 12Y); **fac** → *make!* from **facio**; **i** → *go!* from **eo** (see Unit 12X) and **es**, **este** → *be!* from **sum** (see Unit 12P).

Insight

Here's a way to remember some of the irregular imperatives: '**Dic** says it's a **fac** that a **duc** has **fer**!'

O There is another form of the imperative found in both the 2nd and 3rd persons. Its endings are **-to** (2nd person), **-tote** (3rd person singular) or **-nto** (3rd person plural). These are rarely used outside legal documents and in certain verbs like **esto** → *let him/her/it be* and **sunto** → *let them be*, from **sum** or **memento**, **mementote** → *remember*, from **memini** (see Unit 12K).

P Direct commands

▶ In addition to the plain imperative, a direct command can also be expressed with the imperatives **fac**, **facite** or **cura**, **curate** → *take care that / see to it that* and a subjunctive verb (see also Unit 9H), e.g. **omnes**, *curate* **pontem defendeatis** → *everyone, take care that you defend the bridge*.

▶ For polite commands the **future indicative** may be used, often followed by a **subjunctive verb** (see Unit 9H), e.g. *facies ut donum mittatur* → *please see to it that the gift is sent.*

Q Negative direct commands (prohibitions)

▶ The **imperatives** of the irregular verb **nolo** → *I am unwilling,* followed by an infinitive are used for negative direct commands (see J), e.g. **noli** (or **nolite**) **discedere** → *do not leave.*
▶ **cave ne** → *beware of,* **fac ne** → *see that you do not,* or simply **ne** → *do not,* followed by the subjunctive is also used to express prohibitions (see H).
▶ **ne** *followed by the imperative is used in poetry,* e.g. **equo** *ne* **credite** Teucri → *do **not** trust the horse, Trojans.*

R The imperative is used for the greetings **salve, salvete** → *hello*; **vale, valete** → *goodbye*; **ave, avete** → *hello* or *goodbye.* Compare **apage** → *away with you*! and **age, agite** → *come on*!

1 Write down the active infinitives of the following verbs.
e.g. the perfect active infinitive of **rego** → **rexisse**

  a the present active infinitive of **venio**
  b the perfect active infinitive of **amo**
  c the future active infinitive of **ambulo**
  d the present active infinitive of **teneo**
  e the perfect active infinitive of **sedeo**
  f the perfect active infinitive of **capio**
  g the future active infinitive of **doceo**
  h the future active infinitive of **aperio**
  i the present active infinitive of **frango**
  j the perfect active infinitive of **facio**

2 Write down the passive infinitives of the following verbs.
e.g. the present passive infinitive of **do** → **dari**

  a the future passive infinitive of **trado**
  b the perfect passive infinitive of **sperno**
  c the perfect passive infinitive of **iacio**

d the present passive infinitive of **moveo**
e the future passive infinitive of **rogo**
f the present passive infinitive of **scribo**
g the perfect passive infinitive of **video**
h the future passive infinitive of **vinco**
i the perfect passive infinitive of **vincio**
j the present passive infinitive of **cresco**

3 Translate the following infinitives into English.

e.g. **redditurus esse** → *to be about to give back*

a	cecidisse	**f**	dictum iri
b	sepultum iri	**g**	respondere
c	puniturus esse	**h**	laboraturus esse
d	lavari	**i**	aedificatus esse
e	iussisse	**j**	mitti

4 Translate the following infinitives into Latin.

e.g. *to have broken* → **fregisse**

a	to remain	**f**	to be about to fly
b	to be recognized	**g**	to be found
c	to have been chosen	**h**	to have laughed
d	to be about to be closed	**i**	to have been stretched
e	to have dragged	**j**	to run

5 Translate the following sentences into English.

e.g. **nequivimus portam claudere** → *we were unable to shut the gate*

a Latinam linguam intellegere possum.
b Caesar inimicis ignoscere solebat.
c aviam tuam visitavisse debes.
d malo in Gallia habitare.
e volo prae hospitibus canere.
f caudices omina praetermittere optaverunt.
g iuvenis Metellam in matrimonium ducere cupivit.
h imperator amphitheatrum aedificare constituit.
i non audeo leonem provocare.
j nolo in agris dormire.

6 Translate the following sentences into English.

e.g. **dubitamus sapienti contradicere** → *we hesitate to contradict a wise man*

a perseverabimus terram idoneam quaerere.

b subito canes latrare inceperunt.

c festinamus matrem salutare.

d dubitavisti aquam fundere.

e pueri timebant lupis appropinquare.

f spem habere numquam desinam.

g liberi timent domo discedere.

h legati properabunt bello finem facere.

i Cicero pergebat Catilinam vituperare.

j quando desistes servos exagitare?

7 Translate the following sentences into English.

e.g. **hostes per portas irruere** → *the enemy forced their way in through the gates*

a nemo sciebat illud nodum expedire.

b centurio iuvenes docebit milites esse.

c numquam discam tibiis canere.

d Brutus se necavisse traditur.

e coniuratores Caesarem corripere, ferire, occidere.

f senatores Romulum dilaniavisse narrantur.

g omnes araneae muscas decipere sciunt.

h pistores vicanos veneno necavisse putabantur.

i magister discipulos pacem amare docebat.

j Nero matrem necavisse dicitur.

8 Translate the following sentences into Latin.

e.g. *I want to play in the mud* → **volo in luto ludere**

a We ought to support the candidate.

b I prefer to sleep.

c We are learning to swim.

d You (s.) will cease to shout.

e They have decided to depart.

f He knows how to fight.

g I will teach you to write.

h You (pl.) persist in shouting.

i I dare to resist the Romans.

j We desire to see the statue of the god.

9 Write out the imperatives of the following verbs.

e.g. the passive imperatives of teneo → tenere, tenemini

  a the passive imperatives of **rego**
  b the active imperatives of **parco**
  c the passive imperatives of **lenio**
  d the active imperatives of **amo**
  e the passive imperatives of **agnosco**
  f the passive imperatives of **aperio**
  g the active imperatives of **respondeo**
  h the active imperatives of **vincio**
  i the passive imperatives of **persuadeo**
  j the active imperatives of **rapio**

10 Translate the following sentences into English.

e.g. **semper bonis fidite liberi** → *always trust good men, children*

  a cives, monemini a me.
  b carpe diem.
  c ferte haec onera ad portum.
  d salvete discipuli. salve magister.
  e accipe hoc donum pro fautoribus tuis.
  f ambulate mecum ad forum senatores.
  g da mihi lucernam Aladdin!
  h aut disce aut discede.
  i pax esto in mundo.
  j ave atque vale amice.

11 Translate the following sentences into English.

e.g. **noli ab urbe discedere ante noctem** → *do not leave the city before nightfall*

  a nolite id facere pueri.
  b nolite canes dormientes suscitare.
  c matronae, nolite alibi vestimenta emere.
  d noli sollicitari; gaude.
  e ne fraudamini a tabernariis iuvenes.
  f noli tenebras timere mi fili.
  g noli ullum maius quam caput tuum consumere.
  h noli calceis meis caeruleis de pelle suilla fabricatis insistere.
  i nolite lilia inaurare.
  j nolite in pratulum ambulare.

12 **Translate the following sentences into Latin.**

e.g. *listen to the speaker's words, everyone* → **omnes, verba oratoris audite**

a Citizens, do not punish the priests.
b Children, be brave.
c Away with you, Titus! Nobody believes you.
d Hand me the salt, Sextus.
e Boys, do not mock my little horse.
f Do not ignore the oracles, Caesar.
g Welcome the guests, master.
h Push that rock more quickly, Sisyphus!
i Lead the gladiators into the arena, Maximus.
j Hide your gold in the bedroom, Quintus.

Points to remember

1 The present infinitive active is the second principal part of a verb.

2 The present infinitive passive endings for the four conjugations are: **-ari** (*first*), **-eri** (*second*), **-i** (*third*) and **-iri** (*fourth*).

3 The perfect infinitive active is formed by adding **-isse** to the perfect stem of the verb.

4 The perfect infinitive passive is formed using the perfect passive participle and **esse**, the present infinitive of the verb *to be*.

5 The future infinitive active is formed from the future participle and **esse**, the present infinitive of the verb *to be*.

6 The future infinitive passive is formed from the supine and **iri**, the present passive infinitive of the verb *to go*.

7 Infinitives in Latin are used after verbs very much as they are in English. E.g. **volo currere** (*I want to run*).

8 The imperative mood is used to give direct commands. Common irregular singular forms are **dic** (*tell*), **duc** (*lead*), **fer** (*bring*) and **fac** (*do*).

9 Older forms of the second and third person imperatives, though rare, do occur in legal language.

10 To give a negative direct command, Latin uses the imperatives **noli** or **nolite** (*be unwilling*) plus the infinitive. E.g. **nolite cedere** (*do not yield*).

12

Impersonal, defective and irregular verbs

Impersonal verbs

Impersonal verbs do not have a personal subject and usually have only a 3rd person singular in each tense, an infinitive and a gerund. As in English their subject is the pronoun 'it', e.g. *It is raining.* **The most common impersonal constructions are as follows.**

A Some are used alone to express changes of weather or time, e.g. **fulgurat** → *it lightens*, **ningit** → *it snows*, **pluit** → *it rains*, **tonat** → *it thunders*, **lucescit** → *it dawns*, **vesperascit** → *it grows late*.

B Some are followed by the accusative of person and the infinitive of action, e.g. **decet** → *it is becoming*, **dedecet** → *it is unbecoming*, **iuvat** → *it delights*, **fallit** → *it escapes one's notice*, **fugit** → *it escapes one's notice*, **praeterit** → *it passes one by*, **oportet** → *it behoves one* (*one ought, should*), e.g. **dedecet** vos pugnare → **it is unbecoming** *for you to fight*.

C Some take a dative (sometimes with an infinitive), e.g. **libet** → *it pleases*, **licet** → *it is allowed*, **liquet** → *it is clear*, **contingit** → *it befalls*, **convenit** → *it suits*, **evenit** → *it turns out*, **expedit** → *it is expedient*, **placet** → *it pleases, seems good*, **videtur** → *it seems* (*good*), *it is decided*, e.g. **licet** nobis discedere → *we are allowed to leave* (**it is permitted** *for us to leave*).

D Some take accusative of the person and genitive of cause or infinitive of action, e.g. **miseret** → *it moves to pity* (and **miseritum est**), **piget** → *it vexes* (and **pigitum est**), **paenitet** → *it repents*, **pudet** → *it shames* (and **puditum est**), **taedet** → *it wearies* (and **pertaesum est**), e.g. *paenitet* me erroris → *I repent of my mistake* (*it makes me repent of my mistake*).

E Some are followed by **ad** plus the accusative, for example **pertinet** → *it concerns*, **attinet** → *it concerns, it belongs*, e.g. **nihil ad me** *attinet* → *it concerns me in no respect*.

F The verb **refert** → *it concerns, it matters* is used with the feminine singular ablative of the possessive pronouns **mea, tua** etc. (see Unit 7C) which is to be imagined as agreeing with the ablative singular **re** → *thing*, contained in the verb **re**fert. So **mea refert** → *it bears on my business*. By some oddity, the verb **interest** → *it concerns, it is of importance*, takes the same construction. These verbs are usually followed by an accusative and infinitive, although **interest** also takes the genitive of the person concerned in the case of nouns and 3rd person pronouns, e.g. **mea** *refert* vos effugere → *it concerns me that you escape*.

G est → *it is* can be used in an impersonal sense with adjectives and an infinitive, e.g. **difficile** *est* montem ascendere → *it is difficult to climb the mountain*. **opus est** → *there is need of* takes the dative of person in need and ablative of what is needed, e.g. *opus est* mihi trabe → *I need a plank* (*there is need to me of a plank*).

H The verbs **potest** → *it is possible*, **coepit** → *it begins*, **solet** → *it is customary*, **debet** → *it ought* and **desinet** → *it stops* are also used with an infinitive, e.g. *potest* pontem transire → *it is possible to cross the bridge*.

I Some other verbs also have a special impersonal meaning in their 3rd person, e.g. **accedit** → *it is added*, **accidit** → *it happens*, **apparet** → *it is obvious*, **constat** → *it is agreed*, **delectat** → *it charms* and **restat** → *it remains*.

J The existence of the passive of intransitive verbs seems illogical in English as intransitive verbs do not take a direct object. However, in Latin passive intransitive verbs can be used in the 3rd person singular in an impersonal construction, e.g. **Romam a Bruto** *ventum est* → (literally) *it was gone* to Rome by Brutus. We cannot, of course, translate this literally into English and so we say '*Brutus went to Rome*'. In the Latin the subject of the intransitive verb (Brutus) has become the agent.

Compare this with *pugnatum est* in foro → (literally) *it was fought in the forum*, i.e. *there was a fight in the forum*. In this sentence the subject is omitted altogether.

Likewise, *ventum est* in forum → (literally) *it was gone into the forum*, must be translated according to the context, e.g. *we* (or *they* etc.) *went into the forum*. We find this construction with verbs taking the dative (see Unit 4D1), e.g. **ab oratore** *persuadetur* **omnibus civibus** → *the speaker persuades all the citizens* (literally: *it is persuaded to all citizens by the speaker*).

Intransitive verbs which take an ablative are all deponent and their gerundives are used impersonally, e.g. **omnibus voluptatibus** *fruendum est* → *we should enjoy* all pleasures (literally: *enjoyment should be taken of all pleasures*).

1 Translate the following sentences into English.
e.g. oportet vos captivos liberare → *you ought to set the prisoners free*

a ecce pluit!
b decet Romanos pacem conservare.
c hodie mihi convenit domi manere.
d iuvabit te cantorem audire.
e non licet vobis in triclinium intrare.
f non pudet furem impietatis.
g pueris non placet in horto ludere.
h iam vesperescat.
i taedet nos laboris.
j sapienti convenit tacere.

2 Translate the following sentences into English.

e.g. **dulce et decorum est pro patria mori** → *it is sweet and fitting to die for one's country*

a optimo consilio utendum est.

b facile est in montibus te celare.

c ad Graeciam a Cassio navigatum est.

d necesse est canem ferocem vincire.

e opus erit nobis pecunia.

f a nostris processum est ad hostes.

g non potest Germanis resistere.

h opus erat nautis rudentibus.

i nostra refert eum servari.

j solet mane patronum salutare.

3 Translate the following sentences into Latin.

e.g. *we regret our carelessness* → **paenitet nos neglegentiae**

a You (pl.) will need a ship.

b It snowed yesterday.

c It is unbecoming for us to yield.

d It pleases Caesar to spare the prisoners.

e The girls are weary of the songs.

f It concerns me that we learn.

g It is possible to see the treetops.

h It was difficult to find the caves.

i The women went to the theatre.

j It will soon grow light.

Defective verbs

Defective verbs are those from which some forms are absent.

K **odi odisse** → *I hate* and **memini meminisse** → *I remember* have no present, future or imperfect.

▶ Indicative perfect (present in meaning)

1st person singular	odi → I hate	memini → I remember
2nd person singular	odisti	meministi
3rd person singular	odit	meminit
1st person plural	odimus	meminimus
2nd person plural	odistis	meministis
3rd person plural	oderunt	meminerunt

- ▶ Indicative pluperfect (imperfect in meaning)

1st person singular	oderam →	I hated	memineram → I remembered
2nd person singular	oderas		memineras
3rd person singular	oderat		meminerat
1st person plural	oderamus		memineramus
2nd person plural	oderatis		memineratis
3rd person plural	oderant		meminerant

- ▶ Indicative future perfect (future in meaning)

1st person singular	odero → I shall	hate	meminero → I shall remember
2nd person singular	oderis		memineris
3rd person singular	oderit		meminerit
1st person plural	oderimus		meminerimus
2nd person plural	oderitis		memineritis
3rd person plural	oderint		meminerint

- ▶ Subjunctive perfect

1st person singular	oderim	meminerim
2nd person singular	oderis	memineris
3rd person singular	oderit	meminerit
1st person plural	oderimus	meminerimus
2nd person plural	oderitis	memineritis
3rd person plural	oderint	meminerint

- ▶ Subjunctive pluperfect

1st person singular	odissem	meminissem
2nd person singular	odisses	meminisses
3rd person singular	odisset	meminisset
1st person plural	odissemus	meminissemus
2nd person plural	odissetis	meminissetis
3rd person plural	odissent	meminissent

- ▶ Perfect infinitive: **odisse** → *to hate*; perfect participle: **osus -a -um** → *hating* (active); future participle: **osurus -a -um** → *about to hate*; no imperative
- ▶ Perfect infinitive: **meminisse** → *to remember*; perfect participle: —; future participle: —; imperative: **memento** (s.) **mementote** (pl.) → *remember*

L **coepi coepisse** → *I have begun* has no present, future or imperfect.

▶ Indicative	Perfect	Pluperfect
1st person singular	coepi → I have begun	coeperam → I had begun
2nd person singular	coepisti	coeperas
3rd person singular	coepit	coeperat
1st person plural	coepimus	coeperamus
2nd person plural	coepistis	coeperatis
3rd person plural	coeperunt	coeperant
▶ Indicative	Future perfect	
1st person singular	coepero → I shall have begun	
2nd person singular	coeperis	
3rd person singular	coeperit	
1st person plural	coeperimus	
2nd person plural	coeperitis	
3rd person plural	coeperint	
▶ Subjunctive	Perfect	Pluperfect
1st person singular	coeperim	coepissem
2nd person singular	coeperis	coepisses
3rd person singular	coeperit	coepisset
1st person plural	coeperimus	coepissemus
2nd person plural	coeperitis	coepissetis
3rd person plural	coeperint	coepissent

▶ Perfect infinitive: **coepisse** → *to have begun*; perfect participle: **coeptus -a -um** → *begun*; future participle: **coepturus -a -um** → *about to begin*

M **aio** → *say*, **inquam** → *say* and **for fari fatus sum** (deponent) → *speak* have few forms.

▶ aio: present indicative: aio, ais, ait, — — aiunt imperfect: aiebam, aiebas, aiebat, aiebamus, aiebatis, aiebant present subjunctive: aiat, aiant; participle: aiens, aientis

▶ inquam: present: inquam, inquis, inquit, inquimus, inquitis, inquiunt imperfect: — — inquiebat, — — inquiebant; future: — inquies, inquiet perfect: — inquisti, inquit; imperative: inque, inquito

▶ for: present: fatur; future: fabor, fabitur; imperative: fare; present participle: fantem (acc.); perfect participle: fatus; gerund: fandi, fando; gerundive: fandus -a -um

N The verbs **nosco noscere novi notum** and its compound **cognosco cognoscere cognovi cognitum** both mean 'get to know'. Like **odi** and **memini** their perfect tenses have a present meaning. So **novi** → *I have got to know* and, therefore, *I know*; **novero** → *I shall know*; **noveram** (often syncopated to **noram**) → *I knew*; **novisse** (or **nosse**) → *to know*; **notus** → *known*.

O **queo quire quivi quitum** → *I am able* and **nequeo** → *I am unable* are defective and, where tenses exist, conjugate like compounds of **eo** (see X): queo, quis, quit, quimus, quitis, queunt. (As does the verb **veneo venire venii venitum** → *be sold, be on sale*, which has an active form but a passive meaning.)

Irregular verbs

> **Insight**
>
> Unfortunately, the most commonly used verbs tend to be the most irregular – in English as well as in Latin! Consider the irregular verbs 'to be' and 'to go' and compare them with a regular verb such as 'to walk':
>
> | to be | am, is, are | was, were | have been |
> | to go | go, goes, go | went | have gone |
> | to walk | walk, walks, walk | walked | have walked |

P The finite indicative tenses of the irregular verb **sum esse fui** →
to be, are given at Unit 2X. The other forms are as follows:

Subjunctive	Present	Imperfect
1st person singular	sim	essem
2nd person singular	sis	essem
3rd person singular	sit	esset
1st person plural	simus	essemus
2nd person plural	sitis	essetis
3rd person plural	sint	essent

Subjunctive	Perfect	Pluperfect
1st person singular	fuerim	fuissem
2nd person singular	fueris	fuisses
3rd person singular	fuerit	fuisset
1st person plural	fuerimus	fuissemus
2nd person plural	fueritis	fuissetis
3rd person plural	fuerint	fuissent

Alternative forms exist in the present subjunctive:

1st person singular	**siem** or **fuam**
2nd person singular	**sies** or **fuas**
3rd person singular	**siet** or **fuat**
1st person plural	—
2nd person plural	—
3rd person plural	**sient** or **fuant**

and in the imperfect subjunctive:

1st person singular	**forem**
2nd person singular	**fores**
3rd person singular	**foret**
1st person plural	—
2nd person plural	—
3rd person plural	**forent**

Imperative: 2nd person: **es** or **esto** (s.) **este** or **estote** (pl.);
   3rd person: **esto** (s.) **sunto** (pl.)
Infinitives: present: **esse**; perfect: **fuisse**; future: **futurus esse** or **fore**.
Participles: future: **futurus -a -um** (no present or perfect).
   No gerund or supine.

Q The compounds of sum conjugate as it does:
   absum → *I am absent*, **adsum** → *I am present*, **desum** → *I am
   wanting*, **insum** → *I am in*, **intersum** → *I am among*, **obsum** →
   I hinder, **praesum** → *I am in charge of*, **prosum** → *I am of use*,
   subsum → *I am under* and **supersum** → *I survive*.

In **prosum** the letter **d** appears between the **o** and **e**, as in **prodestis**.

These compounds have active participles like **praesens** → *in charge*,
absens → *absent*.

R **possum posse potui** → *I can* is a shortened compound of
   potens sum → *I am able*. This verb takes the prolative infinitive
   (see Unit 11H).

Indicative	Present	Future
1st person singular	possum	potero
2nd person singular	potes	poteris
3rd person singular	potest	poterit
1st person plural	possumus	poterimus
2nd person plural	potestis	poteritis
3rd person plural	possunt	poterunt

Indicative	Imperfect	Perfect
1st person singular	poteram	potui
2nd person singular	poteras	potuisti
3rd person singular	poterat	potuit
1st person plural	poteramus	potuimus
2nd person plural	poteratis	potuistis
3rd person plural	poterant	potuerunt

Indicative	Future perfect	Pluperfect
1st person singular	potuero	potueram
2nd person singular	potueris	potueras
3rd person singular	potuerit	potuerat
1st person plural	potuerimus	potueramus
2nd person plural	potueritis	potueratis
3rd person plural	potuerint	potuerant

Subjunctive	Present	Imperfect
1st person singular	possim	possem
2nd person singular	possis	posses
3rd person singular	possit	posset
1st person plural	possimus	possemus
2nd person plural	possitis	possetis
3rd person plural	possint	possent

Subjunctive	Perfect	Pluperfect
1st person singular	potuerim	potuissem
2nd person singular	potueris	potuisses
3rd person singular	potuerit	potuisset
1st person plural	potuerimus	potuissemus
2nd person plural	potueritis	potuissetis
3rd person plural	potuerint	potuissent

Infinitives: present: **posse**; perfect: **potuisse**. The participle **potens** is used only as an adjective and there are no imperatives, gerund, gerundive or supine.

S volo velle volui → *wish, want*. This verb takes the prolative infinitive (see Unit 11H).

Indicative	Present	Future
1st person singular	volo	volam
2nd person singular	vis	voles

(Contd)

Indicative	Present	Future
3rd person singular	vult	volet
1st person plural	volumus	volemus
2nd person plural	vultis	voletis
3rd person plural	volunt	volent

Indicative	Imperfect	Perfect
1st person singular	volebam	volui
2nd person singular	volebas	voluisti
3rd person singular	volebat	voluit
1st person plural	volebamus	voluimus
2nd person plural	volebatis	voluistis
3rd person plural	volebant	voluerunt

Indicative	Future perfect	Pluperfect
1st person singular	volueris	volueras
3rd person singular	voluerit	voluerat
1st person plural	voluerimus	volueramus
2nd person plural	volueritis	volueratis
3rd person plural	voluerint	voluerant

Subjunctive	Present	Imperfect
1st person singular	velim	vellem
2nd person singular	velis	velles
3rd person singular	velit	vellet
1st person plural	velimus	vellemus
2nd person plural	velitis	velletis
3rd person plural	velint	vellent

Subjunctive	Perfect	Pluperfect
1st person singular	voluerim	voluissem
2nd person singular	volueris	voluisses
3rd person singular	voluerit	voluisset

Subjunctive	Perfect	Pluperfect
1st person plural	voluerimus	voluissemus
2nd person plural	volueritis	voluissetis
3rd person plural	voluerint	voluissent

Infinitives: present: **velle**; perfect: **voluisse**
Present participle: **volens**
Gerund: **volendum** (no imperatives or gerundive)

T **nolo nolle nolui** → *be unwilling* is a compound of **ne volo** → *I do not want*. This verb takes the prolative infinitive (see Unit 11H).

Indicative	Present	Future
1st person singular	nolo	nolam
2nd person singular	non vis	noles
3rd person singular	non vult	nolet
1st person plural	nolumus	nolemus
2nd person plural	non vultis	noletis
3rd person plural	nolunt	nolent

Indicative	Imperfect	Perfect
1st person singular	nolebam	nolui
2nd person singular	nolebas	noluisti
3rd person singular	nolebat	noluit
1st person plural	nolebamus	noluimus
2nd person plural	nolebatis	noluistis
3rd person plural	nolebant	noluerunt

Indicative	Future perfect	Pluperfect
1st person singular	noluero	nolueram
2nd person singular	nolueris	nolueras
3rd person singular	noluerit	noluerat
1st person plural	noluerimus	nolueramus
2nd person plural	nolueritis	nolueratis
3rd person plural	noluerint	noluerant

Subjunctive	Present	Imperfect
1st person singular	nolim	nollem
2nd person singular	nolis	nolles
3rd person singular	nolit	nollet
1st person plural	nolimus	nollemus
2nd person plural	nolitis	nolletis
3rd person plural	nolint	nollent

Subjunctive	Perfect	Pluperfect
1st person singular	noluerim	noluissem
2nd person singular	nolueris	noluisses
3rd person singular	noluerit	noluisset
1st person plural	noluerimus	noluissemus
2nd person plural	nolueritis	noluissetis
3rd person plural	noluerint	noluissent

Imperatives: 2nd person: **noli** or **nolito** (s.) **nolite** or **nolitote** (pl.)
3rd person: **nolito** (s.) **nolunto** (pl.)
Infinitives: present: **nolle**, perfect: **noluisse**
Present participle: **nolens**
Gerund: **nolendum** (no gerundive or supine)

U malo malle malui → *prefer* is a compound of **magis volo** →
I wish more. It takes the prolative infinitive (see Unit 11H).

Indicative	Present	Future
1st person singular	malo	malam
2nd person singular	mavis	males
3rd person singular	mavult	malet
1st person plural	malumus	malemus
2nd person plural	mavultis	maletis
3rd person plural	malunt	malent

Indicative	Imperfect	Perfect
1st person singular	malebam	malui
2nd person singular	malebas	maluisti
3rd person singular	malebat	maluit
1st person plural	malebamus	maluimus
2nd person plural	malebatis	maluistis
3rd person plural	malebant	maluerunt

Indicative	Future perfect	Pluperfect
1st person singular	maluero	malueram
2nd person singular	malueris	malueras
3rd person singular	maluerit	maluerat
1st person plural	maluerimus	malueramus
2nd person plural	malueritis	malueratis
3rd person plural	maluerint	maluerant

Subjunctive	Present	Imperfect
1st person singular	malim	mallem
2nd person singular	malis	malles
3rd person singular	malit	mallet
1st person plural	malimus	mallemus
2nd person plural	malitis	malletis
3rd person plural	malint	mallent

Subjunctive	Perfect	Pluperfect
1st person singular	maluerim	maluissem
2nd person singular	malueris	maluisses
3rd person singular	maluerit	maluisset
1st person plural	maluerimus	maluissemus
2nd person plural	malueritis	maluissetis
3rd person plural	maluerint	maluissent

Infinitives: present: **malle**, perfect: **maluisse**
Gerundive: **malendum** (no participles or imperatives)

V **fio fieri factus sum** → *become*, *be made* is an irregular defective verb. When it means 'be made', the verb is active in form but passive in meaning and must be used as the passive of **facio facere feci factum** → *make*, which supplies the perfect tense **factus sum** → *I have been made*, the future perfect **factus ero** → *I shall have been made* and pluperfect **factus eram** → *I had been made*. When meaning '*become*' **fio** is followed by a nominative.

Indicative	Present	Future	Imperfect
1st person singular	fio	fiam	fiebam
2nd person singular	fis	fies	fiebas
3rd person singular	fit	fiet	fiebat
1st person plural	—	fiemus	fiebamus
2nd person plural	—	fietis	fiebatis
3rd person plural	fiunt	fient	fiebant

Subjunctive	Perfect	Imperfect
1st person singular	fiam	fierem
2nd person singular	fias	fieres
3rd person singular	fiat	fieret
1st person plural	fiamus	fieremus
2nd person plural	fiatis	fieretis
3rd person plural	fiant	fierent

W **edo ēsse ēdi ēsum** → *eat*. Note the similarity between this and parts of **sum** (see Units 2X and P above). The verb *to eat* is distinguished by the long vowel in ēs- but this will not be apparent when you are reading 'real' Latin. The parts of the verb which are not listed here are regular.

Present indicative	Active	Passive
1st person singular	edo	—
2nd person singular	ēs	—
3rd person singular	ēst	ēstur
1st person plural	edimus	—

Present indicative	Active	Passive
2nd person plural	ēstis	—
3rd person plural	edunt	—

Subjunctive active	Present	Imperfect
1st person singular	edam *or* edim	ēssem
2nd person singular	edas *or* edis	ēsses
3rd person singular	edat *or* edit	ēsset
1st person plural	edamus	ēssemus
2nd person plural	edatis	ēssetis
3rd person plural	edant *or* edint	ēssent

Imperfect subjunctive passive: ēssetur
Imperative active: 2nd person: ēs or ēsto (s.) ēste or ēstote (pl.),
  3rd Person: ēsto (s.) **edunto** (pl.)
Present infinitive: ēsse

X eo ire ii (less commonly ivi) itum → *go*. In the perfect tenses the
  iis- is sometimes contracted to is-, e.g. isti, istis, isse etc.

Indicative	Present	Future	Imperfect
1st person singular	eo	ibo	ibam
2nd person singular	is	ibis	ibas
3rd person singular	it	ibit	ibat
1st person plural	imus	ibimus	ibamus
2nd person plural	itis	ibitis	ibatis
3rd person plural	eunt	ibunt	ibant

	Perfect	Fut. Perfect	Pluperfect
1st person singular	ii	iero	ieram
2nd person singular	iisti	ieris	ieras
3rd person singular	iit	ierit	ierat
1st person plural	iimus	ierimus	ieramus
2nd person plural	iitis	ieritis	ieratis
3rd person plural	ierunt	ierint	ierant

Subjunctive	Perfect	Imperfect	Perfect	Pluperfect
1st person singular	eam	irem	ierim	iissem
2nd person singular	eas	ires	ieris	iisses
3rd person singular	eat	iret	ierit	iisset
1st person plural	eamus	iremus	ierimus	iissemus
2nd person plural	eatis	iretis	ieritis	iissetis
3rd person plural	eant	irent	ierint	iissent

Imperatives: 2nd person: **i**, **ito** (s.) **ite**, **itote** (pl.); 3rd person: **ito** (s.) **eunto** (pl.)

Infinitives: present: **ire**; future: **iturus esse**; perfect: **iisse** or **ivisse**; passive: **iri** (see Unit 11G)

Participles: present: **iens euntis**; future: **iturus -a -um**

Supine: **itum** (acc.) **itu** (abl.). Gerund: **eundum**

3rd person singular passive: present: **itur**; imperfect: **ibatur**; perfect: **itum est**

Compounds of **eo** like **adeo** → *approach* have a full passive form.

Y fero ferre tuli latum → *bring, bear, carry*. Like **fero** goes its compound **auferro auferre abstuli ablatum** → *take away*. It also shares forms with **tollo tollere sustuli sublatum** → *raise*.

Indicative active	Present	Future	Imperfect
1st person singular	fero	feram	ferebam
2nd person singular	fers	feres	ferebas
3rd person singular	fert	feret	ferebat
1st person plural	ferimus	feremus	ferebamus
2nd person plural	fertis	feretis	ferebatis
3rd person plural	ferunt	ferent	ferebant

Indicative active	Perfect	Future perfect	Pluperfect
1st person singular	tuli	tulero	tuleram
2nd person singular	tulisti	tuleris	tuleras
3rd person singular	tulit	tulerit	tulerat
1st person plural	tulimus	tulerimus	tuleramus

Indicative active	Perfect	Future perfect	Pluperfect
2nd person plural	tulistis	tuleritis	tuleratis
3rd person plural	tulerunt	tulerint	tulerant

Indicative passive	Present	Future	Imperfect
1st person singular	feror	ferar	ferebar
2nd person singular	ferris	fereris (or -re)	ferebaris (or -re)
3rd person singular	fertur	feretur	ferebatur
1st person plural	ferimur	feremur	ferebamur
2nd person plural	ferimini	feremini	ferebamini
3rd person plural	feruntur	ferentur	ferebantur

	Perfect	Future perfect	Pluperfect
1st person singular	latus sum	latus ero	latus eram
2nd person singular	latus es	latus eris	latus eras
3rd person singular	latus est	latus erit	latus erat
1st person plural	lati sumus	lati erimus	lati eramus
2nd person plural	lati estis	lati eritis	lati eratis
3rd person plural	lati sunt	lati erunt	lati erant

Subjunctive active	Present	Perfect	Passive: Present	Perfect
1st person singular	feram	tulerim	ferar	latus sim
2nd person singular	feras	tuleris	feraris (or -re)	latus sis
3rd person singular	ferat	tulerit	feratur	latus sit
1st person plural	feramus	tulerimus	feramur	lati simus
2nd person plural	feratis	tuleritis	feramini	lati sitis
3rd person plural	ferant	tulerint	ferantur	lati sint

Subjunctive active	Imperfect	Pluperfect	Passive: Imperfect	Pluperfect
1st person singular	ferrem	tulissem	ferrer	latus essem
2nd person singular	ferres	tulisses	ferreris (or -re)	latus esses

(Contd)

Subjunctive active	Imperfect	Pluperfect	Passive: Imperfect	Pluperfect
3rd person singular	ferret	tulisset	ferretur	latus esset
1st person plural	ferremus	tulissemus	ferremur	lati essemus
2nd person plural	ferretis	tulissetis	ferremini	lati essetis
3rd person plural	ferrent	tulissent	ferrentur	lati essent

Active imperative: 2nd person: **fer/ferto** (s.) **ferte/fertote** (pl.), 3rd person: **ferto** (s.) **ferunto** (pl)

Passive imperative: 2nd person: **ferre/fertor** (s.) **ferimini** (pl.), 3rd person: **fertor** (s.) **feruntor** (pl.)

Infinitives: present active: **ferre**; present passive: **ferri**; perfect active: **tulisse**; perfect passive: **latus esse**; future active: **laturus esse**; future passive: **latum iri**

Participles: present: **ferens ferentis**; perfect: **latus -a -um**; future: **laturus -a -um**

Gerund: **ferendum**; gerundive: **ferendus -a -um**; supine: **latum**

Points to remember

1 Impersonal verbs are found in the third person singular in Latin. They are sometimes used alone, as they are in English. E.g. **pluit** (*it is raining*).

2 Impersonal verbs can govern cases and constructions. They are often found with an accusative and infinitive. E.g. **oportet nos pauperes adiuvare** (*We ought to help the poor*).

3 Impersonal forms can be used with normal verbs. E.g. **est facilius equitare** (*It is easier to ride*).

4 Some impersonal forms of normal verbs have a specialized meaning. E.g. **constat** (*It is agreed*).

5 There is a passive version of impersonal verbs in Latin which is not used in English. E.g. **pugnatum est in foro** (*There was a fight in the forum*).

6 There are some verbs, called defective, which lack a complete set of tenses. The common ones are **odi** (*I hate*), **coepi** (*I begin*) and **memini** (*I remember*), and three verbs meaning *say*: **aio, inquam** and **for, fari, fatus sum**.

7 Be careful not to confuse parts of **fio** (*I become*) with parts of **facio** (*I do* or *make*).

8 Be careful not to confuse parts of **fero** (*I carry or bring*) with parts of **tollo tollere sustuli sublatum** (*I raise*).

9 Be careful not to confuse parts of **volo velle volui** (*I wish*) with **volo-are-avi-atum** (*I fly*).

10 Be careful not to confuse parts of **sum esse fui** (*to be*) with parts of **edo esse edi esum** (*I eat*).

13

Relative and temporal clauses, ablative absolute

Relative clauses

A The relative pronoun **qui quae quod** (*who*, *which*) (Unit 7J) usually introduces relative clauses but they may also be introduced by relative adverbs like **ubi** (*where*).

e.g. **corona quam rex gerebat erat aurea** → *the crown which the king wore was golden*

castra posuerunt ubi flumen latissimum est → *they camped where the river is widest*

B As well as coming after the main clause or even in the middle of it, relative clauses sometimes come before it.

e.g. **quae verba pater tibi dicet ea audi** → *listen to those words which father will say to you*

C If the relative pronoun is the subject of a verb which links a subject with a complement (see Unit 4A3), like **sum** → *I am*, **appareo** → *I appear*, **audio** → *I am called* (lit. I hear [of myself]), **evado** or **existo** → *I turn out* and **videor** → *I seem*, then the relative pronoun often agrees in number and gender with the complement.

e.g. **Roma quod mundi caput est** → *Rome, which is the capital of the world*

D A relative pronoun or an ablative absolute (Q) which uses a relative pronoun is sometimes found at the beginning of a sentence to show a connection with something that has happened previously.

e.g. **quam ob rem** → *for which reason* (often written as one word)
   quo facto → *when this was done* (ablative absolute)
   quod viderunt → *as to that which they saw*

E If the relative clause simply states a fact about the **antecedent** (Unit 7J), then the verb of the relative clause is in the indicative.

e.g. **in silvis sunt multae ferae quas timemus** → *in the woods there are many wild beasts which we fear*

F The relative pronoun can be used to introduce **final clauses** (Unit 14D), in which case the verb is in the subjunctive.

e.g. **imperator legatos misit qui dona regi darent** → *the emperor sent ambassadors to give the king gifts* (lit. *who would give the king gifts*)

When a final clause contains a comparative then it is introduced by **quo**.

e.g. **equos conscenderunt quo celerius ad villam perveniremus** → *we mounted the horses to reach the villa more quickly*

G The relative pronoun can also be used to introduce **consecutive clauses** (Unit 14I) when the verb is also in the subjunctive. The meaning of **qui** in these cases amounts to *of such a kind that* and the clause defines a characteristic of the antecedent. (For **quin** see Units 16H–L.)

e.g. **nemo erat tam fortis qui illis leonibus resisteret** → *no-one was so brave as to resist those lions*

H The relative pronoun can also be used to introduce **causal clauses** (Unit 16B) in which case it is also followed by a subjunctive.

e.g. **te culpo qui hoc facias** → *I blame you for doing this.*

Temporal clauses

I **Temporal clauses** express the time when something happened, is happening or will happen. They are introduced by **temporal conjunctions** (Unit 6F).

J Temporal clauses introduced by **ubi, ut** (*when*), **postquam** (*after*), **simulac, simulatque** (*as soon as*) or **quotiens** (*whenever*) have their verbs in the indicative.
   e.g. **ubi in Gallia habitabam magnam villam habebam** → *when I used to live in Gaul, I had a large country estate*

After **postquam, simulac** or **ubi**, a Latin perfect tense is sometimes best translated by an English pluperfect tense.
   e.g. **postquam Caelius intravit omnes tacuerunt** → *after Caelius had entered everyone fell silent*

K Clauses introduced by **dum, donec, quoad** and **quam diu** (*while, as long as*), have their verbs in the **indicative**.
   e.g. **multi liberorum nostrorum discunt donec ludunt** → *many of our children learn while they are playing*

dum (*while*), is regularly followed by the present tense, even if referring to a past action, to indicate a period of time during which something else happens. (This is called the **historic present**.)
   e.g. **dum Roma incenditur, Nero fidibus canebat** → *while Rome was burning, Nero was playing on the lyre*

L Clauses introduced by **dum, donec, quoad** (*until*), and **antequam, priusquam** (*before*) have their verbs in the indicative if all that is being conveyed is an idea of time.
   e.g. **heri in foro cum amicis manebam donec sol occidit** → *yesterday I stayed in the forum with my friends until the sun set*

Often **antequam** and **priusquam** are split into separate words (**ante ... quam** and **prius ... quam**) which do not need to stand next to each other.

e.g. **Septimus canem ingentem prius vidit quam ille latravit** →
Septimus saw the huge dog before it barked

M Clauses introduced by **dum, donec, quoad** (*until*) and **antequam, priusquam** (*before*) can have their verbs in the subjunctive if the action of the clause is anticipated or has an idea of purpose as well as time.
e.g. **cenam celeriter coquus parat antequam hospites adveniant** →
the cook is preparing dinner quickly before the guests arrive

---

Temporal clauses with cum

N **cum** can mean *when, whenever, since* or *because*, according to its context.

O **cum** can only govern an **indicative** verb under the following circumstances:
▶ When **cum** (*when*) introduces a temporal clause with a verb referring to the present or future.
e.g. **cum aurum invenero dives ero** → *when I find* (lit. *shall have found) the gold, I shall be rich*
▶ When **cum** (*when*) introduces a temporal clause referring to the past which emphasizes the idea of time. (Note the phrase **cum primum** → *as soon as.*)
e.g. **cum nos hostibus appropinquabamus vos terga dabatis** → *at the time when we were approaching the enemy, you were retreating*
▶ When **cum** (*when*) introduces a temporal clause referring to the past which is positioned after the main clause and, although a subordinate clause, expresses the main event of the sentence.
e.g. **navis paene ad portum advenerat cum gubernator excidit** → *the ship had almost reached the harbour when the helmsman fell out*
▶ When **cum** means *whenever*. If the verb in the main clause is in the present tense, then the verb of the temporal clause will be

in the perfect tense. However, if the verb in the main clause is in a past tense, then the verb of the temporal clause will be in the pluperfect tense.

e.g. **cum tuba sonuerat athletae quam celerrime cucurrerunt** → *whenever the trumpet sounds* (lit. *had sounded*), *the athletes ran as quickly as possible*

P When **cum** (*when, since* or *because*) introduces a temporal clause referring to a past action other than those mentioned above, then the verb will be in the **subjunctive**:

▶ If the verb of the temporal clause refers to an action which occurs at the same time as the action of the main clause, then it is in the **imperfect subjunctive**.

e.g. **cum ver appropinquaret peregrinatores ad montes profecti sunt** → *when spring was approaching, the travellers set off for the mountains*

▶ If the verb of the temporal clause refers to an action which occurred before the action of the main verb, then it is in the **pluperfect subjunctive**.

e.g. **cum hospites discessisent Cassius coniurationem patefecit** → *when the guests had left, Cassius revealed the plot*

Ablative absolute

Q The **ablative absolute** construction is a phrase which comes at the beginning of a sentence (or of a subordinate clause) and which is *grammatically* independent of the rest of the sentence, but does have a connection *in sense* with it. The phrase consists of **a noun or pronoun in the ablative and a participle** (Unit 10A–D) (or another noun or adjective) agreeing with it.

R An ablative absolute is not used if the noun in it would refer to either the subject or the object of the main clause.

S It is sometimes possible to translate the ablative absolute literally into English.

e.g. **labore confecto, agricolae domum redierunt** → *with the work finished, the farmers returned home*

T If a participle is used in an ablative absolute, then the phrase can nearly always be translated as a temporal clause in English. The tense of the participle depends not on whether the time of its action is in the present, past or future, but on whether it happens before, during or after the action of the main **verb in its clause:**

▶ **Caesare interfecto Brutus Roma effugit** → *after Caesar was killed, Brutus escaped from Rome*

▶ **spectatoribus tacentibus imperator signum dedit** → *as the spectators were falling silent, the emperor gave the signal*

▶ **fratribus discessuris nuntius regis advenit** → *when the brothers were on the point of departing, the king's messenger arrived*

U In an ablative absolute, participles can take objects and constructions.

e.g. **auriga equos flexuro rota fracta est** → *as the charioteer was about to wheel the horses around, the wheel broke*

V As there is no participle for the verb *to be* in Latin, in an ablative absolute where one would be used if it existed, Latin just has the noun and adjective, or the noun and another noun, without any participle.

e.g. **Pompeio duce legiones Spartacum superaverunt** → *with Pompey as leader the legions overcame Spartacus*

e.g. **ventis adversis, naves aegre in portum intraverunt** → *since the winds were contrary the ships barely got into the harbour*

1 Translate the following sentences into English. They illustrate A and B above.

e.g. **vir quem iudex arcessivit est innocens** → *the man whom the judge sent for is innocent*

  a ille qui in spelunca dormiebat antiquissimus erat.
  b hodie illa templa quae Romani aedificaverunt videre volumus.
  c terra unde peregrinus advenit paene deserta est.

d viros quos elegisti nos iam vidimus.

e quem tu sequeris nos quoque sequemur.

f Claudiam manebam ubi casa arboribus celatur.

g verba quae imperator dixerat milites delectaverunt.

h statim prosiluit ubi hostes densissimi erant.

i bene eum cognovi cuius filius mortuus est.

j candidatum cui favemus numquam amavistis.

2 Translate the following sentences into English. They illustrate C and D above.

e.g. **quod locuti sunt, nemo id intellegit** → *as to what they have said, no-one understands it*

a Londinium, quae urbs maxima videtur, multo minus quam Roma est.

b uxor mea, quod mihi praesidium semper erat, est iam avia.

c Athenae quod est caput Atticae pulcherrima urbs est.

d quam ob rem Cassius etiam divitior factus est.

e quo facto, ille valde iratus e foro discessit.

f ille est Catilina, quod evasit exitium reipublicae.

g quam ob rem non iterum navigabimus.

h quod Caesar faciet, nemo volet parere.

i quo facto Romani multos dies gaudebant.

j Sirius, quae est clarissma stella iam ortus est.

3 Translate the following into Latin.

e.g. *what I have said, everyone has heard* → **quod ego dixi omnes audiverunt**

a He will look for the bird where he saw the nest.

b Have you (s.) seen the young man whom Lucretia loves?

c As to that which we did, everyone will be silent (**taceo**).

d For which reason the procession halted.

e Brutus whose clan (**gens**) is noble, has saved the republic.

f The dog caught the cat which had caught the mouse.

g Augustus, who was the ornament (**decus**) of his time.

h They killed the goose which used to lay (**pario**) the golden eggs.

i Cloelia, who was a model to the Romans.

j When this was done, the spectators applauded.

4 Translate the following sentences into English. They illustrate J above.

e.g. **quotiens tu vocabis ego veniam** → *whenever you (will) call, I shall come*

  a ubi tu in silvis errabas ego in horto laborabam.
  b postquam fures togas abstulerunt ianitor verberatus est.
  c postquam Valeria cecinit omnes plauserunt.
  d simulac taurus intravit nos diffugimus.
  e simulatque patronus advenit, clientes surrexerunt.
  f ut tecta viderunt Romam agnoverunt.
  g ubi haec verba iudex dixit reus tremuit.
  h simulac pons fracta est Horatius in flumen desiluit.
  i postquam Milo Clodium interfecit in exsilium relegatus est.
  j quotiens galli cantabant agricolae expergiscebantur.

5 Translate the following sentences into English. They illustrate K, L and M above.

e.g. **dum liberi ludunt iuvenes coniurabant** → *while the children played, the youths plotted*

  a navem paraveramus priusquam nautae advenerunt.
  b dum sol fulgebat apes mel faciebant.
  c atrium ornabimus antequam hospites advenient.
  d hostes latebant donec agmen in saltum venerit.
  e in castris manebamus donec periculum emotum sit.
  f dum sacerdotes sacrificant sicarius me percussit.
  g poeta recitabat quam diu turba manebat.
  h ignem exstinxit antequam casa flammas conciperet.
  i dum canes dormiunt fures domum intrabunt.
  j tribunus perstiterat donec consul cessisset.

6 Translate the following sentences into Latin.

e.g. *When* (**ubi**) *it snows the water freezes* → **ubi ningit aqua concrescit**

  a While (**dum**) the guards were shouting amongst themselves, the captives escaped.

b Did you (s.) wait until (**quoad**) the poet had recited the story?

c The lion lay hidden for a long time before (**antequam**) he attacked the ram.

d We listened as long as (**quam diu**) the orator was speaking.

e While (**dum**) Decius was approaching, the dog barked.

f Whenever (**quotiens**) I buy a puppy for you (s.) you ask for (**peto**) another.

g We shall knock the door until (**dum**) you (s.) open it.

h After (**postquam**) the earth trembled, the mountain exploded.

i Marcellus, hit the nail as soon as (**simulac**) I nod.

j While (**donec**) Julia was walking on the riverbank, the otters were playing in the river.

7 Translate the following sentences into English. They illustrate O above.

e.g. **cum tuba sonabit pompa discedet** → *when the trumpet sounds, the procession will depart*

a cum domina loquitur ancillae audiunt.

b cum Sulla dictator erat omnes senatores in magno periculo erant.

c coniurati Caesarem tenebant cum Casca eum percussit.

d cum te vidi vox mea deest.

e cum illum gladiatorem vident spectatores plaudunt.

f cum librum leges fabulam intelleges.

g montibus appropinquabamus cum Galli oppugnaverunt.

h cum primum pons deletus est Horatius se in flumen coniecit.

i cum pater intraverat pueri riserunt.

j cum primum porta clausa erat puella puerum osculata est.

8 Translate the following sentences into English. They illustrate P above.

e.g. **cum viam invenissent omnes riserunt** → *when they had found the road everyone smiled*

a cum montes relinquissent peregrinatores gavisi sunt.

b cum hospites advenissent vinum Sextus distribuit.

c cum canes latrarent fures diffugiebant.

d cum sol oriretur custodes dormiebant.

e cum hoc scelus patefecisset Cicero coniuratos comprehendit.

f Romam cum iter fecissemus nusquam hospitium invenire poteramus.

g cum venatores lente reperent aper se celabat.

h Caesar, cum Rhenum transire constituisset, pontem aedificavit.

i cum auditores riderent poeta irascebatur.

j cum litus vidissent nautae navem verterunt.

9 Translate the following sentences into Latin. Use the conjunction cum in each one.

e.g. *the sailors sing when they set sail* → **nautae cantant cum vela dant**

a You (s.) were turning the ship when the pirates attacked us.

b When we had reached the shore, we thanked the gods.

c I was walking home when the dog attacked me.

d As soon as (**cum primum**) the bell rang, the monks departed.

e When they had killed Caesar, the conspirators fled.

f At the time when the young men were ill, the thief stole the gold.

g When they had seen the bear, the boys fled.

h Whenever the moon was bright, the werewolf walked.

i The women used to sing when they span thread.

j At the time when the cook was preparing dinner, the guests arrived.

10 Translate the following sentences into English. They illustrate T above.

e.g. **rotis fractis plaustrum inutile erat** → *after the wheels were broken, the cart was useless*

a auro invento avarus stupefactus est.

b civibus loquentibus te audire non possum.

c sole oriente matrona ancillas arcessivit.

d his verbis dictis legatus celeriter discessit.

e militibus discessuris foedus renovatum est.

f tempestate adventura nautae in portu manebant.

g nuntio locuto portae apertae sunt.

h victoria nuntiata epistulam patri misimus.

i obsidibus necatis sicarius de vita desperabat.
  j nave refecta nautae statim vela dederunt.

11 Translate the following sentences into English. They illustrate U and V above.

e.g. **me duce certe vincemus** → *with me as leader, we will certainly win*

  a illis virginibus cantantibus nautae delirant.
  b Claudio et Aemilio praetoribus, nulli latrones damnati sunt.
  c custodibus captivos comitantibus agmen per silvas erravit.
  d Tarquinio rege Romani Cloacam Maximam construxerunt.
  e civibus secundis statuam patri meo erexi.
  f hostibus urbem oppugnaturis Iuppiter tonuit.
  g Marcello pecuniam adepto fundum comparavimus.
  h imperatore se necaturo milites seditionem fecerunt.
  i Boudicca regina Britanni Camulodunum expilaverunt.
  j filo ductore Theseus e labyrintho effugit.

12 Translate the following sentences into Latin. Use the ablative absolute construction.

e.g. *when the dice had been cast, the gambler smiled* → **aleis iactis aleator risit**

  a As Jupiter was about to hurl a thunderbolt, Juno shouted.
  b While you (s.) were sleeping, I painted the bedroom.
  c After the light had been extinguished, we walked in darkness.
  d When we were on the point of seeing the target, the referee stopped the contest.
  e After the tyrant's brother was slain, the Athenians were severely oppressed.
  f When the water had been drained off, the soldiers crossed the river bed.
  g While the fishermen were bringing the rods, the boys were preparing the food.
  h With Marius as general we shall overcome the barbarians.
  i When camp was pitched (**pono**), the soldiers made bread.
  j With Mercury as our guide we shall reach the land of the dead.

Points to remember

1 The relative pronoun **qui quae quod** (*who, which*) is so called because it *relates* to another word. This other word is referred to as the antecedent of the pronoun.

2 The relative pronoun will be in the same number and gender as its antecedent, but its case will depend on its function in its own clause.

3 Relative pronouns often appear in ablative absolutes.
E.g. **quibus rebus dictis** (*when these things were said*).

4 Relative pronouns can also be used to introduce final and consecutive clauses.

5 Temporal clauses express the time *when* something happens. They are introduced by temporal conjunctions.

6 The verbs of temporal clauses can be in the indicative or the subjunctive, depending on the introductory conjunction and the time reference. The word **cum** can be followed by verbs of either mood, depending on the context.

7 The ablative absolute construction is a way of subordinating an idea, with a noun or pronoun and participle at the beginning of a clause (often with a temporal meaning), by putting everything into the ablative. E.g. **Caesare necato** (*after Caesar was slain*).

8 The tense of the participle in an ablative absolute refers to the time when the event took place. E.g. **militibus profecturis** (*with the soldiers on the point of setting out*).

9 Participles in an ablative absolute can take objects.
E.g. **Aegytiis pyramidas aedificantibus** (*while the Egyptians were building the pyramids*).

10 When an ablative absolute appears without a participle, supply the verb *to be* in English. E.g. **Hannibale puero** (*when Hannibal was a boy*).

14

Final, consecutive and conditional clauses

Final clauses

A Final clauses (commonly called **purpose clauses**) express the purpose for which something is done. They are introduced by **ut** (*so that*), if they are positive and by **ne** (sometimes **ut ne**) (*lest, so that not, in case*), if they are negative. Some are introduced by the relative pronoun **qui quae quod** and some by **quo**. It is common in English to translate a purpose clause with a simple infinitive, e.g. *I opened the box to see the contents.*

B The following phrases can introduce a negative final clause as well as **ne** (*lest*):
    ne quis → *lest anyone, so that no-one*
    ne quid → *lest anything, so that nothing*
    ne umquam → *lest ever, so that never*
    ne usquam → *lest anywhere, so that nowhere*
    ne ullus → *lest any, so that no*

C The verb of the final clause is in the **subjunctive**. The tense of the subjunctive depends upon the **sequence of tenses** (Unit 1Y).

    i If the verb of the main clause is **primary** (in the imperative or the present, future, future perfect or perfect with 'have'), then the verb of the final clause will be in the **present subjunctive**.

e.g. **ianuam claudo ne hi canes effugiant** → *I am closing the door so that these dogs do not escape*

ii If the verb of the main clause is **historic** (perfect without 'have', imperfect or pluperfect), then the verb of the final clause will be in the **imperfect subjunctive**.
e.g. **ianuam clauseram ne hi canes effugerent** → *I had closed the door so that these dogs would not escape*

D A final clause may be introduced by the relative pronoun **qui quae quod** (see Unit 13F).
e.g. **senatores Caesarem misit qui Gallos superaret** → *the senators sent Caesar to overpower the Gauls*

E If a final clause contains a comparative adjective or adverb then it is introduced by **quo** (see Unit 13F).
e.g. **decem dies exercebat quo citius cursum curreret** → *he exercised for ten days so that he might run the race more quickly*

Consecutive clauses

F **Consecutive clauses** (commonly called **result clauses**) express the result (consequence) of an action. They are introduced by **ut** (*with the result that* or *so that*). A negative result is expressed by **ut non** (or **quin** – see Unit 16H). In English we usually use *that* to introduce a consecutive clause, e.g. *We walked so far that we were exhausted*. Sometimes, however, we can omit a conjunction altogether, e.g. *We were so late we missed the boat*.

G A consecutive clause is usually (but not always) signposted in the main clause by one of the following:

tam, sic or **ita** → *so*	**talis -is -e** → *such, of such a kind*
adeo → *to such an extent, so much*	**tot** → *so many*
tantus -a -um → *so great, so big*	**totiens** → *so often*

H The verb of a consecutive clause is in the **subjunctive**. The tense of the subjunctive does not depend on the sequence of tenses but stays for the most part in the same tense as it would appear in English.

i If the result is going to occur in the future, then Latin invents a **future subjunctive** tense. This consists of the **future participle** (Unit 10D), which agrees with whatever it refers to, and the **present subjunctive** of the verb *to be* (Unit 12P).
e.g. **tam sero advenisti ut pompam non visurus sis** → *you have arrived so late that you will not see the procession*

ii If the result occurs in the present, then the **present subjunctive** is used.
e.g. **tam altum est flumen ut transire non possim** → *the river is so deep that I cannot cross*

iii If the result occurred in the past and stress is being laid upon the fact that it actually happened, then the **perfect subjunctive** is used.
e.g. **Cicero Catilinam tam ferociter obtrectavit ut senatores illum evitaverint** → *Cicero disparaged Catiline so fiercely that the senators actually avoided him*

iv If the result occurred in the past and is expressed simply as a consequence of the action in the main clause, then the **imperfect subjunctive** is used.
e.g. **tanta erat tempestas ut velas dare non possemus** → *the storm was so great that we could not set the sails*

I Some consecutive clauses may be introduced by a relative pronoun which has the sense 'of such a kind that' (see Unit 13G).
e.g. **Boudicca non est femina quam irrites** → *Boudicca is not a woman to provoke* (lit. *is not a woman of such a kind that you may provoke her*)

Conditionals

J A conditional statement consists of two elements, either of which can appear first:

▶ A clause, introduced by **si** (*if*) or **nisi** (*unless, if ... not*) which contains a condition. This clause is called the **protasis**.
▶ A main clause containing the consequence of the condition. This is called the **apodosis.**

K Conditional sentences are of two kinds:

▶ A condition which is, was or will be true, and whose consequence will be true in the future, is true in the present or was true in the past is called an **open conditional**. The verb of both clauses is almost always in the **indicative.**
▶ A possible condition, the result of which is not certain to be fulfilled or cannot possibly be fulfilled is represented in English by the words *would* or *should* in the main clause. In Latin the verb of both clauses is in the **subjunctive.**

L The tense of the indicative in an open conditional depends on:

  i If the condition and its consequence refer to the future, then Latin is much more precise than English. As well as using the **future indicative** in the main clause, Latin uses either a **future** or **future perfect** indicative in the protasis. English is rather lazy in these cases and mostly uses the present tense.
    e.g. **nisi hoc facies numquam thesaurum invenies** → *if you do not do this you will never find the treasure* (lit. *If you will not do this ...*)

ii If the condition and its consequence refer to the present, then the **present indicative** is used in both clauses.

e.g. **si gaudes nos quoque gaudemus** → *if you are happy, we are also happy*

iii If the condition and its consequence refer to the past, then both clauses will contain either the **imperfect** or **perfect indicative**.

e.g. **si illo favebas, longe errabas** → *if you were supporting that man, you were far wrong*

e.g. **si tu hoc fecisti, nos perdidisti** → *if you did this, you have ruined us*

iv It is possible for the condition to refer to one time while its consequence refers to another.

e.g. **si umquam vitam servavisti valde laudandus es** → *if you have ever saved a life you are greatly to be praised*

v A **pluperfect indicative** verb in the protasis and an **imperfect indicative** verb in the apodosis refer to something which happened frequently.

e.g. **si umquam templum viderat statim sacrificare parabat** → *if ever he saw a temple he at once prepared to make a sacrifice*

M Occasionally the apodosis contains an **imperative** or a **subjunctive** of will or desire.

e.g. **Minotaurum neca, si audes** → *slay the Minotaur if you dare*

e.g. **si eis licentiam dedisti exeant** → *if you have given them permission, let them leave*

N Conditionals which have *would* or *should* in the main clause in English refer to conditions which are only possible or are contrary to known facts, rather than those which are certain. In Latin the verbs of both clauses are in the **subjunctive** and their tenses depend upon the following.

i If the condition and its consequence refer to the future and the condition expresses something which may or may not be fulfilled, a **present subjunctive** is used in both clauses.

e.g. **si epistulam legas totam rem intellegas** → *if you were to read the letter, you would understand the whole affair*

ii If appropriate, the **perfect subjunctive** can appear also in the protasis of such sentences.

e.g. **si a sociis nostris relicti simus libertatem non servemus** → *if we were deserted by our allies, we would not preserve our freedom*

iii If the condition and its consequence refer to the present and the condition expresses something contrary to known facts, an **imperfect subjunctive** is used in both clauses.

e.g. **si vinum biberes ebrius esses** → *if you were (now) drinking wine, you would be drunk*

iv If the condition and its consequence refer to the past and the condition is contrary to known facts, a **pluperfect subjunctive** is used in both clauses.

e.g. **si cum Caesare pugnavisses, eum vero admiratus esses** → *if you had fought with Caesar, you would have admired him*

v It is possible for the condition to refer to one period of time while its consequence refers to another. In such cases the **imperfect** and **pluperfect subjunctive** are used.

e.g. **nisi pater suus dives fuisset numquam Quintus ignavus esset** → *if his father had not been rich, Quintus would never be idle*

e.g. **nisi ibi aquas dulces invenirentur milites castra non posuissent** → *if fresh water were not found there, the soldiers would not have pitched camp.*

O When conditional clauses are used in an **indirect statement** (Unit 15F), then the verb of the protasis is in the **subjunctive** and the verb of the apodosis becomes an infinitive.

i The tense of the **subjunctive** depends upon the **sequence of tenses** (Unit 1Y) except that the **imperfect** and **pluperfect subjunctives** can be used after a present indicative verb introducing the indirect statement.

ii The tense of the **infinitive** of an open conditional depends on the normal rules for indirect statement (Unit 15C).

iii The **infinitive** of a conditional with *would* or *should* is in the **future** tense and is accompanied by **esse**, for conditionals referring to the future, or **fuisse** for those referring to the present or past.

1 Translate the following sentences into English. They illustrate C i above.

e.g. **ad portum curremus ut naves videamus** → *we shall run to the harbour to see the ships*

a tene speculum ut te videas.
b oves custodio ne leonibus edantur.
c pavimentum puer lavat ut a matre laudetur.
d pictores strenue laborabunt ut atrium uno die pingant.
e tabulam celavi ne illa insula usquam inveniatur.
f canes latrant ne quis domui appropinquet.
g Caesar collem munit ne Galli castra capiant.
h carpe diem ne felicitas te vitet.
i omnia nomina appello ne quis omittatur.
j nonne plaustrum reficies ut frumentum feramus?

2 Translate the following sentences into English. They illustrate C ii above.

e.g. **arborem succidit ut lignum compararet** → *he cut the tree down to get firewood*

a equum conscendi ut artem meam demonstrarem.
b corpora sepeliebat ne quid videretur.
c mercator aediculam occultam fabricavit ut gemmas intus celaret.

d venatores cervis insidiebantur ut cibum liberis praeberent.
e fundos vendiderat ut aes alienum exsolveret.
f canem comparavi ne Claudius usquam se celare posset.
g homo scelestus arborem succidit ne ulla avis ibi nidificaret.
h puellae libros legebant ut carmina antiqua cognoscerent.
i portas clauseramus ne quis admitteretur.
j portam obseravi ne umquam domum iterum reviseremus.

3 Translate the following sentences into English. They illustrate D and E above.

e.g. **legatos mittemus qui foedera renovent** → *we shall send ambassadors to renew the pacts*

a dux novas copias misit quae nobis subveniant.
b fabros conduxeramus qui thermas aedificarent.
c athleta diu exercebat quo facem celerius ferret.
d hunc scribam comparavi qui meos libros scribat.
e medicus potionem exhauserat quo altius dormiret.
f milites collegi qui me defendant.
g Quintia, dona misi quae te delectent.
h oculos magnos habeo quo melius te videam.
i murum diruebat quo plus horti videret.
j pastor ovile aedificavit quo oves tutius protegerentur.

4 Translate the following sentences into Latin.

e.g. *I drink wine to take the pain away* → **vinum bibo ut dolorem emoveam**

a Are you (s.) hiding the bread to annoy mother?
b The farmer was watching the field in case any cow should escape.
c We have sons to avenge us.
d He barred the gate so that no one might open it.
e Sulla had published (**proscribo**) the names of his enemies so that they would be killed.
f I washed the floor so that no mud might be seen.
g I have large teeth so that I may eat you (s.) better.
h I showed everyone the box so that they would not suspect me.

i Did Cicero arrive to hear the speech?

j Taste (s.) the food lest there is any poison inside.

5 Translate the following sentences into English. They illustrate H i above.

e.g. **adeo cunctatur ut omnes perituri sint** → *he is delaying so much that everyone will die*

a tot milites rex comparavit ut expeditio certe victura sit.

b tam laetus erit pater ut nobis dona daturus sit.

c tanta est venti velocitas ut hodie non navigaturi simus.

d adeo ningit ut nihil visuri simus.

e tot pisces feles devorat ut mox dormitura sit.

f totiens decidit ut crura fracturus sit.

g tam esuriens est pauper ut calceos suos esurus sit.

h tam infirmus est pons ut etiam capri non transituri sint.

i talis est Titus ut duci optime subventurus sit.

j tam celeriter currit ut periculum non visura sit.

6 Translate the following sentences into English. They illustrate H ii above.

e.g. **adeo pluit ut flumen inundet** → *it is raining so much that the river is flooding*

a tam alta est turris ut tectum non videam.

b talis est Crassus ut fautores non corrumpat.

c tanta sunt saxa ut asini ea non possint portare.

d terra adeo tremit ut paene cadam.

e tot oves viae obstant ut pastores haereant.

f haec avis totiens cantat ut me semper delectet.

g tam gravia sunt plaustra ut pons frangatur.

h tam clare loquitur ut omnia verba audire possim.

i tanta est fides mea ut inermis pugnem.

j aqua ita calida est ut non bibi possit.

7 Translate the following sentences into English. They illustrate H iii and iv above.

e.g. **tam parvus erat ut in hama sederet** → *he was so small that he used to sit in a bucket*

a mater nostra tam benigna erat ut semper amaretur.
b magistratum totiens vituperaveram ut comprehensus sim.
c tantos montes transiveramus ut defessi essemus.
d puellae adeo lacrimabant ut dictatorem commoverint.
e tot barbari per portas irruerunt ut custodes resistere non possent.
f Tarquinius tam superbe regnaverat ut cives eum expulerint.
g elephanti tam ingentes erant ut Romani valde timerent.
h picturam tam bene pinxit ut multa praemia acciperet.
i tam celeriter equos equitabat ut tandem interfectus sit.
j tot viros vexaverat ut in insula solus derelictus sit.

8 Translate the following sentences into Latin.

e.g. *he was so amazed that he did not speak* → **adeo stupefactus est ut non locutus sit**

a Helen had so many wooers that she could actually choose her husband.
b Marius is so great a general that the soldiers will follow him faithfully.
c Pausanias so (**ita**) liked the temple that he would always praise it.
d We are so many that you (s.) cannot resist us.
e The boy used to cry 'wolf' so often that no-one would believe him.
f Cato was so honest that he would not lie.
g They argued to such an extent that Romulus actually slew Remus.
h Othello used to tell such tales that Desdemona loved him.
i Victoria was not a woman you (s.) might amuse.
j Crassus is so rich that he is unaware of his own wealth.

9 Translate the following into English. They illustrate L i above.

e.g. **si hoc feceris omnes delectabis** → *if you do this, you will amuse everyone*

a si Metella Aemilio nupserit matres amborum laetae erunt.
b si Romani Alexandriam ceperint Aegytum regent.

c nisi nos liberabis nihil de amico tuo audies.

d si Aulus magnum piscem capiet eum hodie edemus.

e nisi donum mihi cras dederis ululabo.

f nisi Fabius curret leporem non capiet.

g domus certe ruet nisi parietes refecti erunt.

h si imperatori epistulam mittes tibi consilium dabit.

i si vacca iuvencum pariet eum non vendam.

j nisi tu ad me venies ego veniam ad te.

10 Translate the following sentences into English. They illustrate L ii and iii above.

e.g. **si paratus es cives manent** → *if you are ready, the citizens are waiting*

a nisi pecuniam comparavisti fundum amisimus.

b nisi praedones cavebant in magno periculo erant.

c si vos disceditis nos laeti sumus.

d si aves canant ver appropinquat.

e si ullam navem vidimus ad portum cucurrimus.

f nisi Neapolim vidisti plane non vixisti.

g si Clodia te amabat felicissimus eras.

h nisi Egnatius ridet uxor misera est.

i nisi in agris laborabant totum diem terebant.

j si magistratum vituperavi stultissimus fui.

11 Translate the following sentences into English. They illustrate L iv, v and M above.

e.g. **si te offendi veniam peto** → *if I have offended you, I beg your pardon*

a roga matrem, si eam invenire potes.

b nisi ianua clausa est canis effugiet.

c si amphoras fractas vendidi pecunia tibi reddetur.

d si pueri aberant poenas dabunt.

e si Quintum Sempronia amat certiorem eum faciat.

f iuvenis, bibe potionem nisi times.

g si umquam tu me aspectaveras erubescebam.

h proditorem neca nisi confitebitur.

i occasionem cape si tibi offertur.

j si illam urbem pulchram vidisti vero felix es.

12 Translate the following sentences into Latin.

e.g. *if you see Milo, greet him for me* → **si Milonem videbis eum saluta pro me**

a If the cook does not burn the peacock, dinner will be excellent.

b If Cyrus has broken the vase, he will be punished.

c If you (s.) drink the draught, you will enjoy (**utor**) eternal youth.

d The city will be captured unless the ambassador renews the treaty.

e If the captives have not been bound, the guards have neglected their duty.

f If the bridge has been broken, the army cannot cross.

g If Titus shows me the map, I will lead you (pl.) to the cave.

h If we ever greeted our patron, he gave us dole money (**sportula**).

i If Valgus is not in the baths, look (s.) for him in the forum.

j If the dogs are asleep, the cat walks proudly around the garden.

13 Translate the following sentences into English. They illustrate N i and ii above.

e.g. **si rota fracta sit currus ruat** → *if the wheel were broken, the chariot would crash*

a si flumen latius sit id non transeamus.

b nisi Manlius adsit conventus not fiat.

c si claves amissi sint coniurati domum non intrent.

d nisi cautus sis capiaris.

e nisi flumen derivetur oppidum inundetur.

f si vas fractum sit aliquis puniatur.

g si Cicero loquatur plurimi adsint.

h si signum detur milites progrediantur.

i si liberi querantur domi maneant.

j nisi praetoriani imperatori faveant sine dubio depellatur.

14 Translate the following sentences into English. They illustrate N iii above.

e.g. **si sapientior esset vobis parceret** → *if he were wiser, he would spare you*

a nisi Romani essemus togas non gereremus.
b si pater miles esset imperium Romanum defenderet.
c si minus cautus essem fures intrarent.
d nisi cives superstitiosi essent deos non colerent.
e si oppugnareris multi tibi subvenirent.
f si in urbe essetis multa spectacula videretis.
g si iunior essem cum athletis currerem.
h nisi legati essemus interficeremur.
i nisi consules adessent milites minus fortiores essent.
j si innocens esses non timeres.

15 Translate the following sentences into English. They illustrate N iv and v above.

e.g. **si fortior fuissem arcam aperuissem** → *if I had been braver, I would have opened the box*

a nisi Caesar Rubiconem transiisset bellum non exarsisset.
b si anulum conservavisset invictus esset.
c nisi vocem eius audivissent Publium non invenissent.
d nisi Cleopatra pulchra esset Antonius eam non amavisset.
e si monachus linguam Graecam intellexisset librum legisset.
f nisi puer esset latro eum interfecisset.
g si epistulam scrutati essetis manum agnovissetis.
h nisi cibum gustavisset veneno necatus esset.
i si ludos spectavisses Spartacum vidisses.
j si luscinia cecinisset valde delectati essemus.

16 Translate the following sentences into Latin.

e.g. *if you were to bribe me, I would support you* → **si me corrumpas tibi faveam**

a If the senators were to expel you (s.), we ourselves would follow you.

b If we had seen the danger, we would not have arrived unarmed.

c If the road were wider, the wagons would not be blocked (**intercludo**).

d If you (pl.) had not believed Lucius, you would have convicted an innocent man.

e If we were to sleep among the tombs, the ghosts would frighten us.

f If Larcius were kinder, the slaves would like him.

g If he were poor, Cassius would be more humble.

h If he had consulted the omens, Caesar would not have left.

i If they were allies, they would shout the password.

j If we were to see the body, we would believe you (s.).

Points to remember

1 Final clauses express purpose. They are introduced but **ut** (*so that*) or **ne** (*lest*) and their verbs are in the subjunctive.

2 If the verb of the main clause is in the present, future, future perfect, perfect with 'have' or imperative, the verb of the final clause is in the present subjunctive.

3 If the verb of the main clause is in the imperfect, pluperfect or perfect without 'have', the verb of the final clause is in the imperfect subjunctive.

4 If a final clause contains a comparative adjective or adverb, it is introduced not by **ut**, but by **quo**.

5 Consecutive clauses express result. A positive result is introduced by **ut** (*with the result that*), a negative one with **ut non**.

6 A consecutive clause if often signposted in the main clause by **tam**, **sic** or **ita** (*so*), **adeo** (*so much*), **tantus-a-um** (*so great*), **talis-is-e** (*such*), **tot** (*so many*) and **totiens** (*so often*).

7 The verb of the consecutive clause is in the subjunctive. Its tense remains much the same as it would in English.

8 If the result is in the future, then Latin invents a future subjunctive consisting of the future participle and the present subjunctive of the verb *to be*.

9 A conditional statement consists of two clauses: the protasis (the condition) and the apodosis (the consequence of the condition).

10 An 'open' conditional statement, referring to certainties, has the verbs of both clauses in the indicative. E.g. *If it rains I will stay indoors*. A 'closed' one, referring to uncertainties, has both verbs in the subjunctive. E.g. *If I were faster I would win*.

15

Indirect speech

Indirect statements

> **Insight**
>
> The Latin 'accusative + infinitive' is a common way of
> expressing an indirect statement: *I know that he is a good man*
> would be rendered *I know <u>him to be</u> a good man*.

A An **indirect statement** is a reported statement which is
introduced either by an impersonal verb (Unit 12B) or a verb
of saying, thinking, perceiving, knowing, believing or denying.
For example, **direct statement** (i.e. the original statement): *the
river is teeming with fish*. Indirect statement (i.e. the reported
statement): *the angler says that the river is teeming with fish*.
Or *I can see that the river is teeming with fish*.

B In English we commonly use the conjunction *that* to link the
main clause with the indirect statement, although we can leave it
out, e.g. *they saw the river was teeming with fish*. In either case
the indirect statement has its own finite verb.

However, we could also say *we know the river to be teeming with
fish*. In this example the subject of the indirect statement (*river*) has
become the object (in the **accusative**) of the main verb (*we know*),
while the verb of the indirect statement has changed from a finite
verb into an **infinitive** (*to be teeming*). This is how the Romans
used to express themselves and that is why the indirect statement is

often called the **accusative and infinitive** construction in Latin. The negative form is introduced by **nego -are -avi -atum** (*I say that ... not, I deny*).

C The tense of the infinitive in an indirect statement is the same as the tense of the original (direct) statement, regardless of the tense of the introductory verb. The tense of the verb of the indirect statement in English *does* depend upon the tense of the introductory verb. You will need to find the correct tense according to the contexts set out below, depending on whether the introductory verb is in the present or future (**a**) or the past (**b**).

 i A **present infinitive** is used in place of the present tense verb in the original statement. If the original statement is *he is carrying* or *he is being carried*, then the indirect forms are:
  e.g. (**a**) **puto eum portare** → *I think that he is carrying*
   (**a**) **dicemus eum portari** → *we shall say that he is being carried*
   (**b**) **dixi eum portare** → *I have said that he is carrying*
   (**b**) **crediderunt eum portari** → *they believed that he was being carried*

 ii A **future infinitive** is used in place of a future tense verb in the original statement. If the original statement is *he will carry* or *he will be carried*, then the indirect forms are:
  e.g. (**a**) **nego eum portaturum esse** → *I say that he will not carry*
   (**a**) **sciunt eum portatum iri** → *they know that he will be carried*
   (**b**) **dicebas eum portaturum esse** → *you used to say that he would carry*
   (**b**) **videramus eum portatum iri** → *we had seen that he would be carried*

 iii A **perfect infinitive** is used in place of any past tense verb in the original statement. If the original statement is *he was carrying* or *he was carried* then the indirect forms are:
  e.g. (**a**) **sentimus eum portatum esse** → *we sense that he was carried*

- (a) **dicam eum portavisse** → *I shall say that he carried*
- (b) **audivistine eum portatum esse?** → *did you hear that he had been carried?*
- (b) **negabamus eum portavisse** → *we denied that he had carried*

iv In the case of future active and perfect passive (and deponent) infinitives, the part of the infinitive which declines agrees in number, gender and case with the accusative it refers to.

e.g. **Valerius dicit eam cras navigaturam esse** → *Valerius says that she will sail tomorrow.*

D When the reflexive pronoun **se** (*himself, herself, itself, themselves*) (Unit 7B) and the possessive pronoun **suus -a -um** (*his, her, its, their*) (Unit 7C) appear in an indirect statement then they refer to the subject of the **main clause**, whereas, e.g. **eum** or **eius** would refer to someone other than the subject of the main clause.

e.g. **custos dicit se discessurum esse** → *the guard says that he (himself) is going to leave*

e.g. **custos dicit eum discessurum esse** → *the guard says that he (someone else) is going to leave*

E The word **esse** is frequently omitted from perfect and future infinitives in an indirect statement.

e.g. **prima luce Caesar Pompeium necatum scivit** → *at first light Caesar knew that Pompey had been killed*

F The infinitive of an indirect statement can govern its own construction (see e.g. Unit 14O).

e.g. **negat se velle equum conscendere** → *he says he is not willing to mount a horse*

e.g. **dixit fabros arcum perfecturos fuisse si strenue laboravissent** → *he said that the workmen would have finished the arch if they had worked hard*

G Indirect statements can depend upon impersonal verbs.

e.g. **constat omnes cives idem consilium cepisse** → *it is agreed that all the citizens adopted the same plan*

H Indirect statements introduced by verbs of hoping, promising, threatening and swearing take the accusative and future infinitive.

e.g. **speramus te mox adventurum esse** → *we hope that you will arrive soon*

I The accusative and infinitive construction can also be found after the verbs **iubeo** (*I order*), **veto** (*I forbid*), **patior** and **sino** (*I allow*).

e.g. **vos vetamus illos captivos tangere** → *we forbid you to touch those captives*

J The construction can also follow **volo** (*I want*), **nolo** (*I do not want*), **malo** (*I prefer*) and **cupio** (*I desire*), if the subject of the indirect statement is different from the subject of the main verb.

e.g. **malo te fundum colere** → *I prefer you to tend to the farm*

K It may also follow verbs of rejoicing and grieving.

e.g. **hostes vinctos esse gaudebant** → *they were rejoicing that the enemy had been beaten*

Indirect questions

> **Insight**
>
> A direct question reproduces the exact words of the question: *'Sam asked me "Have you seen my keys?"'* Compare this with the reported or indirect question *'Sam asked me if I had seen his keys.'*

L An **indirect question** is a reported question which is introduced by a verb of questioning, enquiring, knowing or telling, and the same interrogative word which introduced the direct question, except that **num** (*if, whether*), may be used to replace the interrogative ending **-ne** (see Unit 7U). Note that the word **num** means something else when it introduces a direct question (see Unit 7U).

For example, **direct question** (i.e. the original question): *How did they do that?* **Indirect question** (i.e. the reported question): *We asked how they did that.*

M The verb of the indirect question is in the **subjunctive**. Its tense depends upon its context, the tense of the original question and the tense of the main (introductory) verb. As a general rule, the sequence of tenses (Unit 1Y) is followed, although there is a greater variety of subjunctive tenses available for use in the indirect question. Just remember that a **primary** verb in the main clause is always followed by a **primary subjunctive** verb in the indirect question and a **historic** verb in the main clause is always followed by a **historic subjunctive** in the indirect question. Bear in mind also the difference between the perfect tense with 'have' (primary) and the perfect tense without 'have' (historic).

i If the main verb is **primary**, then the verb of the indirect question will be in the **present subjunctive** if the original question was of the present (**a**), in the **perfect subjunctive** if the original question was of the past (**b**), and in the composite **'future subjunctive'** (see Unit 9A) if the original question was of the future (**c**).

Original question	Possible main verb	Indirect question
(**a**) **quis est?** → *Who is it?*	**rogo** → *I ask*	(**a**) **quis sit** → *who it is*
(**b**) **quis fuit?** → *Who was it?*	**rogabo** → *I shall ask*	(**b**) **quis fuerit** → *who it was*
(**c**) **quis erit?** → *Who will it be?*	**rogavi** → *I have asked*	(**c**) **quis futurus sit** → *who it will be*
	rogavero → *I shall have asked*	
	roga → *ask*	

ii If the main verb is **historic** then the verb of the indirect question will be in the **imperfect subjunctive** if the original question was of the present (**a**), in the **pluperfect subjunctive** if the original question was of the past (**b**), and in the composite 'future perfect subjunctive' (see Unit 9A) if the original question was of the future (c).

Original question	Possible main verb	Indirect question
(a) quis est? → *Who is it?*	rogabam → *I was asking*	(a) quis esset → *who it was*
(b) quis fuit? → *Who was it?*	rogavi → *I asked*	(b) quis fuisset → *who it had been*
(c) quis erit? → *Who will it be?*	rogaveram → *I had asked*	(c) quis futurus esset → *who it would be*

N When the indirect question offers a negative alternative, then necne (*or not*) is used.

e.g. iudex rogavit num Bruti filius patriam prodidisset necne → *the judge asked whether the son of Brutus had betrayed his country or not*

Indirect commands

O An **indirect command** (see also Unit 16G) is a reported command which can be introduced not only by a verb of commanding or demanding but also by any verb which implies an act of the will, like verbs of decreeing, persuading, requesting, warning, entreating, permitting, urging, encouraging, taking care (that) and resolving and some impersonal verbs. In English the indirect command is usually expressed by an infinitive.

For example, **direct command** (i.e. the original command): *Open the doors.*

Indirect command (i.e. the reported command): *I told him to open the doors.*

P In Latin, an indirect command which is introduced by any of the verbs iubeo (*I order*), veto (*I forbid, I order ... not*),

sino (*I allow*) and **patior** (*I allow*), has its verb in the infinitive, as in English.

e.g. **eum vetui hoc facere** → *I forbade him to do this* (or: *I told him not to do this*)

Q Other indirect commands in Latin are introduced by **ut** (negative: **ne**) and a verb in the **subjunctive** which is the equivalent of an infinitive or a 'that' clause in English. The tense of the subjunctive depends upon the **sequence of tenses** (Unit 1Y).

▶ If the verb of the main clause is **primary** (in the imperative or the present, future, future perfect or perfect with 'have'), then the verb of the indirect command will be in the present subjunctive.

e.g. **philosophi nos persuadent ut pacem amemus** → *philosophers persuade us to love peace*

▶ If the verb of the main clause is **historic** (perfect without 'have', imperfect or pluperfect), then the verb of the indirect command will be in the **imperfect subjunctive**.

e.g. **agricola saepe te monebat ne mala surriperes** → *the farmer often used to warn you not to steal the apples*

▶ Sometimes the word **ut** is omitted after **rogo** (*I ask*), **moneo** (*I warn*), **suadeo** (*I persuade*), **impero** (*I order*), **curo** (I take care [*that*]), **necesse est** (*it is necessary*), **licet** (*it is allowed*) and **oportet** (*it behoves*).

e.g. **moneo vos quam celerrime discedatis** → *I warn you to depart as quickly as possible*

Indirect wishes

R An **indirect wish** is a reported wish (compare clauses of fear in Unit 16E). It is introduced by a verb of wishing like **cupio** (*I desire*), **opto** (*I choose*), **volo** (*I want*), **nolo** (*I do not want*) or **malo** (*I prefer)* and by the conjunction **ut** (negative: **ne**) and a subjunctive verb. (Some of these verbs also take the accusative and infinitive construction. See Unit 15J). The verb of the indirect wish is an optative subjunctive (Unit 9H). Present and perfect subjunctives are used to refer to wishes for the future, the imperfect subjunctive is used to refer to wishes for the present and the pluperfect subjunctive is used to refer to wishes for the past.

e.g. **cupivit ut tu mansisses** → *he wished that you had stayed*

1 Translate the following into English. They illustrate C i above.

e.g. **dixit catellas in horto ludere** → *he said that the puppies were playing in the garden*

a nuntiavimus navem desertam appropinquare.
b saepe dico eam felicem esse.
c Galli negaverunt Druides celari.
d dicam te vestiri.
e putasne Septimum animalia alere?
f num dixisti custodes dormire?
g negant Catilinam innocentem esse.
h videbitis me fortissimum esse.
i cives credunt vos praetermitti.
j omnes sciunt Carthaginienses perfidos esse.

2 Translate the following sentences into English. They illustrate C ii above.

e.g. **video Titum pulchrum fore** (or **futurum esse**) → *I see that Titus is going to be handsome*

a sciebamus coniuratos necatum iri.
b puto Catilinam nos relicturum esse.
c putasne meas fabulas ab actoribus notissimis actum iri?
d sciverasne Marium comprehensum iri?
e nonne videtis Gallos vicum censuros esse?
f negabas Caesarem dictatorem fore.
g praedones non crediderunt insulam defensum iri.
h dux nuntiavit exercitum statim profecturum esse.
i tibi dixi Helenam cras discessuram esse.
j negat puellam lectum iri.

3 **Translate the following sentences into English. They illustrate C iii above.**

e.g. **dicit rationes probatas esse** → *he says that the accounts have been approved*

    a dicisne eam Tiberio nupsisse?
    b scimus agricolas vaccas omnes vendidisse.
    c putabamus patriam a Cicerone servatam esse.
    d nonne vides hunc equum lautum esse?
    e exploratores nuntiaverunt novas copias advenisse.
    f negabimus senem aurum invenisse.
    g Valerius dixit haruspicem mentitum esse.
    h negasne te hanc feminam umquam vidisse?
    i videmus hospites bene oblectatos esse.
    j custodes negabant captivum vinctum esse.

4 **Translate the following sentences into English. They illustrate D above.**

e.g. **Caesar dixit suos Gallos superaturos esse** → *Caesar said his men would beat the Gauls*

    a Quintus sciebat se poenas pro scelere suo non daturum esse.
    b Marius putabat se necatum iri.
    c Cato iuvenem castigavit et dixit se eum incusaturum esse.
    d cives nesciunt se a Tarquinio deceptos esse.
    e Marcus negavit se arborem succidisse.
    f milites negaverunt se effugisse.
    g Egnatius dicit se a praedonibus spoliatum esse.
    h senatores nuntiaverant se Pompeium electuros esse.
    i Sempronia putavit se cultrum invenisse.
    j scriba negat se haec verba scripsisse.

5 **Translate the following sentences into English. They illustrate E, F and G above.**

e.g. **fossor scit aurum ibi inventum** → *the miner knows that gold has been found there*

    a dictum est Romanos bello intractabiles esse.
    b nego nos captum iri si lente ambulemus.

c negavistine te captum?

d Horatius dixit se pontem custoditurum.

e constat Marium Romam servavisse.

f dictum est delphinum in portum navisse.

g nesciebamus te picturam picturum.

h negatum erat Augustum aegrum esse.

i non putabam cives Cornelium umquam electuros fuisse nisi ab eo corrupti essent.

j scio te tutum futurum esse si mea verba respicias.

6 Translate the following sentences into English. They illustrate H, I, J and K above.

e.g. **spero vos semper felices fore** (or **futuros esse**) → *I hope that you will always be fortunate*

a nonne promittes te mecum iter facturum esse?

b hostes minantur se urbem incensuros esse.

c iuro me semper fidelem fore.

d patronus pollicitus est se dona clientis daturum esse.

e iubesne me ab urbe discedere?

f magistratus vetavit pistores collegium condere.

g sperabamus vos fundum empturos esse.

h Publius gaudet avum suum convalescere.

i volo te aquam de fonte portare.

j lugemus Ciceronem necatum esse.

7 Translate the following sentences into Latin.

e.g. *Lucius thinks he is being watched by a gnome* → **Lucius putat se a terricula spectari**

a Calpurnia thinks she will be attacked by the dog.

b Catullus knows that he loves Clodia.

c I know that the fox will escape if the gate is opened.

d It has been said that Nero killed his own mother.

e They have promised that the new statue is not going to fall.

f Do you (s.) forbid me to eat beans?

g They are unwilling for us to see the new carpet.

h I rejoice that your wife is pregnant.

i He swears that he will avenge his father.

j We hope that she will catch the tortoise.

8 Translate the following sentences into English. They illustrate Mi and N above.

e.g. **Tullia rogat cur feles in culina ludat** → *Tullia asks why the cat is playing in the kitchen*

a Caelia rogat num fabri cras laboraturi sint.

b rogabo num Hortensius liberos ducturus sit necne.

c rogavi quando regina advenerit.

d Tullius rogabit Decimum num aurum inventum sit.

e Decius non vult rogare quomodo id acciderit.

f pueri, rogate matrem num poetam audire velit.

g rogavistine me num laetus sim?

h rogavimus num Servius Caeciliam amet necne?

i tribuni rogabunt quis consilium patefacturus sit.

j roga quot plaustra sint.

9 Translate the following sentences into English. They illustrate Mii and N.

e.g. **rogavi ubi aurum inventum esset** → *I asked where the gold had been found*

a rogavimus cur puellae non cantarent.

b fossores rogaverunt num mercedes accepturi essent necne.

c num rogavisti num Titus Liviam osculatus esset?

d non rogaveram quem dux electurus esset.

e Romulus non rogavit quid accidisset.

f ductor nos rogaverat quomodo iter faceremus.

g semper rogabant quando ibi adventuri essent.

h rogaveramus quotiens Marius consul fuisset.

i nonne Sulla rogavit num exercitus victus esset?

j volo videre num larva ventura sit necne.

10 Translate the following sentences into Latin.

e.g. *I shall ask whether the guests have arrived* → **rogabo num hospites advenerint**

a Have you (s.) asked whether the gates are closed or not?
b Ask (s.) whether the boys are working in the garden.
c We used to ask whether the statue was alive.
d He had asked whether you (s.) were a farmer.
e The citizens are asking who will be queen.
f Did he ask if I had been wounded?
g They are asking whether the dinner is ready.
h I had asked whether Marius would arrive.
i The maidservant is asking whether you (s.) are asleep or not.
j Who knows what happened?

11 Translate the following sentences into English. They illustrate O, P and Q above.

e.g. **mandata eis dedi ut collem ascendant** → *I have given them orders to climb the hill*

a anus regem monet ut libros emat.
b Stephanus domino persuasit ut Furium manumitteret.
c Holconius curat ut novae thermae aedificentur.
d Sextus vetabatur potionem tangere.
e agricolae postulabunt ut rex se abdicet.
f hortati sumus Plautum ut fabulas scriberet.
g iubebimus Terentium cenam coquere.
h Iuppiter Minervam permiserat ut Graecis subveniret.
i mater nos sinet pullos agitare.
j imperavit nobis ut pavimentum lavemus.

12 Translate the following sentences into English. They illustrate R above.

e.g. **cupit ut tu ibi nunc adesses** → *he wishes that you were there now*

a cupimus ut pater ursum nobis demonstret.
b optaveramus ne Lucius ebrius esset.

c volo ut tu mihi nubas.

d Cicero cupivit ut Catilina interfectus esset.

e omnes malumus ut tu domi maneas.

f baiuli cupiunt ne onera gravia sint.

g volo ut anulum invenissem.

h voluisti ut Cato electus esset.

i visne ut thesaurus inventus esset?

j Hadrianus cupit ut murus aedificetur.

13 Translate the following sentences into Latin.

e.g. *he has warned the citizens not to expect much* → **cives monuit ne multa exspectent**

a I demand (**postulo**) that you (s.) free the slave.

b They are urging (**hortor**) us to attack the camp.

c I took care (**curo**) that the togas would not be dirty.

d Order (**impero**) (s.) the guard not to sleep.

e I implore (**obsecro**) you (pl.) not to kill Caesar.

f We warned (**moneo**) you (s.) not to wander into the woods.

g We desire (**cupio**) that you (s.) depart from the palace.

h They had forbidden (**veto**) the boys to swim in the river.

i She had persuaded (**persuadeo**) him to eat the apple.

j We shall permit (**permitto**) them to buy the horse.

Points to remember

1 An indirect statement is a reported statement introduced not only by verbs of saying but also verbs of perception. The introductory verb is followed by the accusative and infinitive. The tense of the infinitive depends upon the tense of the original statement.

2 When the subjects of indirect statements refer to themselves, the reflexive pronoun is used. E.g. **scit se convalescere** (*He knows he is getting better*).

3 An indirect question is a reported question introduced either by the original question word, or **num** (*whether, if*) with a subjunctive verb. The tense of the verb depends upon its context.

4 If the main verb of an indirect question is primary, the subordinate verb will be in the present, perfect or the invented future subjunctive.

5 If the main verb of an indirect question is historic, the subordinate verb will be in the imperfect, pluperfect or the invented future perfect subjunctive.

6 A indirect command is a reported command introduced not only by verbs of commanding but also verbs of persuading, warning, encouraging, decreeing, urging, taking care that, permitting, etc.

7 Indirect commands which follow **iubeo** (*I order*), **veto** (*I forbid*), **sino** or **patior** (*I allow*) use an infinitive, as in English.

8 Indirect commands which follow other verbs are introduced by **ut** or **ne** (negative) and have a subjunctive verb, in the present or imperfect, according to the sequence of tenses.

9 An indirect wish is a reported wish, introduced by a verb of wishing and the conjunction **ut** (negative **ne**), and followed by a subjunctive verb.

10 Wishes for the future are expressed by a present or perfect subjunctive, those for the present by an imperfect subjunctive and those for the past by a pluperfect subjunctive.

16

Other subordinate clauses

Concessive clauses

A **Concessive clauses** are those which indicate a concession
(*although*). They are introduced by the concessive conjunctions
(Unit 6F) **etsi**, **etiamsi** or **tametsi** (*even if, even though*),
quamquam, **quamvis**, **ut** (negative **ne**), **licet** (*although*) or
cum (*whereas*).

▶ If the clause is introduced by **quamquam**, then its verb will be in
the **indicative**. (Some later writers used it with the subjunctive.)
  e.g. **quamquam pons deletus est, ego flumen transivi** →
    although the bridge was destroyed, I crossed the river
▶ If the clause is introduced by **quamvis**, **licet**, **ut** or **cum** then its
verb will be in the **subjunctive**.
  e.g. **quamvis pons deletus sit, ego flumen transivi** → *although
    the bridge was destroyed, I crossed the river*
▶ If the clause is introduced by **etsi**, **etiamsi** or **tametsi** (even
though), then the mood of its verb is decided by the same rules
as for conditionals (Unit 14J–O). Generally it is in:

  i the **indicative** if the concession did occur, is occurring or will
  occur.
    e.g. **etiamsi pons deletus erat, ego flumen transivi** → *even
      though the bridge had been destroyed, I crossed the river*

or

ii the **subjunctive,** if the concession might have occurred, may be occurring or might occur. The subjunctive verb in the main clause is commonly translated into English by the words *would* or *should*.

> e.g. **etsi pons deletus esset, ego flumen transivissem** → *even if the bridge had been destroyed, I would have crossed the river*

Causal clauses

B **Causal clauses** indicate the reason for something (*because*). They are introduced by **quod, quia, quoniam, quando** → *because, since*, and **cum** → *since*.

▶ In causal clauses introduced by **quod, quia, quoniam** or **quando,** when the person (author or character) stating the reason is also supporting the reason as true, then the verb of the clause is in the **indicative.**

> e.g. **te non vocavi quod dormiebas** → *I did not call you because you were asleep*

However, when the speaker gives a reason with which others, including the speaker, may not agree, then the verb of the clause is in the **subjunctive.**

> e.g. **Romani victi sunt quod perfidi essemus** → *the Romans were beaten (some say) because we were treacherous*

▶ When **cum** introduces a causal clause, then its verb is in the **subjunctive,** whether the speaker vouches for the reason or not.
▶ The verb of a causal clause introduced by the relative pronoun **qui** or **quippe qui** (*since, for in fact, doubtless, because* [often sarcastic]) is in the **subjunctive** (see Unit 13H).

Clauses of proviso

C A **clause of proviso** is introduced by **dum, dummodo** or **modo** (*provided that*). The construction is really an extension of the temporal clause **dum** (*as long as*) (Unit 13K). However, the verb of the clause is in the **subjunctive**. A negative clause of proviso is introduced by **dum ne**.

    e.g. **oderint dum metuant** → *let them hate provided that they fear*

    e.g. **in horto ludant dum flores ne carpant** → *let them play in the garden provided that they do not pick the flowers*

Clauses of comparison

D In a **clause of comparison** the action of the clause is compared with the action of the main clause.

▶ If the comparison is being made with something that is an actual fact then the clause is introduced by **velut, sicut** (*just as*) or **ut** (*as*) (often with **ita** in the main clause), and the verb of the clause is in the **indicative**.

    e.g. **Caesar postridie necatus est, sicut vates praedixerat** → *Caesar was killed on the following day, just as the prophet had predicted*

▶ If the comparison is being made with an event that is imaginary, then the clause is introduced by **quasi, ut si, velut si** (*as if*), or **ceu, tamquam** (*as though*), and the verb of the clause is in the **subjunctive**.

    e.g. **mihi mandata insolenter dedit quasi servus quidam essem** → *he gave me the instructions haughtily, as if I were some slave*

Clauses of fear

E ▶ These are introduced by a verb of fearing such as **timeo,**
vereor or **metuo** and the conjunction **ne.** They express fear
about something that is happening, may happen or has
happened and the verb of the clause is in the **subjunctive.**

▶ The tense of the subjunctive usually depends upon the
sequence of tenses (Unit 1Y) but when you come to translate
extended passages of Latin, it is always necessary to take
account of the context in which these clauses appear in order
to get the most appropriate tense in your English translation.
For example, **vereor ne captivi necentur** can mean either *I am*
afraid that (lest) the captives are being killed or *I am afraid*
that (lest) the captives may be killed.

▶ If the fear is that something will *not* happen, then **ne non**
(or sometimes **ut**) is used.

e.g. **timemus ne milites non adveniant** → *we are afraid that*
the soldiers may not come

Clauses of doubting

F ▶ A clause which expresses positive doubt and is introduced by,
e.g. **dubito** (*I doubt*), **dubium est** (*it is doubtful*) or **incertum**
est (*it is uncertain*), is treated as an **indirect question**
(Unit 15L–M). The verb of the clause is in the **subjunctive.**
e.g. **dubium erat utrum Tiberius adveniret necne** → *it was*
doubtful whether Tiberius would arrive or not

▶ Note the phrases **dubito an** (*I am inclined to think that*), and
dubito num (*I doubt if [or whether]*).
e.g. **dubitavit an Pompeius cederet** → *he was inclined to think*
that Pompey would yield
e.g. **dubitavi num de hoc audires** → *I doubted whether you*
would hear about this

▶ When **dubito, dubium est** or other expressions of doubt
introduce a negative doubt or occur in questions (often
accompanied by the archaic **haud** [*not*]), they are followed

by a clause introduced by **quin** (*but that* or *that ... not*) (see below), which has its verb in the **subjunctive**.

e.g. **haud dubium est quin regina captivis parcant** → *there is no doubt but that the queen will spare the prisoners (or there is no doubt that the queen will spare the prisoners.)*

e.g. **quis dubitat quin Verres innocens sit?** → *who doubts but that Verres is innocent?*

Clauses of hindering, preventing and forbidding

G In English these clauses usually consist of *from* with a participle or an infinitive after *forbid*, e.g. *The storm prevents us from entering the harbour, I forbid you to do that.* Compare the indirect command in Unit 15O–Q.

  i The verb **veto** (*I forbid*), takes the accusative of the person ordered and a prolative infinitive (Unit 11J) of the action forbidden.

   e.g. **Titus vetuit milites oppugnare** → *Titus forbade the soldiers to attack*; or, in more natural English, *Titus told the soldiers not to attack.*

  ii Apart from **veto** and **prohibeo** (*I prevent* – see below), all other verbs of hindering, preventing or forbidding are followed by a clause with a **subjunctive** verb.

 iii If the main clause contains a positive prohibition, then the subordinate clause is introduced by **ne** or **quominus** (*so that ... not*).

   e.g. **luto impedimur ne viam transeamus** → *we are hindered from crossing the road by mud*

 iv If the main clause contains a negative prohibition, e.g. **non impedio** (*I do not hinder*), then the subordinate clause is introduced by **quominus** or **quin**.

   e.g. **non nos impedit quin in via ludamus** → *he is not hindering us from playing in the road*

v The verb **prohibeo** (*I prevent*) can either take the same construction as **veto** or the construction in **iii** or **iv** above.

e.g. **prohibuit agricolas agros arare** → *he prevented the farmers from ploughing their fields*

e.g. **Quintus Fabius milites prohibuit quominus Carthaginienses oppugnarent** → *Quintus Fabius prevented the soldiers from attacking the Carthaginians*

The use of quin

quin (*but that, that ... not*) is the shortened form of an archaic interrogative adverb **quine** (*how not, why not?*). Apart from being used in clauses of doubting (see F) and hindering (see G), **quin** is also used after some other expressions which involve negatives.

H Usually **quin** introduces a consecutive clause (Unit 14F) and some other clauses, when it is used as the equivalent of **ut ... non**. It is followed by the **subjunctive**.

e.g. **nullus tyrannus tam potens est quin deleri possit** → *no tyrant is so powerful that he cannot be destroyed (or no tyrant is so powerful but that he can be destroyed)*

e.g. **non potest fieri quin hic Verres convincatur** → *it cannot happen that this man Verres is not convicted (or it cannot happen but that this man Verres is convicted)*

I In expressions like **nemo est quin** (*There is no-one who ... not*), **quin** acts like a relative pronoun followed by **non** (*not*). It is followed by the **subjunctive**.

e.g. **nemo est his temporibus quin tale scelus admittere audeat** → *there is no-one in these times who would not dare to commit such a crime*

J **quin** can also be used with its original meaning as an adverb (*how not, why not*) to introduce **direct questions**, followed by the **subjunctive**.

e.g. **quin nos clementiam de imperatore petamus?** → *why should we not ask for mercy from the general?*

K **quin** can be used as an emphasizing adverb at the start of a statement which supports or emphasizes something which has been stated previously. Unusually, in this usage **quin** does not have a negative sense. It may be followed by the indicative. It is best translated as *indeed* or *in fact*.

e.g. **multos clientes ille patronus habet quin Cassius interest** →
That patron has many clients. In fact Cassius is among them.

L **quin** may be used as an emphasizing adverb to reinforce an imperative. It is best translated as *well* or *well then*.

e.g. **quin eos oppugnate, milites!** → *well then, attack them, soldiers!*

1 Translate the following sentences into English. They illustrate concessive clauses.

e.g. **quamquam dives sum, te non spernam** → *although I am rich, I shall not spurn you*

a quamquam femina pulchra erat, avarus eam suspicatus est.
b quamvis signum captum esset, legionarii fortiter pugnaverunt.
c licet tabernarii inurbani sint multas tamen stolas emam.
d ut gladius in saxo infixus sit, Arturus eum extrahet.
e quamquam Gaius modo septem annos natus est nihilominus inter iuvenes ludit.
f etsi vesperascit, pueri in silvas repunt.
g etiamsi pater discessit strenue laboramus.
h tametsi gladiator ingens est, cum eo pugnabo.
i quamquam avum meum numquam vidisti eum certe amabis.
j tametsi exercitus non paratus fuisset, barbaros superavissemus.

2 Translate the following sentences into English. They illustrate causal clauses.

e.g. **Iulius abest quod aeger sit** → *Julius is away because, some say, he is ill*

a Aemilia Caelium non amat quod pater eius pauper sit.
b Cicero coniuratos interfecit quia respublica in maximo periculo esset.
c Quintus non venabitur quippe qui feras timeat.

d senex sero adveniet quod sero discessit.

e Cassius Caesarem odit quod Romam amet.

f canem expuli quia felem insequebatur.

g es dives Cassius quoniam felix sis.

h harundines comparaverunt quando cras piscabuntur.

i cum iter certe longum sit tecum ibo.

j pueri altercantur quoniam fessi sunt.

3 Translate the following sentences into Latin. Use the conjunctions provided.

e.g. *we are weeping because the enemy are here* → **lacrimamus quod hostes adsunt**

a Although (**quamvis**) Alexander had been wounded, he fought more fiercely.

b Although (**quamquam**) Gaius is lazy, he will repair the wheel.

c Even if (**etsi**) you (s.) had killed the king, we would not have escaped.

d Even though (**etsi**) the river was very wide, we reached the bank.

e The mice are playing because (**quia**) the cat is away.

f Rome was burnt, some say, because (**quod**) Nero wanted to build a new palace.

g The king has summoned me doubtless because (**quippe qui**) he admires me.

h The prince will come because (**cum**) he loves you (s.).

i Titus will not fight because (**quoniam**) he is gentle.

j Although (**quamquam**) we cannot see you (pl.), we can hear your (pl.) words.

4 Translate the following into English. They illustrate C above.

e.g. **me conducet dum ne stertam** → *he will hire me provided that I do not snore*

a cenent pueri dum se laverint.

b hodie dormiant fabri dummodo cras strenue laborent.

c invita Caecilium dum fratrem ne ducat.

d stolam eligam dummodo tu eam emas.

e liberi loquantur dum inter se ne pugnent.
f illos iuvenes certe vides dummodo puellae quoque adsint.
g pueri fabulam spectent dummodo taceant.
h domum explorate pueri, dum in illam partem ne erretis.
i maritum eligat filia tua dum eum amet.
j canes in atrio ludant dum ne quid frangant.

5 Translate the following into English. They illustrate D above.

e.g. **Caesar se gerebat tamquam rex esset** → *Caesar behaved as if he were a king*

a panem pauper consumit velut si non iterum edat.
b lupa pueros alebat ut si catuli essent.
c pueri ludunt sicut viri laborant.
d cur locutus es quasi Catilina non proditor esset?
e filius meus pecuniam impendit velut si patrimonium exceperit.
f leo in spelunca vero habitat sicut saepe confirmas.
g iuvenes navigant ceu venti non fortes sint.
h candidatus novas thermas aedivicavit ut promisit.
i spectatores plauserunt tamquam fabula conclusa esset.
j poeta viros sapientiores facit sicut magister pueros docet.

6 Translate the following sentences into English. They illustrate E above.

e.g. **timesne ne pater nos non eripiat?** → *are you afraid that father may not rescue us?*

a piscatores metuebant ne retia frangerentur.
b duces timent ne novae copiae non adveniant.
c veremur ne Titus arcam non inveniat.
d pastor veritus est ne agnam lupi cepissent.
e magister timebat ne liberi in silvas ambulavissent.
f athletae metuunt ne praemia non auferant.
g metuebam ne pecuniam non compararem.
h Cassius timuerat ne proditor consilium consulibus patefecisset.
i estne periculum ne capiamur?
j timebam ne Caesar Rubiconem transiisset.

7 Translate the following sentences into Latin.

e.g. *I am afraid that the Trojans may attack* → **timeo ne Troiani oppugnent**

a Rufus carries a sword as though (**tamquam**) he is a soldier.

b Let the young men approach, provided that (**dummodo**) they are unarmed.

c There was a danger that the wall would collapse.

d The conspirator persuaded the assassin just as (**sicut**) the serpent beguiles its prey.

e Let Cicero come in provided that (**dum**) he does not (**ne**) speak.

f Were they afraid that Sulla would find him?

g I shall dine with (**apud**) you tomorrow Titus, provided that your wine is good.

h He looked at me as if (**quasi**) he had seen me before.

i I was afraid that the scouts had not found food.

j He paraded (**traduco**) the captives as though (**ceu**) they were slaves.

8 Translate the following into English. They illustrate F above.

e.g. **dubito num tua verba vera sint** → *I doubt whether your words are true*

a dubitaveramus num ad tempus advenires.

b quis dubitavit quin Cicero servum liberet?

c dubium est num Carthaginienses re vera victi sint.

d dubitaverunt num Valerius testamentum scripsisset.

e incertum est unde advena venerit.

f dubitavisti an talis candidatus pessimus esset.

g dubium erat num Ulysses domum rediret.

h Caesar dubitavit an Cassius non fidelis esset.

i Cloelia dubitavit an virgines sequerentur.

j haud dubium erat quin navis demergeretur.

9 Translate the following into English. They illustrate G above.

e.g. **Titus non me prohibebit quin cantem** → *Titus will not prevent me from singing*

a Valerius deterruit pueros ne iter longum facerent.
b magistratus vetuerunt cives legatos accipere.
c interdictum est nobis ne illum proditorem defendamus.
d rex captivos non prohibuit quin liberentur.
e custodes impediebantur quominus portas aperirent.
f vetabuntne nos sacrificium tangere?
g centurio prohibuit legionarios diu dormire.
h oneribus gravibus asini impediuntur quominus pontem transeant.
i nihil obstat quin nos amici simus.
j num nos impedies ne gladiatores videamus?

10 Translate the following sentences into Latin.

e.g. *why do you doubt but that Titus loves you?* → **cur dubitas quin Titus te amet?**

a The Gauls were hindered (**impedio**) from crossing the river by the flood (**gurges**).
b Portia has forbidden (**veto**) us to annoy the geese.
c There is no doubt but that the Romans will burn the village.
d The omens do not hinder (**impedio**) the general from setting out.
e Cornelius, will you prevent (**prohibeo**) the dogs from attacking my son?
f We were inclined to think that you (s.) would prefer to leave.
g I doubt if Servius is able to ride.
h Certain people doubted whether Augustus would like the poem.
i Magistrates, prevent (**prohibeo**) that man from entering the house.
j It is doubtful whether the workmen have finished the bridge.

11 Translate the following sentences into English. They illustrate H and I above.

e.g. **nemo est quin domum meam amet** → *there is no-one who does not like my house*

a nullus miles tam fortiter pugnabat quin praemia mereat.
b non potest fieri quin Claudius eligatur.
c nulla femina tam dives erat quin prudens esset.

d nemo erat quin Alexandrum Magnum sequeretur.
e nemo est quin Brutum admiretur.
f nullus puer est tam bonus quin mala mea furetur.
g non potest fieri quin Caesar dictator fiat.
h non potest fieri quin Cloelia reddatur.
i nemo est quin oratori illo credat.
j nullus dux est tam durus quin captivis parcat.

12 Translate the following sentences into English. They illustrate J, K and L above.

e.g. **quin Iuliettam petam?** → *why should I not woo Juliet?*

a quin tribunus consuli resistat?
b is gladiator notissimus est; quin libertus mox erit.
c quin serva infantem frater!
d quin fugitivus hic maneat?
e iuvenes fortissimi erant; quin Hercules leonem interfecerat.
f quin emovete gregem pastores.
g quin mater filium amet?
h quin agite pueri, pilam capite.
i quin eam pilam videre potueris?
j quin eos flores carpamus?

13 Translate the following sentences into Latin.

e.g. *I am not so deaf that I cannot hear you* → **non tam surdus sum quin te audire possim**

a Caecilius is not so poor that he cannot buy a bigger house.
b It cannot happen that the treaty is not renewed.
c There was no-one who did not know about the wedding.
d No knot is so complicated that it cannot be undone.
e How should Sextus not believe us?
f Quintus does not like me; in fact yesterday he insulted me.
g Why should Felix not sell the horse?
i There is no soldier who does not fear death.
j Well then, seize the day, children.

Points to remember

1 A concessive clause indicates a concession (*although*). If it is introduced by **quamquam** (*although*), it contains an indicative verb.

2 If a concessive clause is introduced by **quamvis, ut, licet** (*although*) or **cum** (*whereas*), it contains a subjunctive verb.

3 If a concessive clause is introduced by **etsi, etiamsi, tametsi** (*even if*), the mood of the verb is the same as for conditionals.

4 A causal clause indicates the reason for something. If the speaker agrees with the reason, the verb is in the indicative, if not, the verb is in the subjunctive.

5 A clause of proviso is introduced by **dum, dummodo** or **modo** (*provided that*) or **dum ne** (*negative*). The verb is in the subjunctive.

6 In a clause of comparison the action of the clause is compared with the action of the main clause. If the comparison is a fact, the verb is in the indicative, if not the verb is in the subjunctive.

7 A clause of fear is introduced by a verb of fearing followed by **ne** and a subjunctive verb, usually following the sequence of tenses.

8 A clause which expresses positive doubt is introduced by a verb of doubting and has a verb in the subjunctive, as in indirect questions. Negative doubts are introduced by the conjunction **quin** (*but that*) and have a subjunctive verb.

9 In a clause of hindering, preventing or forbidding, if the introductory verb is **veto** (*I forbid*), the accusative and construction is used.

10 In a clause of hindering, preventing or forbidding, if the introductory verb is not **veto** (*I forbid*), the verb of the clause is in the subjunctive, introduced by **ne, quominus** or **quin**.

17

Miscellaneous

A Dates

Roman years can be reckoned **Ab Urbe Condita** (*from the founding of the city* [literally from the founded city]). This is often abbreviated to **AUC**. 753 years must be added to a date CE while a date BCE **must be taken away from 754 to get the Roman year.**

e.g. MMDCCLIV AUC → 2754 years from the founding of the city
→ 2001 CE

Years after the institution of the republic in 510 BCE can also be recorded as 'the year in which x and y were consuls'. In such phrases the names of the consuls are in an ablative absolute with the word **consulibus** (sometimes abbreviated to **coss**) (see Unit 13V).

e.g. **P. Cornelio Scipione Ti. Sempronio Longo coss.** → *When Publius Cornelius Scipio and Tiberius Sempronius Longus were consuls.* → 218 BCE.

B The Roman year was divided into 12 months. The titles of the months are adjectives used in agreement with the implied word **mensis** (*month*), or the special days mentioned in C below. Most of them are the words we still use. The names Quintilis and Sextilis were changed in honour of Julius Caesar and Augustus.

Januarius -a -um	Julius -a -um (Quintilis -is -e)
Februarius -a -um	Augustus -a -um (Sextilis -is -e)
Martius -a -um	September -bris
Aprilis -is -e	October -bris

Maius -a -um	November -bris
Junius -a -um	December -bris

C Roman months were 29 and 30 days long alternately. They had no equivalent of a week but did divide their months up into periods between three significant days in each month. The names of these days are feminine and plural:

- ▶ **Kalendae -arum** *the Kalends*. The first day of the month.
- ▶ **Nonae -arum** *the Nones*. The seventh day of March, July, October and May, but the fifth day of the other months.
- ▶ **Idus -uum** *the Ides*. The fifteenth day of March, July, October and May, but the thirteenth day of the other months.

If a date is one of these days, it is expressed in the ablative with the adjective of the month in agreement with it. It is also normally abbreviated.

e.g. **Id(ibus) Mar(tiis)** → *on the Ides of March* → on 15th March

If a date is the day before one of these days, it is expressed by **pridie** ([*on*] *the day before*), followed by the accusative of the day. It is sometimes abbreviated to prid.

e.g. **prid. Non(as) Mar(tias)** → *on the day before the Nones of March* → on 6th April.

All other dates are reckoned as being so many days **ante diem** (*before the next named day*, normally abbreviated to **a.d.**). The whole phrase is in the accusative. Unusually, when the Romans calculated this they included both the date and the named day in the interval.

e.g. **a.d. III Non. Mar.** → **ante diem tertium Nonas Martias** → three days *before the Nones of March* (including the **Nones** and the date mentioned) → on 5th March

D The following sample months are enough to give a guide to the dates of any month in the year. They have been modified for the Gregorian calendar with months of 30 or 31 days.

	April	May
1st	Kal. Apr.	Kal. Mai.
2nd	a.d. IV Non. Apr.	a.d. VI Non. Mai.
3rd	a.d. III Non. Apr.	a.d. V Non. Mai.
4th	prid. Non. Apr.	a.d. IV Non. Mai.
5th	Non. Apr.	a.d. III Non. Mai.
6th	a.d. VIII Id. Apr.	prid. Non. Mai.
7th	a.d. VII Id. Apr.	Non. Mai.
8th	a.d. VI Id. Apr.	a.d. VIII Id. Mai.
9th	a.d. V Id. Apr.	a.d. VII Id. Mai.
10th	a.d. IV Id. Apr.	a.d. VI Id. Mai.
11th	a.d. III Id. Apr.	a.d. V Id. Mai.
12th	prid. Id. Apr.	a.d. IV Id. Mai.
13th	Id. Apr.	a.d. III Id. Mai.
14th	a.d. XVIII Kal. Mai.	prid. Id. Mai.
15th	a.d. XVII Kal. Mai.	Id. Mai.
16th	a.d. XVI Kal. Mai.	a.d. XVII Kal. Iun.

	April	May
17th	a.d. XV Kal. Mai.	a.d. XVI Kal. Iun.
18th	a.d. XIV Kal. Mai.	a.d. XV Kal. Iun.
19th	a.d. XIII Kal. Mai.	a.d. XIV Kal. Iun.
20th	a.d. XII Kal. Mai.	a.d. XIII Kal. Iun.
21st	a.d. XI Kal. Mai.	a.d. XII Kal. Iun.
22nd	a.d. X Kal. Mai.	a.d. XI Kal. Iun.
23rd	a.d. IX Kal. Mai.	a.d. X Kal. Iun.
24th	a.d. VIII Kal. Mai.	a.d. IX Kal. Iun.
25th	a.d. VII Kal. Mai.	a.d. VIII Kal. Iun.
26th	a.d. VI Kal. Mai.	a.d. VII Kal. Iun.
27th	a.d. V Kal. Mai.	a.d. VI Kal. Iun.
28th	a.d. IV Kal. Mai.	a.d. V Kal. Iun.
29th	a.d. III Kal. Mai.	a.d. IV Kal. Iun.
30th	prid. Kal. Mai.	a.d. III Kal. Iun.
31st		prid. Kal. Iun.

E The Romans frequently had to add days or even months to years in order to make up for the difference between their calendar year and the solar year and in 45 BCE Julius Caesar revised their calendar. In the leap years 24th February (a.d. VI Kal. Mar.) was counted twice and called **dies bissextus**.

F After Constantine legalized Christianity the seven days of the week officially acquired Latin names in 321 CE. Some of these survive in modern European Romance languages today. Even English still has Saturday.

dies **Solis**	*day of the sun*	Sunday
dies **Lunae**	*day of the moon*	Monday
dies **Martis**	*day of Mars* (god of war)	Tuesday
dies **Mercuri**	*day of Mercury* (the messenger god)	Wednesday
dies **Iovis**	*day of Jupiter* (king of the gods)	Thursday
dies **Veneris**	*day of Venus* (goddess of love)	Friday
dies **Saturni**	*day of Saturn* (father of Jupiter)	Saturday

G Money

It is impossible to give modern equivalents for the value of money in ancient times. Not only did it fluctuate considerably during the centuries of Roman history but also the value of today's currency is soon out of date itself. It is possible to get an idea of the value from contemporary writers.

▶ The **as** (**as assis** m.) (*unit*), was the coin of lowest value.
▶ Two and a half asses was worth one **sestertius** (-i m.), a word formed from **semis tertius** (*the third half*, i.e. 2.5). We usually call this a **sesterce** in English. The symbol for a sesterce was HS, an abbreviation for **duo et semis** → *two and a half* (asses). Sometimes the word **nummus** (-i m.) (*coin*), was also used for the sesterce.
▶ Four sestertii made one **denarius**.
▶ Twenty-five denarii made one **aureus**.

H The sesterce was a unit of currency which was mentioned very frequently with reference to large prices or sums of money.

▶ When expressing thousands of sesterces the Romans used the special neuter plural word **sestertia** (*thousands of sesterces*), with a distributive numeral (Unit 6N).
e.g. HS$\overline{\text{V}}$ → **quina sestertia** → *five thousand sesterces*
▶ When expressing hundreds of thousands of sesterces the Romans used the genitive plural **sestertium** (with **centena milia** understood) with a numeral adverb (Unit 6U).
e.g. HS $|\overline{\text{X}}|$ → **decies sestertium** → *one million* (10 x 100,000) *sesterces*

I The Romans also made use of Greek (silver) units of currency.
▶ The smallest unit commonly mentioned by the Romans is the **drachma**.
▶ One hundred drachmae made one **mina**.
▶ Sixty minae made one **talentum** (*talent*).

J Weight
▶ The smallest unit was the **scrupulum** (*Roman scruple*).
▶ Four scrupula made one **sextula**.
▶ Six sextulae made one **uncia** (*Roman ounce*).
▶ Twelve unciae made one **libra** (*Roman pound*, about 11.5 English ounces or 326 grams).

K Liquid capacity
▶ The smallest unit was the **cochlearium**.
▶ Four cochlearia made one **cyathus**.
▶ Twelve cyathi made one **sextarius** (a little less than an English pint or about half a litre).
▶ Six sextarii made one **congius**.
▶ Eight congii made one **amphora**.
▶ Twenty amphorae made one **culleus**.

L Dry capacity
▶ The smallest unit was the **cochlearium**.
▶ Four cochlearia made one **cyathus**.
▶ Twelve cyathi made one **sextarius**.

- ▶ Eight sextarii made one **semodius**.
- ▶ Two semodii made one **modius** (two English gallons or about nine litres).

M Length

- ▶ The smallest unit was the **uncia** (*Roman inch*).
- ▶ Twelve unciae made one **pes** (*Roman foot*, which was slightly less than an English foot or about 30 centimetres).
- ▶ Eighteen unciae (1.5 pedes) made a **cubitum** (*Roman cubit*).
- ▶ Five pedes made one **passus** (*Roman yard* [pace]).
- ▶ One hundred and twenty-five passus made one **stadium** (*Roman furlong*).
- ▶ Eight stadia made one **mille passus** (*Roman mile* [1,000 paces]; about 1,620 English yards or 1,481 metres).

N Area

- ▶ The smallest unit was the **pes quadratus** (*square foot*).
- ▶ One hundred pedes quadrati made one **scripulum** or **decempeda quadrata** (*ten feet square*).
- ▶ One hundred and forty-four scripula made one **actus quadratus**.
- ▶ Two actus quadrati made one **iugerum** (*Roman acre*, about five-eighths of an English acre or 2,529 square metres).
- ▶ Two iugera made one **heredium**.
- ▶ One hundred heredia made one **centuria**.

O Personal names

A Roman man had three names: a **praenomen**, a **nomen** and a **cognomen**, in that order, e.g. Tiberius Sempronius Gracchus. Some even had a fourth or fifth name (**agnomen**).

The **praenomen** (*forename*), is an individual name used by family and close friends. There are not many to choose from and they are written in an abbreviated form when the other names are given. The commonest are:

A.	Aulus	P.	Publius
C.	Gaius	Q.	Quintus
Cn.	Gnaeus	Ser.	Servius
D.	Decimus	S. (or Sex.)	Sextus

L.	Lucius	Sp.	Spurius
M.	Marcus	T.	Titus
M'.	Manius	Ti. (or Tib.)	Tiberius
N.	Numerius		

The **nomen** (*name*), is the **gens** (*clan*, extended family) name and usually ends in **-ius**. Famous Roman clans are the Claudii, Sempronii, Cornelii, Iulii and Iunii.

The **cognomen** (*surname*), is the **familia** (*family*) name. Originally cognomina were individual nicknames, often descriptive of appearance, e.g. Rufus → Redhead, Naso → Big nose, Caligula → Little boots, etc. Eventually cognomina became hereditary and were used to distinguish one branch of a clan from another.

An **agnomen** is a further name added onto the cognomen. It is used either:

▶ As a title of honour, like Augustus → Majestic (His Majesty), Africanus → Conqueror of Africa, Numidicus → Conqueror of Numidia or Macedonicus → Conqueror of Macedonia, etc. Or
▶ As a sign that a person has been adopted into their current gens from another gens. These agnomina of adoption usually end in **-ianus**. The emperor Augustus' **nomen** was originally Octavius. After he had been adopted by his uncle Julius Caesar and granted the title Augustus by the senate he was called Gaius Iulius Caesar Octavianus Augustus.

Roman women generally only used one name; the feminine form of their **nomen**, e.g. Claudia, Sempronia, Cornelia, Iulia and Iunia. If there was a number of sisters in a family then the eldest was called **Maior** (*the Elder*), the second **Minor** (*the Younger*), the third **Tertia** (*the Third*), **Quarta** (*the Fourth*), etc.

Freedmen (ex-slaves) would take their ex-master's **nomen** and add their own **cognomen**, e.g. M. ARTORIUS M. L. PRIMUS ARCHITECTUS → Marcus Artorius Primus, freedman (**libertus**) of Marcus (Artorius): Architect (Inscription in the theatre in Pompeii)

When we write Latin names in English we use anglicized versions of the names of those authors and personalities who are more familiar to us, e.g. Vergil (or Virgil) for Vergilius, Horace for Horatius, Ovid for Ovidius, Pliny for Plinius and Livy for Livius.

P Place names

The Adriatic Sea → mare superum
The Aegean Sea → mare Aegaeum
Africa → Libya, Africa
Alexandria → Alexandria
The Alps → Alpes (f. pl.)
Anglesey → Mona
Antioch → Antiocha
The Apennines → mons Apenninus
Athens → Athenae (f. pl.)
Avignon → Avenio (f.)
Babylon → Babylon (f.)
The Balearic Is. → Baliares insulae (f. pl.)
Barcelona → Barcino (f.)
Bath → Aquae Sulis
Belgium → Belgae (m. pl.)
The Black Sea → Pontus (Euxinus)
Bologna → Bononia
Brindisi → Brundisium
Britain → Britannia
Brittany → Armoricae (f. pl.)
Cadiz → Gades (f. pl.)
Caerleon → Isca
Campagna → Campania
Canterbury → Durovernum
Capri → Capreae (f. pl.)
Cartagena → Carthago Nova
Carthage → Carthago (f.)
Chester → Deva
Chichester → Regnum
China → Seres (m. pl.)

Cirencester → Corinium
Colchester → Camulodunum
Constantinople (Istanbul) → Byzantium
Cordoba → Corduba
Corfu → Corcyra
Corinth → Corinthus
Crete → Creta
Cyrene → Cyrenae (f. pl.)
The (Lower) R. Danube → Ister
The Dardanelles → Hellespontus
Dover → Dubri (m. pl.)
The Straits of Dover → fretum Gallicum
Egypt → Aegyptus (-i f.)
Mt. Etna → Aetna
Florence → Florentia
France (Gaul) → Gallia
Genoa → Genua
Germany → Germania
The Straits of Gibraltar → fretum Gaditanum
Greece → Graecia
Holland → Batavi (m. pl.)
Ireland → Hibernia
Italy → Italia
Jerusalem → Hierosolyma (n. pl.)
Lebanon → Libanus
Lincoln → Lindum

London → Londinium	The R. Rhine → Rhenus
Lyons → Lugdunum	Rhodes → Rhodos (f.)
Malta → Melita	The R. Rhone → Rhodanus
Marseilles → Massilia	Rome → Roma
Milan → Mediolanum	St Albans → Verulamium
Morocco → Mauretania	Scotland → Caledonia
Naples → Neapolis (f.)	The R. Severn → Sabrina
Nice → Nicaea	Seville → Hispalis
The R. Nile → Nilus	Sicily → Sicilia
Padua → Patavium	Spain → Hispania
Paris → Lutetia	Switzerland → Helvetia
The R. Po → Padus	The R. Thames → Tamesis (m.)
Portugal → Lusitania	Thebes → Thebae (f. pl.)
Pozzuoli → Puteoli (m. pl.)	The R. Tiber → Tiberis (m.)
Provence → Provincia	Tuscany → Etruria
The Pyrenees → Pyrenaei montes	Venice → Veneti (m. pl.)
(m. pl.)	York → Eburacum
The Red Sea → sinus Arabicus	

Q Inscriptions

We have no original Latin literary documents but we have many
examples of Latin written on walls or stone which come under the
technical title **epigraphy**. They are generally graffiti or inscriptions
and are valuable evidence for contemporary Latin usage and
spelling. As there was always a limited space to fill abbreviations
were common. These are from Pompeii:

▶ **Record of the building of the amphitheatre c.70 BCE**

Quinctius C[aii] f[ilius] Valgus M[arcus] Porcius M[arci] f[ilius]
duovir[i] quinq[uennales] coloniai honoris caussa spectacula de sua
peq[unia] fac[iunda] coer[arunt] et coloneis locum in perpetuom
deder[unt] → *Quinctius Valgus, son of Gaius, [and] Marcus
Porcius, son of Marcus, censors* (quinquennuial duoviri), *for the
honour of the colony took care that a showground be built out
of their own money and they gave the place to the colonists for
ever.* Note the spelling of **coloniai** for **coloniae, caussa** for **causa,**

pequnia for pecunia, coerarunt for curaverunt, coloneis for colonis and perpetuom for perpetuum. *Showground* (spectacula) is used instead of amphitheatrum. Note the confidence of in perpetuom (*for ever*).

▶ **A graffito scratched on the wall of the basilica**

C[aius] Pumidius Dipilus heic fuit a[nte] d[iem] v Nonas Octobreis M[arco] Lepid[o] Q[uinto] Catul[o] co[n]s[ulibus] → *G. Pumidius Dipilus was here on October 3rd when M. Lepidus and Q. Catulus were consuls* (78 BCE). Note the old spelling of heic for hic and Octobreis for Octobris, and the way of dating a year.

▶ **On the colonnade in front of the Eumachia building (fullers' guild)**

Eumachia L[uci] f[ilia] sacerd[os] publ[ica] nomine suo et M[arci] Numistri Frontonis fili chalcidicum cryptam porticum Concordiae Augustae Pietati sua pecunia fecit eademque dedicavit → *Eumachia, daughter of Lucius, public priestess, had the vestibule, covered walkway and colonnade built with her own money in her name and that of her son Marcus Numistrius Fronto and dedicated the same to the Pietas Concordia Augusta*

This prominent local woman was not only enhancing the fullers' guild with her generosity but also her son's social standing. The dedication associates her with Augustus' political outlook.

▶ **On the plinth of a statue of Holconius in the Via dell' Abbondanza**

M[arco] Holconio M[arci] f[ilio] Rufo trib[uno] mil[itum] a populo duovir[o] i[ure] d[icundo] v quinque[nnali] iter[um] Augusti Caesaris sacerd[oti] patrono coloniae → *To Marcus Holconius Rufus, son of Marcus, tribune of the soldiers [chosen] by the people, duumvir with the right of pronouncing [judgement] five times, censor a second time, priest of Augustus Caesar, patron of the colony*

Most of the abbreviations are standard for inscriptions. Holconius is in the dative because the statue was put up in honour of (to) him. Notice the old form **dicundo** for **dicendo**. A censor (**quinquennalis**) was elected every five years. To be patron of the colony was the highest honour a man could have, rather like having the freedom of a city. Holconius associated himself closely with the imperial family and was active at the start of the Christian era. This inscription is also found in metal letters in the floor of the second row of the theatre.

▶ **In the temple of the Genius of the Emperor (Vespasian in 79 CE) in the forum**

Mamia P[ubli] f[ilia] sacerdos public[a] Genio Aug[usti] solo et pecunia sua → *Mamia daughter of Publius, public priestess, on her own land and with her own money [dedicated a temple] to the Genius of Augustus*

The cult of the Genius of the emperor began in 7 BCE. The public paid for Mamia's tomb.

▶ **On the tomb of Scaurus who got rich producing *garum* (fish sauce), a local speciality**

A[ulo] Umbricio Scauro IIvir[o] i[ure] d[icundo]. Huic decuriones locum monum[enti] et HS … in funere et statuam eques[trem] in f[oro] ponendam censuerunt → *To Aulus Umbricius Scaurus, duumvir with the right of pronouncing [judgement]. The town council decreed the place for the monument to this man and … sesterces for his funeral and an equestrian statue to be placed in the forum*

▶ **The Temple of Isis in Pompeii was restored after an earthquake in 62 CE**

N[umerius] Popidius N[umerii] f[ilius] Celsinus aedem Isidis terrae motu conlapsam a fundamento p[equnia] s[ua] restituit. hunc decuriones ob liberalitatem cum esset annorum sexs ordini suo gratis adlegerunt → *Numerius Popidius Celsinus, son of Numerius with his own money restored from its foundation the temple of Isis which had been destroyed by an earthquake. Because of his generosity the decuriones (the town council) admitted this [boy] to their order free even though he was six years old*

This boy's father was a freedman (the cult of Isis attracted freedmen) and rebuilt the temple in his son's name so that his son would have a social advantage in Pompeian society. Note the spelling of **sexs** → *six*.

Political graffiti survives painted on walls. The aediles (town officials) had not cleaned it off after the previous election before Vesuvius erupted. It can therefore be dated to 79 CE. Note the politeness of the formulaic indirect wish **oramus vos faciatis** which crops up often.

- ▶ A[ulum] Vettium Firmum aed[ilem] o[ramus] v[os] f[aciatis]. dign[us] est. Caparasia cum Nymphio rog[ant] → *We pray that you make Aulus Vettius Firmus aedile. He is worthy. Caparasia asks [this] with Nymphius.*
- ▶ M[arcum] Holconium II vir[um] i[ure] d[icundo] d[ignum] r[e] p[ublica] o[ramus] v[os] f[aciatis] → *We ask that you make the worthy Marcus Holconius duumvir with the right of pronouncing judgement*
- ▶ **Satrium rogant** → *[...] ask for Satrius (to be elected)*

Some of the graffiti, found scratched on walls, is more familiar:

- ▶ **tu es verpa qui istud legis** → *You are a prick if you read this.*

R Timeline
BCE

753	Traditional date of the founding of Rome by Romulus
753–510	Rome traditionally ruled by seven kings: Romulus, Numa Pompilius, Tullus Hostilius, Ancus Martius, Tarquinius Priscus, Servius Tullius and Tarquinius Superbus
510	The expulsion of the royal family. Rome becomes a republic for the next 462 years
498	Larcius was created the first dictator

494	The plebeians retire to Mt Sacer. Office of tribune of the plebs established
458	Cincinnatus dictator
450	The Twelve Tables, a codification of Roman law, established
439	Cincinnatus dictator again
390	Rome captured by the Gauls
367	The first plebeian consul elected
338	Rome subdues the Latin League
281–72	Rome at war with Tarentum and King Pyrrhus of Epirus
264–41	The First Punic War. Rome defeats the Carthaginians thereby gaining Sicily
240	Plays (by Livius Andronicus) first acted at Rome
219	Hannibal attacks Saguntum
218–2	The Second Punic War
217	Quintus Fabius Maximus ('Cunctator') created dictator
216	Hannibal defeats Rome and her allies at the Battle of Cannae
212	Marcellus captures Syracuse during which a Roman soldier murders Archimedes
202	Scipio defeats Hannibal at the Battle of Zama, winning the Second Punic War
197	Rome defeats the Macedonians at the Battle of Cynoscephalae
184	Cato the Elder elected censor. Titus Plautus Maccius, playwright, dies
159	Publius Terentius Afer (Terence), playwright, dies
149–6	The Third Punic War
146	Rome sacks Carthage and Corinth, becoming the supreme power in the Mediterrranean
133	Tiberius Gracchus, reforming tribune, assassinated
123	Gaius Gracchus, Tiberius' brother, tribune
107–100	Gaius Marius holds seven successive consulships to deal with military emergencies from the tribes of the Cimbri and Teutones
91–88	The Social War
88–2	Civil War between Gaius Marius and Cornelius Sulla
86	Sulla conquers Athens

82–79	Sulla dictator
70	First consulate of Gnaeus Pompeius (Pompey) and Marcus Licinius Crassus
73–1	The revolt of Spartacus the gladiator
63	Marcus Tullius Cicero as consul suppresses the Catilinarian conspiracy
60	First Triumvirate of Pompey, Crassus and Julius Caesar formed
58–1	Caesar campaigns in Gaul
55 & 54	Caesar takes military expeditions to Britain
50	Caesar crosses the R. Rubicon. Civil war between Caesar and Pompey begins
c.55	Titus Lucretius Carus, poet, dies
54	Valerius Catullus, poet, dies
48	Caesar defeats Pompey at the Battle of Pharsalus, effectively ending the republic
44	Caesar assassinated by Brutus, Cassius and others
43	Formation of the second Triumvirate: Marcus Antonius (Antony), Octavian and Lepidus. Cicero, orator and man of letters, assassinated at Antony's behest
42	Brutus and Cassius defeated at the Battle of Philippi
35	Gaius Sallustius Crispus (Sallust), historian, dies
31	Octavian defeats Antony and Cleopatra at the Battle of Actium
27	Octavian takes the title Augustus
26	Vitruvius Pollio, architectural writer, dies
25	Cornelius Nepos, biographer, dies
19	Publius Vergilius Maro (Vergil), poet, and Albius Tibullus, poet, die
c.16	Sextus Propertius, poet, dies
8	Quintus Horatius Flaccus (Horace), poet, dies

CE

9	Defeat of the Romans under Varus by Arminius (Herman) in the Teutoburger Wald
14–37	Tiberius emperor
17	Titus Livius (Livy), historian, dies
18	Publius Ovidius Naso (Ovid), poet, dies

37–41	Gaius (Caligula) emperor
41–54	Claudius emperor
43–5	The Romans annex Britain
54–68	Nero emperor
61	Revolt of Boudicca (Boadicea), queen of the Iceni, against the Romans
62	Persius Flaccus, poet, dies
65	Gaius Petronius Arbiter, novelist, and Lucius Annaeus Seneca, philosopher, commit suicide at Nero's behest. Marcus Annaeus Lucanus (Lucan), poet, dies
68–9	Galba, Otho and Vitellius emperors
69–79	Vespasian emperor
79	Pompeii destroyed by Vesuvius. Pliny the Elder, natural scientist, killed in the eruption
79–81	Titus emperor
81–96	Domitian emperor. He was succeeded by Nerva
c.95	Marcus Fabius Quintilianus (Quintilian), orator, dies
c.96	Publius Papinius Statius, poet, dies
98	Nerva dies and Trajan becomes emperor
98–128	The writing career of Decimus Junius Juvenalis (Juvenal), satirist
100	Gaius Plinius Caecilius Secundus (Pliny the Younger), letter writer, governor of Bithynia-Pontus
104	Marcus Valerius Martialis (Martial), poet, dies
109	Roman empire reaches its greatest extent under Trajan
c.113	Pliny the Younger dies
117	Publius Cornelius Tacitus, historian, and Trajan, emperor, die. Hadrian emperor
121	Hadrian builds the wall across the North of Britain
c.155	Lucius Apuleius, novelist, dies
c.160	Gaius Suetonius Tranquillus, historian, dies
180	Marcus Aurelius, emperor and philosopher, dies
274–337	Constantine emperor
285	Division of the Roman empire into Eastern and Western parts by Diocletian
313	Constantine legalizes Christianity
476	Collapse of the Western Roman empire
565	Justinian, Eastern emperor and jurist, dies

S Latin today

It is easier than you might think to find Latin today. Look at the side of a pound coin and you may read **decus et tutamen** → *an object of beauty and a security*. This is a quotation from Vergil (*Aeneid* 5.262) and originally referred to a coat of chain mail (**lorica**), in fact the following two words in the Latin are **in armis** → *in battle*. You may also find the motto of the Most Ancient and Most Noble Order of the Thistle (Scotland's premier order of chivalry) on the side of a pound: **nemo me impune lacessit** → *no-one assaults me and gets away with it*. Those which come from Jersey have **insula Caesarea** which was its Roman name. The American dollar bill has on it **e pluribus unum** → *one (state) out of more*. Coins and notes will probably always be the commonest place to find Latin. You will find it used in the mottos of institutions, especially schools, and Latin inscriptions are still used on buildings today, even if it is only to record the date of construction in Roman numerals. The numerals are also often used on clock faces and to date films and television programmes. Botanical Latin is still used for the correct names of plants and with the increasing popularity of gardening, you can regularly hear it on radio and television programmes devoted to the hobby. Some series of popular children's books are now produced in Latin such as the stories associated with **Asterix Gallus** → *Asterix the Gaul*, **Vinni ille pu** → *Winnie the Pooh* and **Petrus cuniculus** → *Peter Rabbit*. You can even find volumes of Latin joke books. Latin is still the official language of the Vatican and important ecclesiastical documents like official papal letters are written in Latin. The mass is still said in Latin on certain special occasions and the Vatican does much to promote the language, such as publishing its own modern Latin dictionary.

The following are some Latin words and phrases which are still in use today:

ab initio → *from the beginning*, especially of the learning of languages
aegrotat (pl. aegrotant) → *he (she, or they) are ill* (used in university exam notices)

ad hoc → (*for this*) *immediate, spontaneous, improvised*
ad hominem → *for the man* (used of professorships, etc.)
ad infinitum → *to the point of infinity*
ad lib(itum) → *at (your) pleasure*
ad loc(um) → *at the place*
ad nauseam → *to the point of nausea*
bona fides → *good faith*
compos mentis → *sound in mind*
e(xempli) g(ratia) → *for the sake of example*
ex officio → *by virtue of the position one holds*
habeas corpus → lit. *you may have the body*. A right not to be
  detained without charge.
i(d) e(st) → *that is, namely*
in vitro → *in the test tube*
pro bono (publico) → *for the public good*
quid pro quo → *something in return for something*
satis → *sufficient, enough*
s(ub) v(erbum) → *under the word* (referring to dictionary entries)
sub judice → *under the jurisdiction of a judge*, i.e. something which
  cannot be discussed in case the outcome of a trial is prejudiced
sub poena → *under threat of punishment*, i.e. a compulsory
  summons to court
sub rosa → *under the rose*, i.e. secret
ultra vires → *beyond one's jurisdiction*
viva voce → *an oral rather than a written exam* (lit. *with the
  live voice*)

Of particular interest to observers of the modern version of the
language is the Latin news website **nuntii latini** where you will
find the previous week's news in Latin. It is usually updated
on a Monday. This excellent service is provided by the Finnish
Broadcasting Corporation. Since 1989 they had been broadcasting
the news in Latin on the radio for five minutes after their German
and English language news bulletins on a Sunday evening. As a
good short wave radio is needed to get a decent reception, the
arrival of **nuntii latini** on the Internet was very welcome news. The
bulletins cover all major topics of international interest and there

are often items of Finnish news. As the writers say themselves, **nunc primum in historia fit ut lingua Latina iam nullos limites noverit** → *now for the first time in history it happens that the Latin language knows no bounds.*

The writers face the interesting and sometimes amusing challenge of creating Latin words for modern objects or concepts. The following are good examples of their skill:

aeroplanum capacissimum → *jumbo jet*
autocinetum laophoricum → *bus*
bos grunniens → *yak*
Circuitus Galliae → *the Tour de France*
cangurus → *kangaroo*
charta creditoria → *credit card*
chartula postalis → *postcard*
cuniculus viarius → *motorway tunnel*
demoscopia Gallupiana → *Gallup poll*
diploma inventionis → *patent*
exercitia aerobica → *aerobics*
grex motocyclistarum → *motorbike gang*
horologium excitatorium → *alarm clock*
liga pedifollica → *football league*
linea diei → *the International Date Line*
machina vectoria → *locomotive engine*
pellicula documentaria → *documentary film*
pittacium epistulare → *postage stamp*
scacista → *chess player*
statio spatialis → *space station*
syngraphus viatorius → *passport*
systema cursus cambialis → *exchange rate mechanism*
telephonum portabile → *mobile telephone*
tempus suppletorium → *overtime*
tramen rapidum → *express train*
uranium pauperatum → *depleted uranium*
virus grippicum → *inflenza virus*

In addition to the news there are other items on the website menu which are of interest. A list of reading material including modern Latin dictionaries, a background history of the site, the schedule of broadcasts, a questions page, a letters page for e-mail and an archive of old bulletins. The entire site is written in Latin but an English version of some of the pages is available.

Key to the exercises

It is obvious that the sentences in the exercises may be translated in a variety of ways. The basic sense is given here but any sensible variation may be used. It is assumed that where 'he' is used with a verb then 'she' or 'it' would be equally acceptable if the context allows it.

Unit 2 ex. 1–4

1 a they beg **b** he/she/it gives **c** you (s.) care **d** I drink **e** we approve **f** you (pl.) prepare **g** you (s.) give **h** we stand **i** he/she/it works **j** they drink   **2 a** servo servas servat servamus servatis servant **b** comparo comparas comparat comparamus comparatis comparant **c** loco locas locat locamus locatis locant **d** concito concitas concitat concitamus concitatis concitant **e** voco vocas vocat vocamus vocatis vocant **f** computo computas computat computamus computatis computant **g** muto mutas mutat mutamus mutatis mutant **h** pugno pugnas pugnat pugnamus pugnatis pugnant **i** adflo adflas adflat adflamus adflatis adflant **j** amo amas amat amamus amatis amant   **3 a** vocamus **b** laboras **c** probo **d** probat **e** potant **f** curatis **g** vocat **h** ambulat! **i** sto **j** curant   **4 a** putare, to think **b** cogitare, to ponder **c** laniare, to mangle **d** mandare, to command **e** praetervolare, to fly past **f** clarare, to explain **g** demonstrare, to show **h** fatigare, to exhaust **i** coactare, to force **j** appellare, to pronounce

Unit 2 ex. 5–8

5 a fourth **b** second **c** first **d** third **e** third **f** third **g** fourth **h** third **i** second **j** first   **6 a** We run and we win. **b** You sleep and snore. **c** He searches and he saves. **d** You see and believe. **e** They know and are silent. **f** I inspect and approve. **g** They flee and they weep. **h** I teach and you learn. **i** You laugh and play. **j** We dance and sing.   **7 a** aperio aperis aperit aperimus aperitis aperiunt **b** peto petis petit petimus petitis petunt **c** advenio advenis advenit advenimus advenitis adveniunt **d** video vides videt videmus videtis vident

e discedo discedis discedit discedimus disceditis discedunt **f** teneo
tenes tenet tenemus tenetis tenent **g** facio facis facit facimus facitis
faciunt **h** vasto vastas vastat vastamus vastatis vastant **i** libro libras
librat libramus libratis librant **j** fugio fugis fugit fugimus fugitis
fugiunt **8 a** nubere, to marry **b** merere, to deserve **c** arcessere,
to summon **d** claudicare, to limp **e** gerere, to carry **f** implicare,
to entwine **g** placare, to pacify **h** serere, to sew **i** statuere, to set
up **j** vovere, to vow

Unit 2 ex. 9–12

9 a aedificabo aedificabis aedificabit aedificabimus aedificabitis
aedificabunt **b** miscebo miscebis miscebit miscebimus miscebitis
miscebunt **c** ardebo ardebis ardebit ardebimus ardebitis ardebunt
d mulcebo mulcebis mulcebit mulcebimus mulcebitis mulcebunt
e sonabo sonabis sonabit sonabimus sonabitis sonabunt **f** crepabo
crepabis crepabit crepabimus crepabitis crepabunt **g** stabo stabis stabit
stabimus stabitis stabunt **h** fundabo fundabis fundabit fundabimus
fundabitis fundabunt **i** narrabo narrabis narrabit narrabimus
narrabitis narrabunt **j** horrebo horrebis horrebit horrebimus horrebitis
horrebunt **10 a** They will advise and persuade. **b** You will carry but
we shall walk. **c** They will call and save. **d** We shall wait and watch.
e They will announce but we shall be silent. **f** He will weep and mourn.
g I shall burn but you will soothe. **h** They will shudder and we shall
frighten. **i** I shall relate and you will watch. **j** He will build but they
will destroy. **11 a** cogitabo **b** volabimus **c** mutabunt **d** lugebitis
e monebit **f** placebit **g** debebis **h** nuntiabo **i** vocabunt **j** habebitis
12 a They give but you will owe. **b** They beat and I shall call out.
c You are pacifying and they will be silent. **d** We carry but you will
build. **e** You walk but we shall hurry. **f** They build but we shall
destroy. **g** I think but they will fight. **h** He stands and will stay. **i** I am
preparing and you will approve. **j** We shall buy and you will reckon up.

Unit 2 ex. 13–16

13 a cingam cinges cinget cingemus cingetis cingent **b** scribam
scribes scribet scribemus scribetis scribent **c** claudam claudes claudet
claudemus claudetis claudent **d** colam coles colet colemus coletis
colent **e** petam petes petet petemus petetis petent **f** faciam facies
faciet faciemus facietis facient **g** iaciam iacies iaciet iaciemus iacietis
iacient **h** rapiam rapies rapiet rapiemus rapietis rapient **i** dicam

dices dicet dicemus dicetis dicent **j** aperiam aperies aperiet aperiemus aperietis aperient **14 a** I shall say and you will believe. **b** We shall summon but they will not hear. **c** You will dig and I shall drag. **d** He will not sleep. **e** You will begin but you will not finish. **f** They will flee but we shall resist. **g** I shall open but he will close. **h** They will seek but they will not find. **i** You will depart and I shall arrive. **j** We shall agree but you will disagree. **15 a** fodiam **b** non incipient **c** non ludes **d** adsentiet **e** curram sed resistes **f** advenient **g** capiet **h** non credetis **i** non cedemus **j** dormient sed trahemus **16 a** You will resist and you will not yield. **b** I close but they will open. **c** We shall not arrive. **d** He runs but he will not escape. **e** You are playing but I shall dig. **f** They are writing and they will not play. **g** They will not say. **h** I seek and I shall find. **i** He says but you will not believe. **j** You are writing and will not hear.

Unit 2 ex. 17–20

17 a manebam manebas manebat manebamus manebatis manebant **b** muniebam muniebas muniebat muniebamus muniebatis muniebant **c** cenabam cenabas cenabat cenabamus cenabatis cenabant **d** coquebam coquebas coquebat coquebamus coquebatis coquebant **e** regebam regebas regebat regebamus regebatis regebant **f** veniebam veniebas veniebat veniebamus veniebatis veniebant **g** leniebam leniebas leniebat leniebamus leniebatis leniebant **h** ambulabam ambulabas ambulabat ambulabamus ambulabatis ambulabant **i** ponebam ponebas ponebat ponebamus ponebatis ponebant **j** sedebam sedebas sedebat sedebamus sedebatis sedebant **18 a** We were sitting but we were not sleeping. **b** You were fighting and resisting. **c** You were listening and you were watching. **d** I was cooking but they were dining. **e** He was walking and singing. **f** They were holding and shouting. **g** You were saying and they were not keeping quiet. **h** I was dragging and I was groaning. **i** We were playing but we were not laughing. **j** I was building and you were carrying. **19 a** dormiebam sed non tacebant. **b** dicebamus et audiebant. **c** non spectabas. **d** adveniebam sed discedebatis. **e** assentiebat. **f** trahebamus et fodiebant. **g** stabat sed sedebamus. **h** arcessebat et veniebas. **i** ridebamus et flebant. **j** non videbam. **20 a** He was ordering you were obeying. **b** He will not change. **c** I was preparing, you are cooking and they will dine. **d** We were resisting but you are fleeing. **e** He was not writing. **f** We were carrying, we are digging and we shall build. **g** I was running but you are walking. **h** They were shuddering and we were afraid. **i** They were sitting and they will sleep. **j** You gave and I received.

Unit 2 ex. 21–24

21 a timui **b** paravi **c** rexi **d** cubui **e** feci **f** traxi **g** tetigi **h** sparsi **i** fregi **j** sensi   **22 a** demonstravi demonstravisti demonstravit demonstravimus demonstravistis demonstraverunt **b** secuvi secuvisti secuvit secuvimus secuvistis secuverunt **c** dedi dedisti dedit dedimus dedistis dederunt **d** curavi curavisti curavit curavimus curavistis curaverunt **e** vetui vetuisti vetuit vetuimus vetuistis vetuerunt **f** iuvi iuvisti iuvit iuvimus iuvistis iuverunt **g** ambulavi ambulavisti ambulavit ambulavimus ambulavistis ambulaverunt **h** micui micuisti micuit micuimus micuistis micuerunt **i** amavi amavisti amavit amavimus amavistis amaverunt **j** necavi necavisti necavit necavimus necavistis necaverunt   **23 a** you built **b** they gave **c** I have called **d** you have saved **e** we have placed **f** they bought **g** he prepared **h** I prayed **i** you have cut **j** we have forbidden   **24 a** speraverunt **b** amavimus **c** dedi **d** demonstraverunt **e** vetuistis **f** stetit **g** narravit **h** aedificavi **i** navisti **j** vocavit

Unit 2 ex. 25–28

25 a credo → I *believe* **b** veto → I *forbid* **c** venio → I *come* **d** video → I *see* **e** poto → I *drink* **f** vincio → I *bind* **g** sedeo → I *sit* **h** custodio → I *guard* **i** teneo → I *hold* **j** fugio → I *flee*   **26 a** quaesivi quaesivisti quaesivit quaesivimus quaesivistis quaesiverunt **b** cessi cessisti cessit cessimus cessistis cesserunt **c** posui posuisti posuit posuimus posuistis posuerunt **d** effluxi effluxisti effluxit effluximus effluxistis effluxerunt **e** rupi rupisti rupit rupimus rupistis ruperunt **f** lusi lusisti lusit lusimus lusistis luserunt **g** vici vicisti vicit vicimus vicistis vicerunt **h** cucurri cucurristi cucurrit cucurrimus cucurristis cucurrerunt **i** risi risisti risit risimus risistis riserunt **j** delevi delevidti delevit delevimus delevistis deleverunt   **27 a** invenit **b** viderunt **c** mansistis **d** traxi **e** coluimus **f** dixisti **g** duxerunt **h** cepit **i** tonuit **j** cogitaverunt   **28 a** he flowed out **b** you have pressed **c** I played **d** they have searched **e** you laughed **f** he led **g** we arranged **h** we put **i** they took **j** you have placed

Unit 2 ex. 29–32

29 a momorderam momorderas momorderat momorderamus momorderatis momorderant **b** titillaveram titillaveras titillaverat titillaveramus titillaveratis titillaverant **c** solveram solveras solverat solveramus solveratis solverant **d** postulaveram postulaveras postulaverat postulaveramus postulaveratis postulaverant **e** emanaveram emanaveras emanaverat emanaveramus emanaveratis emanaverant **f** captaveram captaveras captaverat captaveramus captaveratis captaverant **g** miseram miseras miserat miseramus miseratis miserant **h** reduxeram reduxeras reduxerat reduxeramus reduxeratis reduxerant **i** statueram statueras statuerat statueramus statueratis statuerant **j** verberaveram verberaveras verberaverat verberaveramus verberaveratis verberaverant **30 a** you had warned **b** they had bought **c** I had taken **d** we had loved **e** you had run **f** he had played **g** you had inspected **h** they had yielded **i** you had dug **j** I had forbidden **31 a** steteramus **b** manseras **c** putaveram **d** ceperant **e** effugerat **f** dormiverat **g** ieceratis **h** sederam **i** custodiverat **j** posueramus **32 a** I had not hidden but they wept. **b** He slept and you had worked. **c** We had built but they destroyed. They had carried and we had dug. **e** He had closed but I opened. **f** They walked but we had run. **g** He had taught and they had heard. **h** You had watched but you did not see. **i** You had not changed. **j** I had cooked and they dined.

Unit 2 ex. 33–36

33 a cecinero cecineris cecinerit cecinerimus cecineritis cecinerint **b** accepero acceperis acceperit acceperimus acceperitis acceperint **c** vertero verteris verterit verterimus verteritis verterint **d** tetendero tetenderis tetenderit tetenderimus tetenderitis tetenderint **e** tradidero tradideris tradiderit tradiderimus tradideritis tradiderint **f** praebuero praebueris praebuerit praebuerimus praebueritis praebuerint **g** complevero compleveris compleverit compleverimus compleveritis compleverint **h** vexero vexeris vexerit vexerimus vexeritis vexerint **i** surrexero surrexeris surrexerit surrexerimus surrexeritis surrexerint **j** discessero discesseris discesserit discesserimus discesseritis discesserint **34 a** you will have led **b** you will have stayed **c** I shall have called **d** they will have warned **e** you will have made **f** we shall have walked **g** I shall have taken **h** they will have come **i** you will have put **j** we shall have left **35 a** senserit **b** mutaverit **c** spectaverint **d** debuero **e** fleverit **f** feceritis **g** vixerimus **h** petiveris **i** convenerint **j** vertero **36 a** I was afraid and you will have been afraid. **b** You have stayed but they will have fled. **c** We shall have worked and you will have slept. **d** I shall have given and he will have received. **e** They will have departed but you have not arrived. **f** You will have run but I shall have walked. **g** He narrated and they will have heard. **h** He ordered

and they will have obeyed. **i** You have asked and he will have replied.
j He cooked and i shall have eaten.

Unit 2 ex. 37–39

37 a ero **b** non est **c** eramus **d** erant **e** eritis **f** fueras **g** fuerit **h** eram
i fui **j** fuimus **38 a** they were **b** they will have been **c** they have been
d he will be **e** they are **f** we are **g** we were **h** I had been **i** you are
j they will be **39 a** imperfect **b** present **c** perfect **d** future **e** present
f perfect **g** pluperfect **h** future perfect **i** future **j** imperfect

Unit 3 ex. 1–4

1 a chartae f. *paper*, map **b** insulae f. *island* **c** nautae m. *sailor*
d agricolae m. *farmer* **e** ancillae f. *maidservant* **f** areae f. *building
site* **g** incolae m. *inhabitant* **h** viae f. *road* **i** nebulae f. *cloud* **j** mensae
f. *table* **2 a** Sing. ripa ripa ripam ripae ripae ripa. Pl. ripae ripae ripas
riparum ripis ripis **b** Sing. regina regina reginam reginae reginae regina.
Pl. reginae reginae reginas reginarum reginis reginis **c** Sing. carina carina
carinam carinae carinae carina. Pl. carinae carinae carinas carinarum
carinis carinis **d** Sing. matrona matrona matronam matronae matronae
matrona. Pl. matronae matronae matronas matronarum matronis
matronis **e** Sing. taberna taberna tabernam tabernae tabernae taberna.
Pl. tabernae tabernae tabernas tabernarum tabernis tabernis **f** Sing. porta
porta portam portae portae porta. Pl. portae portae portas portarum
portis portis **g** Sing. clementia clementia clementiam clementiae
clementiae clementia. Pl. clementiae clementiae clementias clementiarum
clementiis clementiis **h** Sing. dea dea deam deae deae dea Pl. deae deae
deas dearum deabus deabus **i** Sing. cauda cauda caudam caudae caudae
cauda. Pl. caudae caudae caudas caudarum caudis caudis
j Sing. femina femina feminam feminae feminae femina. Pl. feminae
feminae feminas feminarum feminis feminis **3 a** sagittas **b** rosarum
c vaccam **d** sapientiae **e** hastis **f** sellis **g** ballistae **h** alis **i** iustitia
j ferae **4 a** acc. sing. **b** 1 dat. pl. 2 abl. pl. **c** acc. pl. **d** 1 gen. sing.
2 dat. sing. 3 nom. pl. 4 voc. pl. **e** 1 dat. pl. 2 abl. pl. **f** acc. pl.
g 1 nom. sing. 2 voc. sing. 3 abl. sing. **h** acc. sing. **i** gen. pl. **j** 1 gen.
sing. 2 dat. sing. 3 nom. pl. 4 voc. pl.

Unit 3 ex. 5–8

5 a discipuli m. *pupil* **b** frumenti n. *grain* **c** venti m. *wind* **d** mariti
m. *husband* **e** coli f. *distaff* **f** anni m. *year* **g** somni m. *sleep* **h** eventi

n. *outcome* **i** belli n. *war* **j** umeri m. *shoulder* **6 a** Sing. oculus ocule oculum oculi oculo oculo Pl. oculi oculi oculos oculorum oculis oculis **b** Sing. legatus legate legatum legati legato legato. Pl. legati legati legatos legatorum legatis legatis **c** Sing. lapillus lapille lapillum lapilli lapillo lapillo. Pl. lapilli lapilli lapillos lapillorum lapillis lapillis **d** Sing. rostrum rostrum rostrum rostri rostro rostro. Pl. rostra rostra rostra rostrorum rostris rostris **e** Sing. praefectus praefecte praefectum praefecti praefecto praefecto. Pl. praefecti praefecti praefectos praefectorum praefectis praefectis **f** Sing. ludus lude ludum ludi ludo ludo Pl. ludi ludi ludos ludorum ludis ludis **g** Sing. stilus stile stilum stili stilo stilo. Pl. stili stili stilos stilorum stilis stilis **h** Sing. pullus pulle pullum pulli pullo pullo Pl. pulli pulli pullos pullorum pullis pullis **i** Sing. animus anime animum animi animo animo. Pl. animi animi animos animorum animis animis **j** Sing. iocus ioce iocum ioci ioco ioco. Pl. ioci ioci iocos iocorum iocis iocis **7 a** digiti **b** officiis **c** camele **d** somnio **e** campum **f** odia **g** initiorum **h** medicis **i** funambulos **j** ferro **8 a** 1 gen. sing. 2 nom. pl. 3 voc. pl. **b** 1 dat. pl. 2 abl. pl. **c** acc. sing. **d** 1 nom. pl. 2 voc. pl. 3 acc. pl. **e** 1 dat. sing. 2 abl. sing. **f** 1 nom. sing. 2 voc. sing. 3 acc. sing. **g** gen. pl. **h** 1 dat. sing. 2 abl. sing. **i** gen. sing. **j** 1 gen. sing. 2 nom. pl. 3 voc. pl.

Unit 3 ex. 9–12

9 a Austri m. *the South wind* **b** Histri m. *The Lower Danube* **c** capri m. *goat* **d** cancri m. *crab* **e** administri m. *assistant* **f** aquiliferi m. *eagle-bearer* **g** cultri m. *knife* **h** apri m. *boar* **i** furciferi m. *rogue* **j** lanigeri m. *sheep* **10 a** Sing. arbiter arbiter arbitrum arbitri arbitro arbitro. Pl. arbitri arbitri arbitros arbitrorum arbitris arbitris **b** Sing. Lucifer Lucifer Luciferum Luciferi Lucifero Lucifero **c** Sing. ingenium ingenium ingenium ingenii ingenio ingenio. Pl. ingenia ingenia ingenia ingeniorum ingeniis ingeniis **d** Sing. Cornelius Corneli Cornelium Cornelii Cornelio Cornelio. Pl. Cornelii Cornelii Cornelios Corneliorum Corneliis Corneliis (members of the family) **e** Sing. Alexander Alexander Alexandrum Alexandri Alexandro Alexandro **f** Sing. socer socer socerum soceri socero socero. Pl. soceri soceri soceros socerorum soceris soceris **g** Sing. liber liber librum libri libro libro. Pl. libri libri libros librorum libris libris **h** Sing. socius soci socium socii socio socio Pl. socii socii socios sociorum sociis sociis **i** Sing. armiger armiger armigerum armigeri armigero armigero. Pl. armigeri armigeri armigeros armigerorum armigeris armigeris

j Sing. studium studium studium studii studio studio. Pl. studia studia studia studiorum studiis studiis **11 a** liberorum **b** trifurcifero **c** ministrum **d** pueris **e** oleastris **f** fibri **g** Tiberi **h** fabri **i** magistros **j** semiviro **12 a** acc. pl. **b** 1 nom. sing. 2 voc. sing. **c** 1 dat. sing. 2 abl. sing. **d** 1 gen. sing. 2 nom. pl. 3 voc. pl. **e** 1 voc. sing. 2 gen. sing. 3 nom. pl. 4 voc. pl. **f** 1 acc. sing. 2 gen. pl. **g** 1 gen. sing. 2 nom. pl. 3 voc. pl. **h** 1 gen. sing. 2 nom. pl. 3 voc. pl. **i** 1 dat. pl. 2 abl. pl. **j** 1 nom. pl. 2 voc. pl. 3 acc. pl.

Unit 3 ex. 13–16

13 a temporis n. *time* **b** consulis m. *consul* (chief magistrate) **c** capitis n. *head* **d** militis m. *soldier* **e** coniugis m. or f. *spouse* **f** iudicis m. *judge* **g** tempestatis f. *storm* **h** clamoris m. *shout* **i** operis n. *work* **j** doloris m. *pain* **14 a** amor → *love* **b** paries → *wall* (of a house) **c** aetas → *age* **d** custos → *guard* **e** nomen → *name* **f** sal → *salt, wit* **g** virtus → *valour* **h** pecus → *beast, head of cattle, sheep, herd animal* **i** aequor → *a level surface* (*plain, sea* etc.) **j** homo → *human being* **15 a** Sing. flos flos florem floris flori flore. Pl. flores flores flores florum floribus floribus **b** Sing. dignitas dignitas dignitatem dignitatis dignitati dignitate. Pl. dignitates dignitates dignitates dignitatum dignitatibus dignitatibus **c** Sing. pes pes pedem pedis pedi pede. Pl. pedes pedes pedes pedum pedibus pedibus **d** Sing. aestas aestas aestatem aestatis aestati aestate. Pl. aestates aestates aestates aestatum aestatibus aestatibus **e** Sing. princeps princeps principem principis principi principe. Pl. principes principes principes principum principibus principibus **f** Sing. anser anser anserem anseris anseri ansere. Pl. anseres anseres anseres anserum anseribus anseribus **g** Sing. laus laus laudem laudis laudi laude. Pl. laudes laudes laudes laudum laudibus laudibus **h** Sing. virgo virgo virginem virginis virgini virgine. Pl. virgines virgines virgines virginum virginibus virginibus **i** Sing. sol sol solem solis soli sole. Pl. soles soles soles solum solibus solibus **j** Sing. carmen carmen carmen carminis carmini carmine. Pl. carmina carmina carmina carminum carminibus carminibus **16 a** acc. sing. **b** abl. sing. **c** dat. sing. **d** gen. pl. **e** 1 nom. sing. 2 voc. sing. 3 acc. sing. **f** 1 nom. pl. 2 voc. pl. 3 acc. pl. **g** gen. sing. **h** 1 nom. pl. 2 voc. pl. 3 acc. pl. **i** 1 dat. pl. 2 abl. pl. **j** 1 nom. pl. 2 voc. pl. 3 acc. pl.

17 a cladis f. *disaster* **b** ignis m. *fire* **c** imbris m. *rain cloud, shower*
d amnis m. *river* **e** vectigalis n. *tax* **f** sedilis n. *chair* **g** avis f. *bird*
h vallis f. *valley* **i** clavis f. *key* **j** iubaris n. *sunbeam* **18 a** aries *ram*
b ensis *sword* **c** cutis *skin* **d** securis *axe* **e** ovis *sheep* **f** crinis *hair*
g axis *axle* **h** frons *foliage* **i** orbis *globe, circle* **j** conclave *room*
19 a Sing. puppis puppis puppim puppis puppi puppe. Pl. puppes
puppes puppis puppium puppibus puppibus **b** Sing. moles moles
molem molis moli mole. Pl. moles moles moles molium molibus
molibus **20 a** dat. sing. **b** gen. sing. **c** 1 nom. sing. 2 voc. sing. 3 acc.
sing. **d** 1 nom. sing. 2 voc. sing. 3 gen. sing. 4 acc. pl. (alternative)
e acc. sing. **f** 1 nom. sing. 2 voc. sing. 3 gen. sing. 4 acc. pl.
(alternative) **g** gen. pl. **h** abl. sing. **i** 1 nom. pl. 2 voc. pl. 3 acc. pl.
j 1 dat. pl. 2 abl. pl.

21 a Sing. saltus saltus saltum saltus saltui saltu. Pl. saltus saltus
saltus saltuum saltibus saltibus **b** Sing. portus portus portum portus
portui portu. Pl. portus portus portus portuum portibus portibus
c Sing. cornu cornu cornu cornus cornu cornu. Pl. cornua cornua
cornua cornuum cornibus cornibus **d** Sing. tribus tribus tribum tribus
tribui tribu. Pl. tribus tribus tribus tribuum tribubus tribubus **e** Sing.
porticus porticus porticum porticus porticui porticu. Pl. porticus
porticus porticus porticuum porticibus porticibus **f** Sing. ictus ictus
ictum ictus ictui ictu. Pl. ictus ictus ictus ictuum ictibus ictibus **g** Sing.
gemitus gemitus gemitum gemitus gemitui gemitu. Pl. gemitus gemitus
gemitus gemituum gemitibus gemitibus **h** Sing. exitus exitus exitum
exitus exitui exitu. Pl. exitus exitus exitus exituum exitibus exitibus
i Sing. impetus impetus impetum impetus impetui impetu. Pl. impetus
impetus impetus impetuum impetibus impetibus **j** Sing. manus manus
manum manus manui manu. Pl. manus manus manus manuum
manibus manibus **22 a** gen. pl. **b** acc. sing. **c** 1 dat. pl. 2 abl. pl.
d abl. sing. **e** 1 nom. sing. 2 voc. sing. 3 gen. sing. 4 nom. pl. 5 voc.
pl. 6 acc. pl. **f** dat. sing. **g** 1 dat. pl. 2 abl. pl. **h** abl. sing. **i** 1 nom.
sing. 2 voc. sing. 3 gen. sing. 4 nom. pl. 5 voc. pl. **6** acc. pl. **j** gen.
pl. **23 a** 4th **b** 2nd **c** 4th **d** 2nd **e** 4th **f** 4th **g** 2nd **h** 2nd **i** 4th
j 4th **24 a** census **b** circumiectibus **c** currus **d** electus **e** anuum
f usui **g** fructibus **h** cursum **i** domitu **j** rictus

25 a progeniei *progeny, descendants, children* **b** pauperiei *poverty*
c caesariei *hair* **d** tristitiei *sorrow* **e** permitiei *ruin* **f** congeriei
heap **g** temperiei *mildness, temperature, due proportion* **h** materiei
matter, substance, timber **i** maciei *meagreness, leanness* **j** planitiei
level ground, plain **26 a** Sing. glacies glacies glaciem glaciei glaciei
glacie **b** Sing. canities canities canitiem canitiei canitiei canitie
c Sing. acies acies aciem aciei aciei acie. Pl. acies acies acies acierum
aciebus aciebus **d** Sing. effigies effigies effigiem effigiei effigiei effigie.
Pl. effigies effigies effigies effigierum effigiebus effigiebus **e** Sing.
superficies superficies superficiem superficiei superficiei superficie.
Pl. superficies superficies superficies superficierum superficiebus
superficiebus **f** Sing. fides fides fidem fidei fidei fide. Pl. fides fides
fides fiderum fidebus fidebus **g** Sing. meridies meridies meridiem
meridiei meridiei meridie. Pl. meridies meridies meridies meridierum
meridiebus meridiebus **h** Sing. spes spes spem spei spei spe. Pl.
spes spes spes sperum spebus spebus **i** Sing. species species speciem
speciei speciei specie. Pl. species species species specierum speciebus
speciebus **j** Sing. diluvies diluvies diluviem diluviei diluviei diluvie. Pl.
diluvies diluvies diluvies diluvierum diluviebus diluviebus **27 a** acc.
sing. **b** gen. pl. **c** 1 dat. pl. 2 abl. pl. **d** 1 gen. sing. 2 dat. sing. **e** abl.
sing. **f** 1 nom. sing. 2 voc. sing. 3 nom. pl. 4 voc. pl. 5 acc. pl.
g acc. sing. **h** abl. sing. **i** acc. sing. **j** abl. sing.

28 a Hylas Hyla Hylan Hylae Hylae Hyla **b** Daphne Daphne
Daphnen Daphnes Daphnae Daphne **c** Sing. Atrides Atrides (or
Atride) Atriden Atridae Atridae Atride. Pl. Atrides Atrides Atridas
Atridum Atridis Atridis **d** Hecate Hecate Hecaten Hecates Hecatae
Hecate **e** Sing. harpe harpe harpen harpes harpae harpe. Pl. harpae
harpae harpas harparum harpis harpis **f** Boreas Borea Borean
Boreae Boreae Borea **g** Sing. crambe crambe cramben crambes
crambae crambe. Pl. crambes crambes crambas crambarum crambis
crambis **h** Cybele Cybele Cybelen Cybeles Cybelae Cybele **i** Cyrene
Cyrene Cyrenen Cyrenes Cyrenae Cyrene **j** Hebe Hebe Heben
Hebes Hebae Hebe **29 a** Sing. lampas lampas lampada lampadis
lampadi lampade. Pl. lampades lampades lampadas lampadum
lampadibus lampadibus **b** Sing. lynx lynx lyncem lyncis lynci lynce.

Pl. lynces lynces lynces or lyncas lyncum lyncibus lyncibus
c Babylon Babylon Babylonem Babylonis Babyloni Babylone
d Agamemnon Agamemnon Agamemnona Agamemnonis Agamemnoni
Agamemnone **e** Pericles Pericles (or Pericle) Periclen Periclis (or
Pericli) Pericli Pericle **f** Rhodos Rhodos Rhodon Rhodi Rhodo
Rhodo **g** Paris Pari (or Paris) Parin (or Parim, Paridem or Parida)
Paridis (or Paridos) Paridi Paride **h** Orpheus Orpheus (or Orpheu)
Orphea Orphei (or Orpheos) Orphei Orpheo **i** Chios Chios Chion
Chii Chio Chio **j** Sing. heros heros heroa (or heroem) herois heroi
heroe. Pl. heroes heroes heroas heroum heroibus heroibus
30 a 1 dat. sing. 2 abl. sing. **b** acc. sing. **c** gen. sing. **d** gen. sing.
e acc. sing. **f** acc. pl. **g** voc. sing. **h** 1 gen. sing. 2 dat. sing. 3 nom. pl.
4 voc. pl. **i** acc. sing. **j** gen. sing. **31 a** poematis n. poem **b** Euripidis
m. Euripides, an Athenian tragedian **c** Phlegethontis m. Phlegethon,
a river in Hades (the Underworld) **d** Trois m. Tros, a king of
Phrygia (after whom Troy was named) **e** Sophoclis m. Sophocles,
an Athenian tragedian **f** Euridices f. Eurydice, wife of Orpheus
g psephismatis n. decree of the people, vote **h** Diones f. Dione,
mother of Venus **i** Theseos (or Thesei) m. Theseus, the Greek hero
who slew the Minotaur **j** Lemni f. Lemnos, an Aegean island

Unit 3 ex. 32–33

32 a acc. sing. from vis **b** 1 dat. pl. 2 abl. pl. from vir **c** acc. pl. from
vir **d** acc. sing. or alternative gen. pl. from vir **e** 1 dat. pl. 2 abl. pl.
from vis **f** gen. pl. from vir **g** abl. sing. from vis **h** 1. gen. sing.
2 nom. pl. 3 voc. pl. from vir **i** gen. pl. from vis **j** 1 nom. pl. 2 voc.
pl. 3 acc. pl. from vis **33 a** Sing. frater frater fratrem fratris fratri
fratre. Pl. fratres fratres fratres fratrum fratribus fratribus **b** Sing.
iuvenis iuvenis iuvenem iuvenis iuveni iuvene. Pl. iuvenes iuvenes
iuvenes iuvenum iuvenibus iuvenibus **c** Sing. mater mater matrem
matris matri matre. Pl. matres matres matres matrum matribus
matribus **d** Sing. canis canis canem canis cani cane. Pl. canes canes
canes canum canibus canibus **e** Sing. pater pater patrem patris patri
patre. Pl. patres patres patres patrum patribus patribus **f** Sing. sedes
sedes sedem sedis sedi sede. Pl. sedes sedes sedes sedum sedibus
sedibus **g** Sing. accipiter accipiter accipitrem accipitris accipitri
accipitre. Pl. accipitres accipitres accipitres accipitrum accipitribus
accipitribus **h** Sing. mensis mensis mensem mensis mensi mense. Pl.
menses menses menses mensum mensibus mensibus **i** Sing. volucris

volucris volucrem volucris volucri volucre. Pl. volucres volucres
volucres volucrum volucribus volucribus **j** Sing. vates vates vatem
vatis vati vate. Pl. vates vates vates vatum vatibus vatibus

Unit 4 ex. 1–4

1 a box **b** pirates **c** we **d** it **e** onions, cabbages **f** Marius **g** diamonds
h ostriches **i** you **j** dish   **2 a** The foot soldiers walked but the
commander rode. **b** The cranes had flown away. **c** The emperor is not
laughing. **d** The hare did not win. **e** We are gladiators. **f** Cassius is
asleep. **g** The soldier and the sailor were drinking. **h** The high priest
has spoken and the people will obey. **i** The teacher was teaching but the
pupils were not listening. **j** Hercules laboured for a long time.
3 a Merlin was a wizard. **b** The pauper will be a prince. **c** The dog is a
nuisance. **d** Pheidias was a master craftsman. **e** Temples are buildings.
f The looters are prisoners. **g** Public speakers are liars. **h** The Romans
were victors. **i** The praetorian guardsmen will be the assassins.
j Brutus had been consul.   **4 a** Master, the guests are departing. **b** Hello
farmers! **c** Valeria, Titus, the boy is falling. **d** Centurion, the captives
have escaped. **e** The enemy are arriving, soldiers! **f** Valerius, Julius and
Tiberius are running. **g** Hello son. **h** Father, spring is on the way.
i Where are you, Marcus? **j** Fortune, you are a goddess.

Unit 4 ex. 5–8

5 a dog **b** boxes **c** misery **d** boats **e** mother **f** dung **g** wall **h** signal
i orders **j** disease   **6 a** The hunters heard the shouts. **b** The teachers
were teaching the boys. **c** The druids have sacrificed a bull. **d** Master,
the slaves are carrying the bread. **e** The squirrels were hiding nuts.
f The workmen are building a wall. **g** The soldiers made Claudius
emperor. **h** The girls applauded the actor. **i** The miser loves money.
j The ship has struck a rock.   **7 a** senator socios vocat. **b** flumen agros
inundavit. **c** Hercules hydram oppugnavit. **d** Aemiliam pueri amant.
e Galli Romanos timent. **f** custodes portas clauserunt. **g** canes
pastorem spectant. **h** agricola aves liberavit. **i** aurum celant. **j** feles
aquam non amant.   **8 a** Oh unbelievable foulness! **b** I am well in (my)
body. **c** He walked for twenty paces. **d** O wonderful courage! **e** The
soldier is six feet tall. **f** I was wounded in the hands. **g** The lake was a
hundred feet deep. **h** The horse is lame in the leg. **i** O fickle glory!
j His limbs were bare (lit. He was bare in the limbs).

Unit 4 ex. 9–10

9 a The boy is reciting the verses of Vergil. **b** I am learning the art of riding. **c** I never open the door of the house. **d** The shepherd loves the daughter of the king. **e** You have heard the children's voices. **f** The barber is counting the hairs of the old man's head. **g** We fear the troop of soldiers. **h** It is the job of a doctor to cure the sick. **i** The threats of the enemy were frightening the children. **j** Heaps of dung are blocking the road. **k** The maidservants heard the sounds of thunder. **l** The citizens approve a man of honesty. **m** Hannibal lost the sight of an eye. **n** The waters of the river flowed slowly. **o** The crown of jewels shone. **p** It is the duty of a leader to look after the city. **q** The elephants are carrying masses of rocks. **r** We do not see the soldiers' wounds. **s** The scouts were looking at the peaks of the mountains. **t** They were learning the language of the Romans. **10 a** onera terga asellorum premunt. **b** Cassius est vir crudelitatis capax. **c** viri oppidi non pugnabunt. **d** servi togas dominorum lavant. **e** undas maris amamus. **f** amor belli humanitatem delet. **g** lucem ignis non viderunt. **h** halitum canis non amo. **i** sapientia reginae navem servavit. **j** pondus argenti habeo. **k** est nautae navigare. **l** praemium virtutis gloria est. **m** domum poetae amabis. **n** amor pecuniae radix mali est. **o** acervum ovorum invenimus. **p** amor matris liberos sustinet. **q** Romani nomen regis non amabant. **r** thesaurum magi quaerimus. **s** mater Bruti dormiebat. **t** virum centum annorum scio.

Unit 4 ex. 11–12

11 a The farmer is mindful of the war. **b** The citizens value dignity at a great price. **c** The miners have found some gold. **d** Where in the world were we? **e** For how large a price did you buy the house? **f** The poor men used to lack shoes. **g** A thief values honesty little. **h** The senator had swallowed a lot of poison. **i** He is carrying enough burdens. **j** The climbers had too little rope. **k** The general saw less of the battle. **l** The girls were carrying some bread. **m** The fox has taken so much cheese. **n** We destroyed part of the wall. **o** Do you have any money? **p** The children have drunk too much water. **q** Many of the gladiators were fighting. **r** Several of the captives are ill. **s** Part of the procession halted. **t** They bought the ships at a great price. **12 a** satis domuum cupimus. **b** equi nimis ligni trahunt. **c** aliquid novi habes? **d** lacus est plenus piscium. **e** corvus aliquid frumenti cepit. **f** memor periculi est. **g** pax multum divitiarum facit. **h** multi liberorum ludebant. **i** nimis fletus vidi. **j** aquae indigemus. **k** hoc temporis custodies dormiunt. **l** parvi pretii fundum emit. **m** pastor partem gregis custodit. **n** pars aciei appropinquabat. **o** puer plus fructus portat. **p** parum salis habemus. **q** quantum fabulae sciunt? **r** partem arboris servavimus. **s** imperator ignavos parvi aestimat. **t** complures nostrum dissensimus.

Unit 4 ex. 13–14

13 a You are telling a story to the children. **b** We have sent help to our allies. **c** The election agent will not persuade the voters. **d** I have promised gifts for the ladies. **e** The poets were reciting to the citizens. **f** The senators did not believe the speaker. **g** The poor do not envy the rich. **h** The sisters were coming to help their brothers. **i** Caesar has spared his enemies. **j** Arminius was pre-eminent over the Germans. **k** We do not favour the candidate. **l** The conjurers pleased the guests. **m** The citizens trust the priests. **n** The barbarians resisted the Romans for a long time. **o** Vitellia was like her mother. **p** The guards were failing in their duty to the prisoners. **q** The masters gave orders to the slaves. **r** Sulla harmed his enemies. **s** We shall not serve the soldiers. **t** The teacher gave the books to the pupils. **14 a** reginae fidebas. **b** venatores vestigiis cervi studiebant. **c** cursores glaciei diffidunt. **d** feminae spectatoribus intererunt. **e** sociis non persuasistis. **f** victoribus invideo. **g** ignavi pueris non subvenient. **h** dominus servis indulget. **i** oves plaustris obstant. **j** mandata militibus non placuerunt. **k** matri favet. **l** vulpes pullis non nocebunt. **m** matrona anulos filiabus misit. **n** sacerdotes sacrificia deis dederunt. **o** iudex sicario non ignoscet. **p** Portia Bruto nupsit. **q** iuvenes nuntio crediderunt. **r** feles canibus diffidunt. **s** moles undis resistet. **t** testes iudici verum dicunt.

Unit 4 ex. 15–18

15 a The boys were collecting charcoal for the workmen. **b** We shall make peace for future generations. **c** The Romans built baths for the inhabitants. **d** The elephants dragged the tree trunks for the foresters. **e** Father has bought horses for his daughters. **f** You have prepared an ambush for the enemy. **g** He is carrying the bread for his wife. **h** Brutus slew Caesar for the republic. **i** The enemy have devastated the fields for the farmers. **j** The girl plucked apples for her sister.   **16 a** The stranger's name was Ulysses. **b** The Carthaginians have elephants. **c** I have sent the gems to my grandmother for a gift. **d** The citizens had a brave leader. **e** They boys chose a place for a fight. **f** The artists sought out the building for its beauty. **g** The summits of the mountains have snow. **h** Thescouts have found a place for the camp. **i** The Greeks have a hundred ships. **j** The workmen were sweeping the stadium for the contest.   **17 a** The ships were of benefit to the Carthaginians. **b** Brutus was a source of honour to the Romans. **c** The prisoners are a burden to the soldiers. **d** Milo was a source of hatred to Clodius. **e** Cloelia is an example to the girls. **f** The husband will be a source of support to his wife. **g** Snares are a danger to bears. **h** The river was a source of safety to the travellers. **i** The son was a concern to his mother. **j** Catiline was a disgrace to the senators.   **18 a** pullos ioco portamus. **b** principes oneri erant civibus. **c** seni dormimus. **d** fornaces pistoribus usui sunt. **e** Romani amphitheatrum spectaculis aedificaverunt. **f** viginti equi sunt aurigae. **g** suffragatoribus candidatus non audiebat. **h** fures aurum avaro surripuerunt. **i** fustes sunt comissatoribus. **j** impedimenta pompae amovebis.

Unit 4 ex. 19–22

19 a We shall free the citizens from slavery. **b** The looters stripped the armour from the bodies. **c** The senators deprived the traitor of his titles. **d** The hostages lack food and water. **e** The boxer fights nude, without clothes. (lit. nude from clothes). **f** The soldiers are keeping the enemy away from the city. **g** The philosopher always used to abstain from wine. **h** The girls are driving the wasps away from the baby's toys. **i** I am acquitting the defendant from the charge. **j** We lack planks and nails.   **20 a** The merchants made the farmers rich with their money. **b** The senate supplied the citizens with bread. **c** The river was born from springs. **d** The maidservants will fill the jugs with water. **e** The ambassadors presented the consuls with a crown. **f** Romulus was born of a god. **g** The butler filled the guests with wine. **h** Once the mine was rich in silver. **i** The wizard satisfied the king's greed with gold. **j** Mars made the woman pregnant with twins.   **21 a** The sailor is steering the ship in a storm. **b** Caesar was wounded in the back. **c** The geese do not fly in silence. **d** The bears attacked the people with speed. **e** The cowards trembled in the knees. **f** The robbers procured the money by fraud. **g** The dog was lame in the foot. **h** The miser surpasses the poet in greed. **i** Cassius is a man of significant public standing. **j** The children were playing with delight. **22 a** exsules terra non expellemus. **b** Achilles dea natus est. **c** loca deserta aqua egent. **d** bello patres filios sepeliunt. **e** fundus pecudibus abundat. **f** Horatius existimatione dignus est. **g** flumen formidine transimus. **h** cupam lacte implevistis. **i** victores vi abstinebunt. **j** Marcus Titum capite pulsavit.

Unit 4 ex. 23–26

23 a The fishermen are catching fish with nets. **b** The pupils were writing with pens. **c** The senators reproached Catiline with insults. **d** The boys were playing with dice. **e** The cowherds are driving the oxen on with sticks. **f** The gardeners have decorated the garden with roses. **g** The orator was urging the citizens on with his words. **h** We shall defend our freedom with axes. **i** They burnt the cottages with torches. **j** The priest struck the victim with a knife. **24 a** He is not opening the gate for fear of the dark. **b** They were walking slowly on account of the speed of the wind. **c** Cassius is no better than Brutus. **d** I have hidden the gold in expectation of robbers. **e** The children are jumping for joy. **f** The snake is longer than the worm by twenty feet. **g** They laid down their arms out of their love of peace. **h** Dogs like grass much less than asses (do). **i** How much bigger is a toad than a frog? **j** The Romans expelled Tarquin because of their hatred of kings. **25 a** I bought the estate for a hundred talents. **b** A ship is sailing on the sea. **c** The assassin hid the body in the garden. **d** Tarquin bought the books for gold. **e** The friends are meeting in the baths. **f** The horses cost twenty talents. **g** He sold the cow for five beans. **h** The legions will spend the winter in cities. **i** The nightingale was singing in the top of the tree. **j** He completed the victory with blood and the sword. **26 a** philosophus inimicos benignitate superavit. **b** Aeneas paulo optimus erat. **c** fragore aves terruisti. **d** equites campo equitabant. **e** tabulas quattuor talentis vendidi. **f** dei consilium ominibus probant. **g** mater liberos mele alit. **h** metallum parvo ememus. **i** Romani Carthaginienses terra marique oppugnaverunt. **j** Horatius amore patriae pugnavit.

Unit 4 ex. 27–30

27 a The bishop's palace was at Antioch. **b** The conspirators met at the house of Brutus. **c** I shall stay in London for three days.

d Claudius used to live at Rome. **e** The Romans pitched camp at Veii. **f** The old man used to sleep on the ground. **g** Foxes and hares are playing in the countryside. **h** We are waiting for the fleet at Brundisium. **i** The end of the world is at Cadiz. **j** Plato and Aristotle used to teach at Athens. **28 a** Tomorrow we shall walk to the country. **b** The boys were hurrying home in terror. **c** Soon we shall depart from Sicily. **d** The ambassadors came to Sparta from Athens. **e** The doctor fled from Alexandria. **f** The merchants sailed to Carthage. **g** In Summer we always send the children to Marseilles. **h** The messenger ran from home. **i** The Romans did not always win in war. **j** The king sent ships to Tyre and Sidon. **29 a** The camels will arrive in four days. **b** They cultivated the farm for five years. **c** You received your inheritance in the third year. **d** In Winter the trees do not have leaves. **e** The youths will guard the bridge for seven days. **f** In the morning the farmer ploughs the field. **g** We shall be parents in nine months. **h** The phoenix will rise in a hundred years. **i** In the evening the sky grows red. **j** The geese were honking for six nights. **30 a** donum domi reliqui. **b** octo dies piscatores fluitabant. **c** quinque diebus Delphos perigrinatores venerunt. **d** patrem Lutetiae exspectabitis. **e** hieme philosophus Athenis habitat. **f** cras cantor Corintho veniet. **g** Londinio non vesperi discedemus. **h** sex mensibus fabri domum perfecerint. **i** testudo centum annos vixit. **j** naves frumentum Ostia portabant.

Unit 5 ex. 1–4

1 a acc. f. s. **b** 1 nom. f. pl. 2 voc. f. pl. **c** gen. f. pl. **d** 1 dat. f. pl. 2 abl. f. pl. **e** acc. m. pl. **f** 1 gen. m. s. 2 nom. m. pl. 3 voc. m. pl. **g** 1 dat. m. pl. 2 abl. m. pl. **h** acc. m. s. **i** 1 nom. n. pl. 2 voc. n. pl. 3 acc. n. pl. **j** abl. m. s. **2 a** I have found beautiful gems in a wooden chest. **b** Good men do not approve of wicked crimes. **c** Yesterday I bought five white horses. **d** The children are afraid of the black night. **e** The shaggy bears are hibernating in thick woods. **f** The sailors saw dark clouds above the sea. **g** The wretched fugitives wandered through the lands. **h** Caesar cut off the right hands of the Gauls. **i** The youths will fight at the red rocks. **j** The little ship is lying on the bottom of the sea. **3 a** malefica umbra in imo puteo habitavit. **b** magni et boni nonnumquam ignavi sunt. **c** suffragatores irati togam candidati sordidam non amant. **d** ursi fulvi iuxta flumen pulchrum ambulant. **e** magus callidus in libro occulto scripsit. **f** rex superbus colonos miseros neglegebat. **g** deae dirae scelestos

punient. **h** arbor longaeva in summo colle stetit. **i** pulli teneri in nido alto dormiunt. **j** cras feminae fessae ad portam primam advenient.
4 a a bonis **b** boni **c** bonorum **d** boni or bonos **e** bone **f** bono **g** bono **h** bonarum **i** bonum **j** bonam

Unit 5 ex. 5–8

5 a The bold youths swam across the river. **b** The boys were touching the toga of the lucky man. **c** The boxers fought with equal strength. **d** They built huge walls around the city. **e** The caves of fierce beasts are in the mountains. **f** The old man was walking through the streets with the youth. **g** Women approve of a prudent husband. **h** The magistrates were powerless. **i** The citizens resisted the vicious king. **j** The philosopher has a mind capable of genius. **6 a** I hear the cries of the brave. **b** The minstrel sang sad tales. **c** The citizens obey the famous orator. **d** The journey is easy for the strong. **e** I love the taste of sweet honey. **f** Father gave gifts to all the children. **g** The Athenians used to have a common treasury. **h** Grand parades were marching through the streets. **i** Donkeys are carrying the heavy burdens across the bridge. **j** I have hidden the jewels in a safe place. **7 a** I hear the sound of fierce horses. **b** Augustus renovated the ancient temples. **c** Jason fought with winged monsters. **d** We drink clean water at the spring. **e** The race is not always to the swift. **f** We are applauding the famous actor in the theatre. **g** The poor man was sitting at the gates of the rich man. **h** The pilgrims arrived at the shrine safe and sound. **i** The messengers hurried with swift steps. **j** Elephants are mindful of everything. **8 a** cursor celer tristem civem salutavit. **b** epistulam tyranno crudeli mittam. **c** Marcus est pauperis filius. **d** domus in colle viridi est. **e** Pericles omnibus persuasit. **f** iuvenes veteres observant. **g** leones saporem liberorum audacium amant. **h** Galli viam saxis ingentibus obstiterunt. **i** fortes non superabitis. **j** equum celerem petimus.

Unit 5 ex. 9–10

9 a It is the egg of a larger bird. **b** I have never seen a worse play. **c** The girl loves the son of a richer man. **d** Nothing is harder than diamond. **e** The journey is longer by road than by sea. **f** The Alps are much higher than the hills of Rome. **g** The Romans withstood stronger enemies than the Greeks. **h** We hear the shouts of more horsemen. **i** The Romans have better buildings than the Gauls. **j** A sheep is a little smaller than a goat. **10 a** Socrates was the wisest of men. **b** The traitor's words were very doubtful. **c** The monster has very sharp teeth. **d** Blood is thicker than water. **e** Some very graceful cranes were flying over the roofs. **f** The pen is mightier than the sword. **g** Gardens are more ideal than fields. **h** The girl was collecting as many roses as possible for her mother. **i** Very many of the citizens searched for the gold. **j** Elephants are much heavier than bulls.

Unit 5 ex. 11–13

11 a The girls jumped down into the lake spontaneously. **b** The miser fed his children too little. **c** The workmen repaired the crane badly. **d** The old man instructed the youths wisely. **e** The defendant fiercely denied the charge. **f** Marcus was easily the tallest. **g** You praised Cicero greatly. **h** The Greeks had about a thousand ships. **i** They were not doing business well. **j** Romeo loved Juliet very much.
12 a We shall always be faithful to the citizens. **b** Master, the guests will arrive soon. **c** Nowhere have I seen a more beautiful woman. **d** We shall attack the enemy elsewhere. **e** He had prepared dinner not long before. **f** I did not stay in the bedroom for long. **g** Cicero has abused Catiline for a second time. **h** Tomorrow perhaps you will see Caesar. **i** He summoned his son again and again. **j** The ambassadors will certainly sue for peace. **13 a** The assassins have very wickedly killed the senator. **b** The poet had finally finished his poem. **c** The priests fled in the greatest safety from the temple. **d** I hurried to the guards as quickly as possible. **e** I walk more easily than I run. **f** Varus waged war worse than Caesar. **g** We have waited for the messenger for too long. **h** The Cyclops was less clever than Ulysses. **i** The horsemen arrived at the city more quickly than the foot soldiers. **j** The maidservant dances much better than she sings.

Unit 6 ex. 1–4

1 a The boys are sitting in the goats' way. **b** The does ran to the woods. **c** At Marcus' house jugglers are pleasing the guests. **d** The old man had built a wall around his garden. **e** The crows are flying over the tops of the trees. **f** The horses were swimming across the river. **g** The slave hid the cup behind the seat. **h** Cicero wrote speeches against Mark Antony. **i** The valley lay between the mountains. **j** The leaders met on this side of the city. **2 a** Horatius withstood the Etruscans in sight of the citizens. **b** The speaker stood in front of the

crowd. **c** The judge spoke on behalf of the defendant. **d** I am walking without companions. **e** Cicero denounced Catiline in the presence of the senators. **f** The miser has buried the gold under the floor. **g** We had an argument about the farm. **h** Water flowed out of the spring. **i** The boys were playing with the girls in the yard. **j** A dolphin was swimming in the harbour. **3 a** The baker put the bread upon the table. **b** The Gauls ravaged the fields as far as the city. **c** The camels do not drink before noon. **d** They are placing the jewels next to the crown. **e** She gave the boy a kiss in front of her parents.
f We are running to the tavern because of the rain. **g** The crocodile lies hidden underneath the river bank. **h** You are seeking power for the sake of money. **i** In the Summer the children will sleep outside their bedrooms. **j** We are looking for the treasure in the caves.
4 a poema honoris gratia scribes. **b** inter casas equitavit. **c** clam custodes portas aperuerunt. **d** cras e silvis discedemus. **e** pro mercatoribus laboro. **f** animalia dormiebant, praeter anseres.
g subter ripam ambulamus. **h** statuae prae templo stant. **i** insulae ultra mare iacent. **j** post meridiem sub sole dormimus.

Unit 6 ex. 5–6

5 a The emperor provided bread and circuses for the citizens.
b I think, therefore I am. **c** They were not only building bridges but also aqueducts. **d** Milo is standing outside the gates for he is a guard.
e The actors recited badly; nevertheless the spectators applauded. **f** I have found neither gold nor silver. **g** Everyone was silent for the master was ill. **h** Both Brutus and Cassius attacked Caesar. **i** Surely you will visit the temple? **j** We have finished our work and so we are walking home.
6 a The crows fly away as often as the dogs bark. **b** At the same time as the trumpet sounded, the enemy made their attack. **c** As the climate warms, so the seas will expand. **d** Children learn while they play. **e** After their mother left, the boys were crying. **f** Because he has produced the games we praise Caesar. **g** Even if the mountain is high, we shall climb it. **h** Because their enemies are everywhere, so the Romans are always fighting. **i** Whether you will stay or leave, I shall always be true to the citizens. **j** Titus fell down because he was running too quickly.

Unit 6 ex. 7

7 a We shall have finished the building within two days. **b** 1966.
c The king reigned for thirty-seven years. **d** The chieftain gave his

brothers three horses each. **e** The animals went into the ship two by two. **f** In the ninetieth year the Greeks renewed the treaty. **g** The scouts saw twenty thousand soldiers. **h** The citizens feared the board of ten very much.

Unit 7 ex. 1–4

1 a Salvius visited me yesterday. **b** We shall walk to the farm with you. **c** I love you. **d** Father told me a story. **e** The Romans' hatred of us is very well known. **f** I shall give you the gold. **g** The judges will forgive you. **h** The knights were approaching us slowly. **i** Several of you are present. **j** We shall stay but you will leave. **2 a** We turn (ourselves) to the North. **b** The robbers have hidden themselves in caves. **c** You favour yourselves for the sake of money. **d** Why will you not forgive yourself? **e** You have disgraced yourself in front of the citizens. **f** I shall keep the gift for myself. **g** We shall never blame ourselves. **h** I always shave (myself) in the morning. **i** They built the house for themselves. **j** Titus has hurt himself with the knife. **3 a** I have bought new clothes for your children. **b** The Romans have devastated our farm. **c** Your horse is bigger than mine. **d** My geese were honking throughout the night. **e** He defended the bridge with his brothers. **f** O my son, at last I have found you. **g** It is through your fault that the thief entered the house. **h** I do not approve of your plans. **i** He loves the sound of his own voice. **j** Our men will fight against the Gauls. **4 a** villam pulchram meam tibi ostendi. **b** nos equitabimus sed vos ambulabitis. **c** Narcissus se nimis amavit. **d** feminae ad forum nobiscum venerunt. **e** Hercules, gloria tua sempiterna est. **f** gladiatores nostros superaverunt. **g** captivi se servabunt. **h** proditor me non servabit. **i** pater nobis ratem fecit. **j** nautae cibum sibi collegerunt.

Unit 7 ex. 5–8

5 a Portia loves him very much. **b** Those girls are playing in the garden. **c** We were at home at that time. **d** We love the same woman. **e** I do not support that candidate. **f** I saw the same monster yesterday. **g** I am looking for their clothes. **h** That picture is of the same boys. **i** I have never seen those men. **j** I saved her but I abandoned him. **6 a** These words are unbelievable. **b** The footprints of this wild beast are very large. **c** This day we shall fight for our freedom. **d** I have often heard this story. **e** We have been expecting these men for a long time. **f** Lions live in this cave. **g** We shall run far from this place. **h** Cassius envies this man. **i** The sculptor is making statues of these citizens. **j** We shall not buy this farm. **7 a** We do not approve of that. **b** Those senators have killed Caesar. **c** We shall enter the city through that gate. **d** The speaker pleaded the case eloquently on behalf of that defendant. **e** I shall not defend the son of that robber. **f** The painters were decorating those houses. **g** The leaders of those nations support the Romans. **h** The youth is watching that woman intently. **i** We saw that man yesterday in the forum. **j** That dog of yours has bitten me. **8 a** eam mox videbimus. **b** hae sunt eaedem arbores. **c** illud aratrum gravius hoc est. **d** nemo ista vestimenta amat. **e** id non audivi. **f** haec cena optima est. **g** togam huius lavavi. **h** eodem die ad templum advenimus. **i** sonitum illorum tintinnabulorum amo. **j** eam epistulam ei dederunt.

Unit 7 ex. 9–11

9 a Who will guard those very guards? **b** She chose the dress herself. **c** Dido killed herself with this very sword. **d** These captives are the children of the king himself. **e** I saw the very same ghost again yesterday. **f** I have given the money to my uncle himself. **g** I cooked dinner myself. **h** The soldiers of the praetorian guard themselves slew the emperor. **i** The crime itself revealed the perpetrator. **j** I have seen the goddess herself in the temple. **10 a** Those whom you love, I love too. **b** Those men are people whom I shall never support. **c** The dinner which you had prepared was very bad. **d** He who dares will win. **e** There are two choices, neither of which is good. **f** Titus is the judge before whom we shall stand. **g** That man is the leader whom we shall always obey. **h** This is the senator whose son Vitellia loves. **i** The gold which I have found is very heavy. **j** That man shall be king who will have pulled the sword out of the stone. **11 a** aurum ipsum quod avarus ipse celavit inveni. **b** fures qui te spoliaverunt capiemus. **c** domum quam cupis aedificabunt. **d** quod vidi non amo. **e** monstrum ipsum non inimicum est. **f** pericula quae timuimus ea ipsa vitavit. **g** viro diffidimus cuius pater proditor erat. **h** feminae urbem ipsam servabunt. **i** fures ipsos capietis. **j** non omne quod fulget est aurum.

Unit 7 ex. 12–14

12 a Someone's horse has jumped over the fence. **b** A certain traveller saw someone on the road. **c** I supported a certain candidate whom I

shall not name. **d** They hid the treasure underneath a certain tree.
e The soothsayer whispered certain ill-omened words. **f** The assassin
killed the senator with certain poisons. **g** The hunters watched some
stags. **h** We have adopted a certain dangerous plan. **i** The refugees
will depart from the city secretly on a certain day. **j** We shall never
know the names of some conspirators. **13 a** What news have you
heard? **b** I have asked each man about the gold. **c** Who, pray, freed
that troll? **d** The Romans slew each single one of the villagers.
e What secret symbols do magicians have? **f** I shall give you whatever
money I have got. **g** Surely the miser has not left anything to his
son? **h** Is there any woman who will love Antony? **i** What witnesses
will you call to the court? **j** Whose farm is this? **14 a** quis est
ea femina? **b** Titus Romam quibusdam amicis veniet. **c** fabulam
quandam a sene audivi. **d** Melissa aliquid de domino mihi dixit.
e quisque templum vidit. **f** cuius donum cepisti? **g** quos legatus
eliget? **h** quemqam hodie vidisti? **i** cum quibus regina ambulabat?
j feminae quaedam tibi non favebunt.

Unit 7 ex. 15–17

15 a Which consul have the Carthaginians killed? **b** We shall climb
the mountains by any means. **c** Cloelia alone resisted the enemy.
d I prefer the one brother to the other. **e** We shall adopt another
plan. **f** We have seen no ships in the harbour. **g** Cicero received the
praise of the entire senate. **h** Neither girl recognized the actor.
i Hercules feared no-one. **j** Clodia loves the husband of another
woman. **16 a** The guards have killed one or other of the prisoners.
b With such words the orator persuaded the citizens. **c** What sort
of gifts are these? **d** How big is an elephant? **e** I shall support
whichever of the two consuls will give bribes. **f** I have got some
money from father. **g** Such a youth will never be a soldier. **h** With
what sort of companions will you make your journey? **i** Petronius
always produces such great plays. **j** The cook has seasoned the dinner
with a little spice. **17 a** quali viro Cloelia nubet? **b** quanta est
potestas deorum? **c** nemo Cassandrae credidit. **d** alter consul alterum
graviter vituperavit. **e** ego solus Lepido favebo. **f** cras templa alius
urbis videbimus. **g** utram sororem amas? **h** desperati ulla consilia
capient. **i** non saepe tales thesauros vidimus. **j** neutrum fratrem hodie
viderunt.

18 a Has Caesar really been killed? **b** Have you seen my dog?
c Did that man really steal the money? **d** Surely Titus will not come
tomorrow? **e** You have fed the cat, haven't you Septimus? **f** Have
you seen that gladiator before? **g** Did Cassius really say that?
h Are the boys playing in the sand? **i** Surely you do not support that
candidate? **j** The flowers are beautiful, aren't they? **19 a** When will
my prince come? **b** How did Caesar cross the Rhine? **c** Why don't
you love her? **d** By what way did the thief come into the hall?
e Where are the chairs, maidservants? **f** How long were you lying in
the bedroom Quintus? **g** How did you find the ancient city? **h** How
firm is this sword? **i** How many sheep are in the fields? **j** Where did
Claudius get that toga from? **20 a** Have you finished the shield,
craftsman? **b** Do you love Tiberius or Quintus? **c** How many times
does he say these words? **d** Will you prepare dinner or not? **e** Are
you nineteen or twenty years old? **f** Why is the slave shutting the
door? **g** Have you visited Vesuvius or not? **h** For what reason are the
Romans attacking the Gauls? **i** Do you prefer nuts or grapes? **j** Will
Tullius ride or will Julius? **21 a** cur milites pontem delent? **b** nonne
aurum celavisti? **c** ubi sunt gemmae mercatoris? **d** estne Marcus
domi? **e** utrum Colosseum an Circum Maximum visitabimus? **f** quot
elephantos habuit Hannibal? **g** an canis te momordit? **h** num fundum
vendidit? **i** utrum Aemilia Romam veniet annon? **j** ubi sunt putei in
hoc vico?

Unit 8 ex. 1–4

1 a ducar duceris ducetur ducemur ducemini ducentur **b** facior faceris
facitur facimur facimini faciuntur **c** regebar regebaris regebatur
regebamur regebamini regebantur **d** servor servaris servatur servamur
servamini servantur **e** capiar capieris capietur capiemur capiemini
capientur **f** docebar docebaris docebatur docebamur docebamini
docebantur **g** custodior custodiris custoditur custodimur custodimini
custodiuntur **h** iubebor iubeberis iubebitur iubebimur iubebimini
iubebuntur **i** dicebar dicebaris dicebatur dicebamur dicebamini
dicebantur **j** moneor moneris monetur monemur monemini
monentur **2 a** you are being persuaded **b** I shall be dragged
c we shall be cut **d** you will be loved **e** it was being felt **f** they will be
seized **g** they are given **h** we are summoned **i** you were being moved
j you were being destroyed **3 a** The ram was held by the thickets.

b Caesar will be warned by Artemidorus. **c** Gifts will be given to you by your grandchildren. **d** The dinner was being cooked by the cook. **e** The general will be captured by the enemy. **f** We are hindered by the mountains. **g** The column will be led by Tiberius. **h** Aeneas is wounded by an arrow. **i** We were being praised by the consuls. **j** The seeds are being scattered by the farmers. **4 a** ab omnibus audiar. **b** ab optimis magistris docebimini. **c** orator a multis creditur. **d** fabula a sene narrabatur. **e** canibus spectantur. **f** a servis portae claudebantur. **g** serpente puella mordebitur. **h** navis undis scopulisque frangebatur. **i** cras nuntiabitur. **j** liber a scriba callidissimo scribebatur.

Unit 8 ex. 5–8

5 a habitus sum habitus es habitus est habiti sumus habiti estis habiti sunt **b** actus ero actus eris actus erit acti erimus acti eritis acti erunt **c** auditus eram auditus eras auditus erat auditi eramus auditi eratis auditi erant **d** captus ero captus eris captus erit capti erimus capti eritis capti erunt **e** ductus eram ductus eras ductus erat ducti eramus ducti eratis ducti erant **f** monitus sum monitus es monitus est moniti sumus moniti estis moniti sunt **g** custoditus sum custoditus es custoditus est custoditi sumus custoditi estis custoditi sunt **h** factus eram factus eras factus erat facti eramus facti eratis facti erant **i** laudatus sum laudatus es laudatus est laudati sumus laudati estis laudati sunt **j** exspectatus sum exspectatus es exspectatus est exspectati sumus exspectati estis xspectati sunt. **6 a** it had been done **b** she has been praised **c** it will have been finished **d** she has been betrayed **e** it had been written **f** she will have been forgiven **g** she had been saved **h** it has been noted **i** she has been punished **j** it will have been built **7 a** The gifts had been given by the king. **b** The asses were oppressed by the burdens. **c** The letters will have been sent by the ambassadors. **d** The crop had been spoilt by the storms. **e** Tomorrow the city will have been captured. **f** The kings were expelled by the citizens. **g** The gems had been stolen by thieves. **h** The very famous knot was cut down the middle by Alexander. **i** The lamb has been snatched off by an eagle. **j** The plans will have been revealed by the traitors. **8 a** lucernae a ministro accensae erunt. **b** fundi a vilico venditi erant. **c** mater crocodilis comsumpta est. **d** rosae pulcherrimae a puella carptae erant. **e** lepus testudine victus erit. **f** a mercatoribus fraudati sumus. **g** umbra a pueris numquam visa erat. **h** agri a militibus vastati erant. **i** haec terra a mago recta est. **j** cives a barbaris excitati erunt.

9 a The philosophers were thinking about the nature of wisdom. **b** Don't dawdle, children. **c** Let us encourage the athletes, citizens! **d** We shall suffer nothing worse than death. **e** The king died in his sixtieth year. **f** In the morning we shall set out from home. **g** The workmen are testing the bridge. **h** The horses stepped nervously through the river. **i** The girls followed the procession joyfully. **j** The Gauls had come in through the gates of Rome. **10 a** The tree nymphs were sprung from trees. **b** Tomorrow the Romans will advance on the Greeks. **c** Let us rejoice, therefore, while we are young. **d** The girl is fourteen years old. **e** That master craftsman only used the best marble. **f** The merchant obtained a luxurious house. **g** The slaves had the use of their kind master's garden. **h** In winter the farmer had used up his hay. **i** After the disaster the emperor used to grow very angry. **j** The consuls will discharge their duty very well. **11 a** The sun will soon rise. **b** The cows feed on the grass. **c** The woman has dared to contradict Caesar. **d** Do not ever tell a lie my son. **e** The muggers attacked the old man. **f** Once, the girls had been accustomed to meet at the spring in the morning. **g** The miser has never trusted me. **h** All the boys are frightened of the bull. **i** The guards will not talk about the prisoners. **j** Why are you threatening the young men, judge? **12 a** cur magistratus de pecunia mentitus est? **b** librisne potitus es? **c** noli tenebras vereri mi fili. **d** animalium non oblitus sum. **e** cervum ingentem venemur. **f** cras de consilio loquemur. **g** hostes trans campum lente progrediuntur. **h** non soles diligenter laborare. **i** cives oratori semper fisi sunt. **j** captivi e carcere non egredientur.

Unit 9 ex. 1–2

1 a faciar faciaris faciatur faciamur faciamini faciantur **b** secem seces secet secemus secetis secent **c** regam regas regat regamus regatis regant **d** tenear tenearis teneatur teneamur teneamini teneantur **e** moveam moveas moveat moveamus moveatis moveant **f** capiar capiaris capiatur capiamur capiamini capiantur **g** aperiar aperiaris aperiatur aperiamur aperiamini aperiantur **h** cedam cedas cedat cedamus cedatis cedant **i** amem ames amet amemus ametis ament **j** veniar veniaris veniatur veniamur veniamini veniantur **2 a** traderer tradereris traderetur traderemur traderemini traderentur **b** viderem videres videret videremus videretis viderent **c** rogarer rogareris rogaretur rogaremur rogaremini rogarentur **d** verterem verteres verteret

verteremus verteretis verterent **e** iacerem iaceres iaceret iaceremus
iaceretis iacerent **f** sentirer sentireris sentiretur sentiremur sentiremini
sentirentur **g** iuberem iuberes iuberet iuberemus iuberetis iuberent
h ducerer ducereris duceretur duceremur duceremini ducerentur **i** starer
stareris staretur staremur staremini starentur **j** frangerem frangeres
frangeret frangeremus frangeretis frangerent

Unit 9 ex. 3–4

3 a risus sim risus sis risus sit risi simus risi sitis risi sint **b** luserim
luseris luserit luserimus luseritis luserint **c** pepercerim peperceris
pepercerit pepercerimus peperceritis pepercerint **d** cupitus sim
cupitus sis cupitus sit cupiti simus cupiti sitis cupiti sint **e** dormiverim
dormiveris dormiverit dormiverimus dormiveritis dormiverint
f pugnatus sim pugnatus sis pugnatus sit pugnati simus pugnati sitis
pugnati sint **g** missus sim missus sis missus sit missi simus missi sitis
missi sint **h** suaserim suaseris suaserit suaserimus suaseritis suaserint
i paratus sim paratus sis paratus sit parati simus parati sitis parati
sint **j** reppererim reppereris reppererit reppererimus reppereritis
reppererint   **4 a** relictus essem relictus esses relictus esset relicti
essemus relicti essetis relicti essent **b** delevissem delevisses delevisset
delevissemus delevissetis delevissent **c** laboratus essem laboratus
esses laboratus esset laborati essemus laborati essetis laborati
essent **d** custodivissem custodivisses custodivisset custodivissemus
custodivissetis custodivissent **e** accepissem accepisses accepisset
accepissemus accepissetis accepissent **f** pulsus essem pulsus esses
pulsus esset pulsi essemus pulsi essetis pulsi essent **g** dixissem dixisses
dixisset dixissemus dixissetis dixissent **h** doctus essem doctus esses
doctus esset docti essemus docti essetis docti essent **i** clausissem
clausisses clausisset clausissemus clausissetis clausissent **j** sepultus
essem sepultus esses sepultus esset sepulti essemus sepulti essetis
sepulti essent

Unit 9 ex. 5–8

5 a Let the gates be opened O guards. **b** Love conquers all; let us too
yield to love. **c** Citizens, let us greet the victorious general. **d** Do not
wake the dogs. **e** Let us live as happily as possible. **f** Let the hunters
beware of the boar. **g** Do not fight in the garden boys. **h** Now let
us work carefully. **i** Let the ambassadors approach. **j** Let us hear
Cicero. **6 a** Where are we to go now? **b** Granted that Clodia killed

her husband. **c** Suppose a monster lives in the cave. **d** How might I have helped you? **e** Why should we support you? **f** Granted that Cassius was afraid of Caesar. **g** Where should I build my villa? **h** Suppose that Britain has been conquered by the Romans. **i** Why should I work for so many years? **j** To whom should I bequeath my books? **7 a** Long live the king! **b** Tomorrow I should like to visit you. **c** May the state flourish! **d** Yesterday you would have seen Brutus laughing. **e** I would not want to see a ghost in the dark. **f** Let our enemies fall! **g** O if only Caesar had not crossed the river. **h** Who would believe Catiline? **i** If only Cato were alive now. **j** I would prefer to ride rather than to walk.   **8 a** quis avarum amet? **b** ne ad litus ambulemus. **c** semper pulchre cantes. **d** ne senex equum laedat. **e** quid senatori dicam? **f** utinam ne anserem interfecisses. **g** cur librum celares? **h** nos imperator ipse ducat. **i** e foro discedamus. **j** amet Caesar Antonium.

Unit 10 ex. 1–3

1 a The farmers sang as they reaped the grain in the fields. **b** The crocodiles attacked the animals which were jumping through the river. **c** I see a boy running towards the gates. **d** The sun melted the boy's wings as he flew. **e** We heard the shouts of people celebrating the holiday. **f** We were wading carefully across the roaring river. **g** The speaker persuaded the doubting citizens. **h** I have sent gifts to my mother who is recovering. **i** The cat was watching the mouse hiding in the grass. **j** We greeted the pilgrims who were approaching the city.   **2 a** The workmen were repairing the broken wheel. **b** The defeated soldiers ran to the camp. **c** At last we heard the messenger we were expecting. (the expected messenger) **d** I found bones in the rubble of the ruined temple. **e** The orator spoke eloquently on behalf of the cheated citizens. **f** The spies, having been seen by the guards, at once fled in different directions. **g** I often visit my beloved girl. **h** The priests were carrying a decorated image of the goddess. **i** The boy likes the shine of polished stones. **j** The words written in the book were very beautiful.   **3 a** I reproached the boy who was going to jump into the mud. **b** The son got in the way of the soldier who was going to kill his father. **c** I caught the vase as it was about to fall. **d** We fear the coming storm. **e** On the point of crossing the bridge, they dismounted from their horses. **f** They keenly applauded the gladiators who were going to fight. **g** The ladies were walking to the forum, going to buy dresses. **h** This is the lyre of the poet who is going to sing. **i** We were standing before the orator who was about to speak. **j** I hear the voices of those about to arrive.

Unit 10 ex. 4–7

4 a sessum **b** effugiendum **c** excusandum **d** intextum **e** sperandum **f** adductum **g** valendum **h** sopitum **i** perdomandum **j** statutum **5 a** The sailors were preparing the ship for sailing. **b** Quintilian used to teach the art of speaking. **c** By putting on games the emperor delighted the citizens. **d** Fabius saved the state by delaying. **e** The refugees did not reach the citadel on account of the fighting. **f** Icarus did not have a fear of flying. **g** Claudius entered the dining room to have dinner. **h** The prince is not suitable for ruling. **i** The workmen had finished the temple by working hard. **j** We did not hear the speaker's words among the shouting. **6 a** The boys have dived down into the river to swim. **b** The tale was wonderful in the telling. **c** The girls ran into the fields to play. **d** The knight went into the temple to keep vigil. **e** The king uttered threats cruel to hear. **f** The soldiers journeyed to the town to spend the winter. **g** The thing will be easy to do. **h** I walked alone through the wood to be quiet. **i** The secret is wrong to reveal. **j** The chest was hard to open. **7 a** servando dominum servus libertatem obtinuit. **b** amor noster navigandi maximus est. **c** cantus avis dulcis auditu erat. **d** celeriter festinando ad tabernam pervenimus. **e** fas dictu est. **f** Romani fortiter pugnando Gallos superaverunt. **g** Iulius canendo matrem delectat. **h** cutis monstri foeda tactu erat. **i** poena Mettii terribilis visu erat. **j** Turnus oppugnandum irruit.

Unit 10 ex. 8–10

8 a Cato was a candidate worthy of election. **b** My wife is truly loveable. **c** The speaker's words are worth hearing. **d** Brutus was a man worthy of praise among the Romans. **e** I used to collect many jewels which were worth having. **f** The very small fly is not to be seen. **g** The consuls put on games worth watching. **h** Yesterday I saw certain horses worth buying. **i** The huge knot was not to be unravelled. **j** The very good cook was preparing a meal worth eating. **9 a** I have proved the argument which had to be demonstrated. **b** Now you must be quiet. **c** Carthage must be destroyed. **d** As she had to be punished, the citizens threw Tarpeia down from the rock. **e** You must beware. **f** We must always respect our parents. **g** Claudius saw to it that an aqueduct be built. **h** We must not be afraid of the enemy. **i** I have said nothing about the plan which must be hidden. **j** Now is the time to drink. **10 a** The citizens were gathering in the forum to elect magistrates. **b** I have hired a Greek teacher of rhetoric to educate my son. **c** The boys climbed onto the roofs to watch the procession. **d** Pliny sought ease to write his books. **e** The hunters journeyed into the mountains to catch wild beasts. **f** The athlete ran very quickly to win the prize. **g** Sulla laid down his dictatorship for the sake of preserving the laws. **h** We have sent a gift to delight mother. **i** Spartacus rebelled for the sake of freeing the slaves. **j** The artist was working carefully to make a beautiful statue.

Unit 11 ex. 1–4

1 a venire **b** amavisse **c** ambulaturus esse **d** tenere **e** sedisse **f** cepisse **g** docturus esse **h** aperturus esse **i** frangere **j** fecisse **2 a** traditum iri **b** spretus esse **c** iactus esse **d** moveri **e** rogatum iri **f** scribi **g** visus esse **h** victum iri **i** vinctus esse **j** cresci **3 a** to have fallen **b** to be about to be buried **c** to be about to punish **d** to be washed **e** to have ordered **f** to be about to be said **g** to answer **h** to be about to work **i** to have been built **j** to be sent **4 a** manere **b** agnosci **c** electus esse **d** clausum iri **e** traxisse **f** volaturus esse **g** inveniri **h** risisse **i** tensus esse **j** currere

Unit 11 ex. 5–8

5 a I can understand the Latin language. **b** Caesar used to forgive his enemies. **c** You ought to have visited your grandmother. **d** I prefer to live in Gaul. **e** I am willing to sing in front of the guests. **f** The idiots chose to overlook the omens. **g** The young man wished to marry Metella. **h** The emperor decided to build an amphitheatre. **i** I do not dare to provoke the lion. **j** I do not want to sleep in the fields. **6 a** We shall persist in searching for a suitable land. **b** Suddenly the dogs began to bark. **c** We are hurrying to greet mother. **d** You hesitated to pour the water. **e** The boys feared to approach the wolves. **f** I shall never cease to have hope. **g** The children are afraid to leave the house. **h** The ambassadors are hurrying to put an end to the war. **i** Cicero continued to slander Catiline. **j** When will you stop scolding your slaves? **7 a** No-one knew how to untie that knot. **b** The centurion will teach the young men to be soldiers. **c** I shall never learn to play on the pipes. **d** Brutus is said to have killed himself. **e** The conspirators grabbed, struck and killed Caesar. **f** The senators are said to have torn Romulus apart. **g** All spiders know how to catch flies. **h** The bakers were thought to have killed the villagers with poison. **i** The teacher used to teach his pupils to love peace. **j** Nero is said to have killed his mother. **8 a** candidato favere debemus. **b** dormire malo. **c** nare discimus. **d** clamare desines. **e** discedere constituerunt. **f** scit pugnare. **g** te scribere docebo. **h** clamare perseveratis. **i** audeo Romanis resistere. **j** effigiem dei videre cupimus.

Unit 11 ex. 9–12

9 a regere regimini **b** parce parcite **c** lenire lenimini **d** ama amate **e** agnoscere agnoscimini **f** aperire aperimini **g** responde respondete **h** vinci vincite **i** persuadere persuademini **j** rape rapite **10 a** Citizens, be warned by me. **b** Seize the day. **c** Bring these burdens to the harbour. **d** Hello pupils. Hello teacher. **e** Accept this gift on behalf of your supporters. **f** Walk with me to the forum senators. **g** Give me the lamp Aladdin! **h** Either learn or leave. **i** Let there be peace in the world. **j** Hello and goodbye friend. **11 a** Don't do that boys. **b** Do not wake sleeping dogs. **c** Ladies, do not buy clothes somewhere else. **d** Don't worry; be happy. **e** Do not be cheated by the shopkeepers, young men. **f** Don't be afraid of the dark my son. **g** Do not eat anything bigger than your head. **h** Don't you step on my blue suede shoes (lit. on my shoes made from blue pig skin). **i** Do not gild the lilies. **j** Do not walk on the lawn. **12 a** cives, nolite sacerdotes punire. **b** liberi, fortes este. **c** apage Tite! nemo tibi credit. **d** da mihi sal Sexte. **e** pueri, nolite ridere meum equum parvum. **f** noli oracula praetermittere Caesar. **g** excipe hospites domine. **h** id saxum pelle celerius Sisyphe. **i** duc gladiatores in arenam Maxime. **j** aurum tuum in cubiculo cela Quinte.

Unit 12 ex.1–3

1 a Look it's raining! **b** It is becoming for the Romans to keep the peace. **c** Today it suits me to stay at home. **d** It will please you to hear the singer. **e** You are not allowed to go into the dining room. **f** The thief is not ashamed of his disloyalty. **g** It does not please the boys to play in the garden. **h** It is already growing late. **i** We are bored with our work. **j** It suits a wise man to keep quiet.

2 a Use must be made of the best plan. **b** It is easy to hide yourself in the mountains. **c** Cassius must sail to Greece. **d** It is necessary to tie the fierce dog up. **e** We shall need money. **f** Our men advanced towards the enemy. **g** It is not possible to withstand the Germans. **h** The sailors needed ropes. **i** It concerns us that he is saved. **j** In the morning he is in the habit of greeting his patron. **3 a** opus erit vobis nave. **b** heri ninguit. **c** dedecet nos cedere. **d** Caesari placet captivis parcere. **e** taedet puellas carminum. **f** mea refert nos discere. **g** potest cacumina arborum videre. **h** difficile erat speluncas invenire **i** a feminis ventum est ad theatrum. **j** mox lucescet.

Unit 13 ex. 1–3

1 a That man who was sleeping in the cave was very old. **b** Today we want to see those temples which the Romans built. **c** The land from where the stranger has come is almost uninhabited. **d** We have already seen the men whom you have chosen. **e** Whom you will follow we shall follow too. **f** I was waiting for Claudia where the cottage is concealed by the trees. **g** The words which the general had said delighted the soldiers. **h** He leapt in immediately where the enemy were thickest. **i** I know well that man whose son has died. **j** You have never liked the candidate we support. **2 a** London, which seems a very large city, is much smaller than Rome. **b** My wife, who was always a tower of strength to me, is already a grandmother. **c** Athens, which is the capital of Attica, is a very beautiful city. **d** For this reason Cassius became even richer. **e** When this was done, that man departed from the forum very angrily. **f** That man is Catiline who turned out to be a disaster for the state. **g** For this reason we shall not go sailing again. **h** As for what Caesar will do, no-one will be willing to obey. **i** When this was done the Romans rejoiced for many days. **j** Sirius, which is the brightest star, has already risen. **3 a** avem petet ubi nidum vidit. **b** iuvenemne quem Lucretia amat vidisti? **c** quod fecimus, omnes tacebunt. **d** quam ob rem pompa constitit. **e** Brutus, cuius gens nobilis est, rempublicam servavit. **f** canis felem quae murem ceperat cepit. **g** Augustus, quod erat decus temporis sui. **h** anserem quae ova auri pariebat necaverunt. **i** Cloelia quod erat exemplar Romanis. **j** quo facto spectatores plauserunt.

Unit 13 ex. 4–6

4 a When you were wandering in the woods, I was working in the garden. **b** After the thieves stole the togas the doorman was beaten.

c After Valeria had sung, everyone clapped. **d** As soon as the bull came in, we scattered. **e** As soon as their patron arrived, the clients got up. **f** As soon as they saw the buildings they recognized Rome. **g** When the judge said these words the defendant trembled. **h** As soon as the bridge was broken, Horatius dived into the river. **i** After Milo had killed Clodius, he was sent into exile. **j** As often as the cocks crowed, the farmers used to wake up. **5 a** We had prepared the ship before the sailors arrived. **b** While the sun was shining, the bees were making honey. **c** We shall decorate the hall before the guests arrive. **d** The enemy lay hidden until the column came into the pass. **e** We stayed in the camp until the danger was removed. **f** While the priests were sacrificing, the assassin struck me. **g** The poet recited as long as the crowd remained. **h** He put out the fire before the house caught fire. **i** While the dogs are asleep, the thieves will enter the house. **j** The tribune had persisted until the consul had given way.
6 a dum custodes inter se clamabant captivi effugerunt. **b** mansistine quoad poeta fabulam recitavisset? **c** leo diu latebat antequam arietem oppugnaverit. **d** audiebamus quam diu orator loquebatur. **e** dum Decius appropinquat canis latravit. **f** quotiens catellam tibi emo, aliam petis. **g** ianuam pulsabimus dum eam aperias. **h** postquam terra tremuit, mons diruptus est. **i** Marcelle, clavum percute simulac adnuo. **j** donec Iulia in ripa ambulabat, lutrae in flumine ludebant.

Unit 13 ex. 7–9

7 a When the mistress speaks the maidservants listen. **b** When Sulla was dictator, all the senators were in great danger. **c** The conspirators were holding Caesar when Casca struck him. **d** Whenever I see you my voice fails. **e** When they see that gladiator the spectators clap. **f** When you (will) read the book you will understand the story. **g** We were approaching the mountains when the Gauls attacked. **h** As soon as the bridge was destroyed, Horatius hurled himself into the river. **i** Whenever father entered, the boys laughed. **j** As soon as the gate had been closed, the girl kissed the boy. **8 a** When they had left the mountains behind, the travellers rejoiced. **b** When the guests had arrived Sextus handed out the wine. **c** Since the dogs were barking the thieves scattered. **d** When the sun was rising the guards were asleep. **e** Since Cicero had uncovered this crime he arrested the conspirators. **f** When we had made the journey to Rome we could not find an inn anywhere. **g** Because the hunters were creeping slowly, the boar hid. **h** When Caesar had decided to cross the Rhine he built a bridge. **i** Since the listeners were laughing the poet grew angry.

j Since they had seen the shore the sailors turned the ship.
9 a navem vertebas cum praedones nos oppugnaverunt. **b** cum ad litus pervenissemus deis gratias egimus. **c** domum ambulabam cum canis me oppugavit. **d** cum primum tintinnabulum sonavit monachi discederunt. **e** cum Caesarem interfecissent coniurati diffugerunt. **f** cum iuvenes aegri erant fur aurum abstulit. **g** cum ursum vidissent pueri diffugerunt. **h** cum luna clara fuisset versipellis ambulavit. **i** feminae cantabant cum fila deducerent. **j** cum coquus cenam parabat hospites advenerunt.

Unit 13 ex. 10–12

10 a When the gold was found the miser was stunned. **b** I cannot hear you while the citizens are talking. **c** As the sun was rising, the lady summoned her maidservants. **d** When these words were spoken, the ambassador left quickly. **e** As the soldiers were about to depart, the treaty was renewed. **f** Since a storm was about to arrive, the sailors stayed in the harbour. **g** When the messenger had spoken, the gates were opened. **h** After the victory was announced we sent a letter to our father. **i** After the hostages were killed, the assassin began to despair for his life. **j** When the ship had been repaired the sailors immediately set sail. **11 a** As those maidens sing the sailors go mad. **b** When Claudius and Aemilius were praetors no robbers were convicted. **c** The column wandered through the woods as the guards accompanied the prisoners. **d** When Tarquin was king the Romans constructed the Cloaca Maxima (Great Sewer). **e** As the citizens are in favour, I have put up a statue to my father. **f** As the enemy were about to attack the city, Jupiter thundered. **g** When Marcellus had obtained the money we bought the farm. **h** As the emperor was on the point of killing himself the soldiers mutinied. **i** With Boudicca as queen the Britons sacked Colchester. **j** With a thread as his guide Theseus escaped from the labyrinth. **12 a** Iove fulmen coniecturo Iuno exclamavit. **b** te dormienti cubiculum pinxi. **c** lumine exstincto in tenebris ambulabamus. **d** nobis scopam visuris, arbiter certamen finivit. **e** fratre tyranni necato Athenienses vehementer opprimebantur. **f** aqua exhausta milites alveum transibant. **g** piscatoribus harundines ferentibus pueri cibum parabant. **h** Mario imperatore barbaros superabimus. **i** castris positis milites panem fecerunt. **j** Mercurio duce ad terram mortuorum perveniemus.

1 a Hold the mirror to see yourself. **b** I am guarding the sheep in case they are eaten by lions. **c** The boy is washing the floor to be praised by his mother. **d** The painters will work hard to paint the hall in one day. **e** I have hidden the map lest that island ever be found. **f** The dogs are barking so that no-one approaches the house. **g** Caesar is fortifying the hill so that the Gauls do not capture the camp. **h** Sieze the day so that happiness does not avoid you. **i** I am calling out all the names so that no-one is left out. **j** Surely you will mend the plough so that we may bring the grain? **2 a** I mounted the horse to show off my skill. **b** He was burying the bodies so that nothing would be seen. **c** The merchant made a secret chamber to hide the gems inside. **d** The hunters were stalking the stags to provide food for their children. **e** He had sold the farms to pay off the debt. **f** I bought the dog that Claudius might never be able to hide. **g** The wicked man cut the tree down so that no bird would build its nest there. **h** The girls were reading the books to learn the ancient poems. **i** We had closed the gates so that no-one would be let in. **j** I bolted the door so that we would never revisit the house again. **3 a** The leader has sent reinforcements to help us. **b** We had hired workmen to build the baths. **c** The athlete trained for a long time to carry the torch more quickly. **d** I have hired this scribe to write my books. **e** The doctor had drained the draught to sleep more deeply. **f** I have gathered soldiers to defend me. **g** Quintia, I have sent gifts to delight you. **h** I have large eyes so that I may see you better. **i** He was demolishing the wall to see more of the garden. **j** The shepherd built a sheepfold so that the sheep would be protected more safely. **4 a** panemne celas ut matrem irrites? **b** agricola agrum spectabat ne ulla vacca effugeret. **c** filios habemus qui nos ulciscantur. **d** portam observavit ne quis eam aperiret. **e** Sulla nomina hostium proscripserat ut interficerentur. **f** pavimentum lavavi ne ullum lutum videretur. **g** magnos dentes habeo ut te melius consumam. **h** omnibus arcam demonstravi ne me suspicarentur. **i** advenitne Cicero ut orationem audiret? **j** cibum gusta ne quid veneni insit.

5 a The king has procured so many soldiers that the expedition will certainly be victorious. **b** Father will be so happy that he will give us presents. **c** The speed of the wind is so great that we shall not sail today. **d** It is snowing so much that we shall see nothing. **e** The cat is scoffing so many fish she will soon be asleep. **f** He is falling down so many times that he will break his legs. **g** The pauper is so hungry that he will eat his own shoes. **h** The bridge is so weak that even the goats will not cross it. **i** Titus is such a man that he will help the leader very well. **j** She is running so quickly that she will not see the danger. **6 a** The tower is so high that I do not see the roof. **b** Crassus is such a man that he does not bribe supporters. **c** The rocks are so big that the asses cannot carry them. **d** The ground is trembling so much that I am almost falling. **e** So many sheep are blocking the road that the shepherds are at a loss. **f** This bird sings so often that it always delights me. **g** The wagons are so heavy that the bridge is being broken. **h** He speaks so clearly that I can hear all the words. **i** So great is my faith that I am fighting unarmed. **j** The water is so hot that it cannot be drunk. **7 a** Our mother was so kind that she was always loved. **b** I had insulted the magistrate so many times that I was actually arrested. **c** We had crossed such great mountains that we were exhausted. **d** The girls were crying so much that they actually moved the dictator. **e** So many barbarians rushed through the gates that the guards could not resist them. **f** Tarquin had ruled so arrogantly that the citizens actually drove him out. **g** The elephants were so enormous that the Romans feared them greatly. **h** He painted the picture so well that he received many prizes. **i** He used to ride horses so quickly that at last he was actually killed. **j** He had annoyed so many men that he was actually marooned alone on an island. **8 a** Helena tot procos habebat ut maritum deligere potuerit. **b** Marius tantus imperator est ut milites eum fideliter secuturi sint. **c** Pausanias templum ita amavit ut semper id laudaret. **d** tot sumus ut nobis resistere non possis. **e** puer totiens 'lupus' clamabat ut nemo ei crederet. **f** Cato tam probus erat ut non mentiretur. **g** adeo dissenserunt ut Romlus Remum necaverit. **h** tales fabulas Othello narrabat ut Desdemona eum amaret. **i** Victoria non erat femina quam delectares. **j** tam dives est Crassus ut divitias suas ignoret.

Unit 14 ex. 9–12

9 a If Metella marries Aemilius, the mothers of both will be happy. **b** If the Romans take Alexandria, they will rule Egypt. **c** Unless you free us you will hear nothing of your friend. **d** If Aulus catches a large fish we shall eat it today. **e** If you do not give me a present tomorrow

I shall howl. **f** Unless Fabius runs he will not catch the hare. **g** The house will certainly collapse unless the walls are repaired. **h** If you send the emperor a letter he will give you advice. **i** If the cow gives birth to a bullock I shall not sell him. **j** Unless you come to me, I shall come to you.   **10 a** Unless you have got the money, we have lost the farm. **b** If the brigands were not careful they were in great danger. **c** If you are leaving, we are happy. **d** If the birds are singing, Spring is on the way. **e** If we saw any ship we ran to the harbour. **f** If you have not seen Naples you clearly have not lived. **g** If Clodia loved you, you were very fortunate. **h** Unless Egnatius smiles his wife is wretched. **i** If they were not working in the fields they wasted the whole day. **j** If I have insulted the magistrate I have been very foolish.   **11 a** Ask mother, if you can find her. **b** If the door has not been closed the dog will escape. **c** If I have sold broken jars, the money will be returned to you. **d** If the boys were absent they will pay the penalty. **e** If Sempronia loves Quintus let her inform him. **f** Young man, drink the potion, unless you are afraid. **g** If you ever looked at me I used to blush. **h** Kill the traitor unless he confesses. **i** Seize the opportunity if it is being offered to you. **j** If you have seen that beautiful city, you are truly fortunate.   **12 a** nisi coquus pavonem accendet, cena optima erit. **b** si Cyrus vas fregit, punietur. **c** si potionem biberis iuventute sempiterna uteris. **d** urbs capietur nisi legatus foedus renovaverit. **e** si captivi non vincti sunt, custodes officium neglexerunt. **f** si pons fractus est, exercitus transire non potest. **g** si Titus mihi tabulam patefaciet, vos ad speluncam ducam. **h** si umquam patronum salutaveramus, nobis sportulam dabat. **i** si Valgus non est in thermis, eum pete in foro. **j** si canes dormiunt, feles superbe circum hortum ambulat.

Unit 14 ex. 13–16

13 a If the river were wider we would not cross it. **b** If Manlius were not here the meeting would not take place. **c** If the keys were lost, the conspirators would not be entering the house. **d** Unless you are careful, you will be caught. **e** If the river were not being diverted, the town would be flooded. **f** If the vase were broken, someone would be punished. **g** If Cicero were speaking, very many people would be present. **h** If the signal were given, the soldiers would advance. **i** If the children complain, let them stay at home. **j** Unless the praetorian guard support the emperor, he would without doubt be expelled.   **14 a** If we were not Romans we would not wear togas.

b If father were a soldier he would defend the Roman empire. **c** If I were less careful the thieves would come in. **d** If the citizens were not superstitious they would not worship the gods. **e** If you were attacked, many people would come to help you. **f** If you were in the city, you would see many sights. **g** If I were younger, I would run with the athletes. **h** If we were not ambassadors we would be killed. **i** If the consuls were not here, the soldiers would be less brave. **j** If you were innocent you would not be afraid.

15 a If Caesar had not crossed the Rubicon, war would not have broken out. **b** If he had kept the ring safe he would be invincible. **c** If they had not heard his voice they would not have found Publius. **d** If Cleopatra were not beautiful, Antony would not have loved her. **e** If the monk had understood the Greek language, he would have read the book. **f** If he were not a boy, the robber would have killed him. **g** If you had examined the letter you would have recognized the handwriting. **h** If he had not tasted the food he would have been killed by the poison. **i** If you had watched the games you would have seen Spartacus. **j** If the nightingale had sung we would have been greatly delighted. **16 a** si senatores te expellant, nos ipsi te sequamur. **b** si periculum vidissemus non inermes advenissemus. **c** si via latior esset plaustra non intercluderentur. **d** si Lucium non credidissetis, innocentem damnavissetis. **e** si inter busta dormiamus, umbrae nos terreant. **f** si Larcius benignior esset, servi eum amarent. **g** si pauper esset, Cassius humilior esset. **h** si omina consuluisset, Caesar non discessisset. **i** si socii esset, tesseram clamarent. **j** si corpus videamus, tibi credamus.

Unit 15 ex. 1–3

1 a We announced that an abandoned ship was approaching. **b** I often say that she is lucky. **c** The Gauls have said that the Druids are not being concealed. **d** I shall say that you are dressing. **e** Do you think that Septimus is feeding the animals? **f** You did not say that the guards were asleep, did you? **g** They deny that Catiline is innocent. **h** You will see that I am very brave. **i** The citizens believe that you are being overlooked. **j** Everyone knows that the Carthaginians are treacherous. **2 a** We knew that the conspirators would be killed. **b** I think that Catiline will abandon us. **c** Do you think that my plays will be performed by very famous actors? **d** Had you known that Marius would be arrested? **e** Surely you see that the Gauls are going to burn the village? **f** You used to say that Caesar would not be dictator. **g** The bandits did not believe that the island would be defended. **h** The leader announced that the army would set off immediately. **i** I have told you that Helen will leave tomorrow. **j** He denies that the girl will be chosen. **3 a** Are you saying that she has married Tiberius? **b** We know that the farmers have sold all their cows. **c** We used to think that the fatherland had been saved by Cicero. **d** Surely you see that this horse has been washed? **e** The spies announced that reinforcements had arrived. **f** We shall deny that the old man had found the gold. **g** Valerius said that the soothsayer lied. **h** Do you deny that you have ever seen this woman? **i** We see that the guests have been well entertained. **j** The guards were denying that the prisoner had been tied up.

Unit 15 ex. 4–7

4 a Quintus knew that he would not pay the penalty for his crime. **b** Marius used to think that he would be killed. **c** Cato scolded the young man and said that he would prosecute him. **d** The citizens do not know that they have been tricked by Tarquin. **e** Marcus said that he had not cut the tree down. **f** The soldiers denied that they had run away. **g** Egnatius says that he was robbed by bandits. **h** The senators had announced that they were going to choose Pompey. **i** Sempronia thought that she had found a knife. **j** The scribe is denying that he wrote these words. **5 a** It has been said that the Romans are intractable in war. **b** I say that we shall not be caught if we walk slowly. **c** Did you say that you had not been captured? **d** Horatius said that he would guard the bridge. **e** It is agreed that Marius saved Rome. **f** It was said that a dolphin had swum into the harbour. **g** We did not know that you were going to paint a picture. **h** It had been denied that Augustus was ill. **i** I used not to think that the citizens would ever have voted for Cornelius unless they had been bribed by him. **j** I know you will be safe if you heed my words. **6 a** Surely you will promise that you will make the journey with me? **b** The enemy are threatening that they will burn the city. **c** I swear that I will always be faithful. **d** The patron promised that he would give his clients gifts. **e** Are you ordering me to leave the city? **f** The magistrate forbade the bakers to form a guild. **g** We were hoping that you would buy the farm. **h** Publius is happy that his grandfather is recovering. **i** I want you to carry the water from the spring. **j** We are grieving that Cicero has been killed. **7 a** Calpurnia putat se cane oppugnatum iri. **b** Catullus scit se Clodiam amare. **c** scio vulpem effugiturum esse si porta

aperiatur. **d** dictum est Neronem maturem suam necavisse.
e me promiserunt novam statuam non casuram esse. **f** vetasne me fabas
consumere? **g** nolunt nos tapetam novam videre. **h** gaudeo uxorem
tuam gravidam esse. **i** iurat se patrem ulturum esse **j** speramus eam
testudinem capturam esse.

Unit 15 ex. 8–10

8 a Caelia is asking whether the workmen will be working tomorrow.
b I shall ask whether Hortensius is going to bring his children or not.
c I have asked when the queen arrived. **d** Tullius will ask Decimus
whether the gold has been found. **e** Decius does not want to ask how
it happened. **f** Boys, ask your mother whether she wants to hear the
poet. **g** Have you asked me whether I am happy? **h** We have asked
whether Servius loves Caecilia or not. **i** The tribunes will ask who is
going to reveal the plan. **j** Ask how many wagons there are. **9 a** We
asked why the girls would not sing. **b** The miners asked whether they
were going to receive their wages or not. **c** You surely did not ask
whether Titus had kissed Livia? **d** I had not asked whom the leader
would choose. **e** Romulus did not ask what had happened. **f** The guide
had asked us how we were making the journey. **g** They were always
asking when they would arrive there. **h** We had asked how many times
Marius had been consul. **i** Surely Sulla asked whether the army had
been beaten? **j** I want to see whether the ghost will come or not.
10 a rogavistine num portae clausae sint necne? **b** roga num pueri in
horto laborent. **c** rogabamus num statua viveret. **d** rogaverat num
agricola esses. **e** cives rogant quis regina futura sit. **f** rogavitne num
vulneratus essem? **g** rogant num cena parata sit. **h** rogaveram num
Marius adventurus esset. **i** ancilla rogat num dormias necne. **j** quis scit
quid acciderit?

Unit 15 ex. 11–13

11 a The old woman is advising the king to buy the books. **b** Stephanus
persuaded his master to free Furius. **c** Holconius is seeing to it that the
new baths are being built. **d** Sextus was forbidden to touch the drink.
e The farmers will demand that the king abdicates. **f** We encouraged
Plautus to write plays. **g** We shall order Terence to cook dinner.
h Jupiter had allowed Minerva to help the Greeks. **i** Mother will allow
us to chase the chickens. **j** He has ordered us to wash the floor.
12 a We wish that father would show us the bear. **b** We had wished

that Lucius would not be drunk. **c** I want you to marry me. **d** Cicero wished that Catiline had been killed. **e** We all prefer you to stay at home. **f** The porters long for the burdens not to be heavy. **g** I wish I had found the ring. **h** You wished Cato had been elected. **i** Do you wish that the treasure had been found? **j** Hadrian desires that a wall be built. **13 a** postulo ut servum manumittas. **b** nos hortantur ut castra oppugnemus. **c** curavi ne togae sordidi essent. **d** impera custodi ne dormiat. **e** vos obsecro ne Caesarem interficiatis. **f** te monuimus ne in silvas errares. **g** cupimus ut ab aula discedas. **h** vetuerant pueros in flumine natare. **i** ea ei persuaserat ut malum consumeret. **j** eos permittemus ut equum emant.

Unit 16 ex. 1–3

1 a Although the woman was beautiful, the miser suspected her. **b** Although the standard had been captured, the legionaries fought bravely. **c** Although the shopkeepers may be unsophisticated, yet I shall buy many dresses. **d** Although the sword is fixed in the stone, Arthur will withdraw it. **e** Although Gaius is only seven years old, he nevertheless plays among the youths. **f** Even though it is growing late, the boys are creeping into the woods. **g** Even though father has left, we are working hard. **h** Even if the gladiator is huge, I shall fight with him. **i** Although you have never seen my grandfather, you will certainly like him. **j** We would have beaten the barbarians even if the army had not been prepared. **2 a** Aemilia does not love Caelius because, no doubt, his father is poor. **b** Cicero slew the conspirators because, he said, the state was in the greatest danger. **c** Quintus will not go hunting, doubtless because he is afraid of the wild beasts. **d** The old man will arrive late because he left late. **e** Cassius hates Caesar because, no doubt, he loves Rome. **f** I sent the dog out because he was chasing the cat. **g** You are rich Cassius because, some say, you are lucky. **h** They have bought rods because they will be fishing tomorrow. **i** Since the journey is certainly long I shall go with you. **j** The boys are quarrelling because they are tired. **3 a** quamvis Alexander vulneratus esset, ferocius pugnavit. **b** quamquam Gaius ignavus est, rotam reficiet. **c** etsi regem necavisses, non effugissemus. **d** etsi flumen latissimum erat, ad ripam pervenimus. **e** mures ludunt quod feles abest. **f** Roma incensa est quod Nero aulam novam aedificare vellet. **g** rex me arcessivit quippe qui me admiretur. **h** princeps veniet cum te amet. **i** Titus non pugnabit quoniam mitis est. **j** quamquam vos videre non possumus, nihilominus verba vestra audire possumus.

4 a Let the boys eat dinner, provided that they have washed. **b** Let the workmen sleep today provided that they work hard tomorrow. **c** Invite Caecilius, provided that he does not bring his brother. **d** I shall choose a dress provided that you buy it. **e** Let the children talk as long as they are not fighting among themselves. **f** You will certainly see those young men, provided that the girls are also there. **g** Let the boys watch the play, provided that they are quiet. **h** Explore the house boys, provided that you do not wander into that part. **i** Let your daughter choose a husband, as long as she loves him. **j** Let the dogs play in the atrium provided that they do not break anything. **5 a** The poor man is eating the bread as if he may not eat again. **b** The she-wolf nourished the boys as if they were cubs. **c** The boys are playing just as the men are working. **d** Why have you spoken as if Catiline were not a traitor? **e** My son spends money as if he had received his inheritance. **f** A lion really does live in the cave, just as you often assert. **g** The young men are going sailing as if the winds are not strong. **h** The candidate built new baths, as he promised. **i** The spectators clapped as though the play had ended. **j** A poet makes men wiser just as a teacher teaches boys. **6 a** The fishermen were afraid that the nets would be broken. **b** The leaders are afraid that the reinforcements may not arrive. **c** We fear that Titus may not find the chest. **d** The shepherd was afraid that the wolves had taken the lamb. **e** The teacher was afraid that the children had walked into the woods. **f** The athletes fear that they will not win the prizes. **g** I was afraid that I would not get the money. **h** Cassius had been afraid that the traitor had revealed the plan to the consuls. **i** Is there a danger that we may be captured? **j** I was afraid that Caesar had crossed the Rubicon. **7 a** Rufus gladium gerit tamquam miles sit. **b** appropinquent iuvenes dummodo inermes sint. **c** periculum erat ne murus rueret. **d** coniurator sicario persuasit sicut serpens praedam decipit. **e** veniat Cicero dum ne loquatur. **f** timueruntne ne Sulla eum inveniret? **g** cras apud te cenabo Tite, dummodo vinum tuum bonum sit. **h** me aspexit quasi me prius vidisset. **i** timebam ne exploratores cibum non invenissent. **j** captivos traduxit ceu servi essent.

8 a We had doubted whether you would arrive on time. **b** Who doubted but that Cicero would free the slave. **c** There is a doubt as to

whether the Carthaginians have really been beaten. **d** They doubted whether Valerius had written the will. **e** It is uncertain where the stranger has come from. **f** You were inclined to think that such a candidate would be very bad. **g** There was a doubt about whether Ulysses returned home. **h** Caesar was inclined to think that Cassius was not loyal. **i** Cloelia was inclined to think that the maidens would follow. **j** There was no doubt but that the ship was sinking.
9 a Valerius discouraged the boys from making a long journey. **b** The magistrates forbade the citizens to receive the ambassadors. **c** It is forbidden for us to defend that traitor. **d** The king did not prevent the prisoners from being freed. **e** The guards were being hindered from opening the gates. **f** Will they forbid us to touch the sacrifice? **g** The centurion prevented the soldiers from sleeping for a long time. **h** The asses are hindered by heavy burdens from crossing the bridge. **i** Nothing stands in the way of us being friends. **j** Surely you will not prevent us from seeing the gladiators? **10 a** Galli a gurgite impediti sunt ne flumen transierint. **b** Portia nos vetuit anseres vexare. **c** haud dubium est quin Romani vicum incendant. **d** omina non impediunt imperatorem ne proficiscatur. **e** Corneli, prohibebisne canes ne filium meum oppugnent? **f** dubitavimus an discedere malles. **g** dubito num Servius equitare possit. **h** quidam dubitaverunt num Augustus versus amaret. **i** magistratus, prohibite illum ne domum intret. **j** dubium est num fabri pontem perfecerint.

Unit 16 ex. 11–13

11 a No soldier was fighting so bravely but that he deserves a prize. **b** It can not happen that Claudius is elected. **c** No woman was so rich that she was not prudent. **d** There was no-one who would not follow Alexander the Great. **e** There is no-one who does not admire Brutus. **f** No boy is so good that he does not steal my apples. **g** It cannot happen that Caesar becomes dictator. **h** It cannot happen that Cloelia be given back. **i** There is no-one who does not believe that speaker. **j** There is no leader so harsh as not to spare prisoners.
12 a Why should the tribune not stand up to the consul? **b** That gladiator is very famous; indeed he will soon be a freedman. **c** Well then brother, save the infant! **d** Why should the refugee not stay here? **e** The young men were very strong; indeed Hercules had killed a lion. **f** So move the flock then, shepherds. **g** Why should a mother not love her son? **h** Well come on boys, catch the ball. **i** How couldn't you have seen that ball? **j** Why should we not pick those

flowers? **13 a** Caecilius non tam pauper est quin maiorem domum emere possit. **b** non potest fieri quin foedus renovetur. **c** nemo erat quin de nuptiis non cognoverit. **d** nullus nodus tam implicatus est quin solvi possit. **e** quin Sextus nos credat? **f** Quintus me non amat; quin heri me vituperavit. **g** quin Felix equum vendat? **h** nullus miles est quin mortem timeat. **i** quin carpite diem liberi. **j** quin dominum tam crudelem adverser?